Budgeting for Not-for-Profit Organizations

BUDGETING FOR NOT-FOR-PROFIT ORGANIZATIONS

Robert D. Vinter
Rhea K. Kish

THE FREE PRESS
A Division of Macmillan, Inc.
NEW YORK

Collier Macmillan Publishers
LONDON

The Free Press
A Division of Macmillan, Inc.
866 Third Avenue, New York, N. Y. 10022

Collier Macmillan Canada, Inc.

Printed in the United States of America

printing number

   3   4   5   6   7   8   9   10

Library of Congress Cataloging in Publication Data

Vinter, Robert D.
  Budgeting for not-for-profit organizations.

  Bibliography: p.
  Includes index.
  1. Corporations, Nonprofit—Accounting. 2. Corporations, Nonprofit—Finance. 3. Budget in business.
I. Kish, Rhea K. II. Title.
HF5686.N56V56 1984   658.1′5   84–47855
ISBN 0–02–933410–1

CONTENTS

ACKNOWLEDGMENTS

Like so many others, we backed into budgeting more by
accident than by design. We are considerably indebted to
those who were our guides and to the many others in
numerous organizations who continue to keep us informed
about budgeting in the real world.

Separately and sometimes together we have served in a
broad variety of public and private organizations, mainly in
the not-for-profit sector. Our duties have usually involved
administrative and fiscal matters, sometimes as professional staff, sometimes on governing boards, and sometimes
as consultants. Participation in operating organizations and
on review and funding bodies—from the local to the federal
level—has helped us recognize the common processes
among these diverse groups, which we attempt to document
throughout the book. We are thankful for these experiences
and for their contributions to our understanding of the
kinds and range of problems faced by such organizations.

As we gained skill and confidence, we began to train
others and, recognizing the widespread interest in this subject, developed a graduate–professional course at The
University of Michigan School of Social Work. The course at-
tracted students from numerous professional disciplines

and stimulated a parallel series of short workshops for new and experienced administrators.

Our greatest debt is to the hundreds of students whom we have been privileged to teach in courses and workshops. They have pressed us to focus on basic procedures and their applications to concrete real-life situations and tasks. These interactions have helped to sharpen our thinking and to formulate and explain the reasons for seemingly arbitrary procedures. They have greatly influenced the emphasis we place on learning budgeting step by step and working with actual fiscal materials. We have been helped perhaps as much by those with less experience as by those with more. Their quandaries and uncertainties have stimulated and guided us, while the enthusiasm of students and the experiences of graduates have sustained our prolonged work on the book.

Effective teaching depends heavily on the availability of systematic knowledge and of good instructional materials. We were dismayed to discover the dearth of adequate and comprehensive guides, manuals, or texts, aside from a few basic references. And this impelled us to develop new instructional materials, which were regularly evaluated by students. Preparation of these materials was later assisted by an award from The University of Michigan's Center for Research on Learning and Teaching. We gratefully acknowledge that important support, which enabled us to complete a series of six "Fiscal Packs" for use in classes and workshops.

The continuously revised materials have been shared with instructors on numerous other campuses, and their responses and exchange of materials have both challenged and affirmed our own approach. Robert Elkin at the University of Maryland has been especially helpful, and his important work has contributed much to our thinking. We have also conducted sessions to prepare others to teach these subjects and have benefited by their insights and suggestions.

Colleagues and deans at the School of Social Work of The University of Michigan have given us encouragement throughout the writing of this book, for which we are grateful.

The entire text has been prepared through computer word-processing equipment, our own and that of The University of Michigan. Mary Ann Rodgers has handled our drafts with great diligence, skill, and unfailing good humor, and we express special appreciation for her assistance. We are greatly indebted to Estelle Titiev for her exceptional help with the proofreading.

Finally, our spouses and families deserve more than a word of thanks for their support and forbearance over the many months consumed in this writing. Their patience has been all the more remarkable considering that they do not share our fascination with budgeting!

ROBERT D. VINTER
RHEA K. KISH

INTRODUCTION

This book is a guide to the principal budgeting and fiscal processes common to small and midsize not-for-profit organizations. It is practical and nontheoretical and focuses on the administrative tasks associated with those processes. Some readers will be old hands at administration, many will be newcomers to these tasks, and still others will be only contemplating a move into management. The characteristics, ranks, ranges of duties, and titles of these persons will vary greatly. All, however, are engaged in a variety of roughly analogous tasks that involve both program and fiscal matters. Thus we concentrate on *the tasks and responsibilities* and do not differentiate among levels of positions and titles or among the various ways organizations are structured.

The organizations in which these administrators work may be separate entities, subunits, or affiliates; they may be units of government or entirely private. They are generally supported by combinations of public and private funds but may be supported solely by either. They report to a board of directors, an executive committee, a city council, a county commission, a state department, or a federal agency.

These organizations serve all manner of people—young, old, poor, rich, well educated, illiterate—in limited or widespread locations. They offer equally diverse kinds of services—education, housing, health, community development, recreation, personal wellbeing, social responsibility—which may be given to individuals, families, small groups, whole communities, or a mixture of these.

For simplicity and economy we usually refer to all these organizations as *agencies* with subsidiary programs that provide services to *clients*. An agency thus can be a day care center, legal services, a crisis intervention hot line, a community mental health center, a planned parenthood clinic, and the like (human services). It can also mean the department of public health, the consumer information or protection center, the local library, the housing authority (government departments or units). Or it means a civic theater, a symphony orchestra, a city museum, and so on (the arts), or a national association of dental technicians, of city administrators, of language teachers (professional associations). "Clients," then, means the *beneficiaries* of the services of these agencies and their programs, who may be called residents, enrollees, members, target groups, patrons, or audiences. Our aim is to clarify and explain how the budget and fiscal processes are related to each other and to the primary service objectives of all such organizations. Thus we have chosen a step-by-step, how-to approach, wedded to real-life situations, because we believe this will best serve these purposes.

The text moves from the more simple or elementary procedures, as we see them, to the more complex and demanding. Whether cost control is more complicated than cost estimating, or whether preparing the budget application is less demanding than, say, setting user charges, may be debatable. Regardless of their comparative difficulties, however, we have tried to shape the presentation by leading the reader progressively from understanding each procedure, through acquiring some skill in its particular techniques, to applying each to problems that simulate actual situations. Information is developed gradually; the learning from one chapter serves as a foundation for later chapters; and technical details can be mastered in a orderly way.

We have combined discussion of general principles with illustrations of techniques for solving specific problems. The exercises we present are designed to reinforce understanding of those basic principles, and readers will participate in applying the currently acceptable procedures associated with them. To underscore the reality and representativeness of the information, we have developed an illustrative service program that faces and resolves—as best it can—the real-life problems with which we deal. Many other examples are interspersed throughout the text to show the wide applicability of the material.

Different readers will, or course, proceed at different paces, but we recommend that those with less experience work through the book chapter by chapter, including the exercises. Those more experienced will probably prefer to select particular chapters or parts of chapters for thorough study. We urge them, however, to scan for information and techniques new to them and to become completely familiar with the illustrative program, since the procedures and problems are framed in that context. The self-instruction format allows readers to advance as rapidly or slowly as needed, with options to study topics selectively. However, it should be even more rewarding to share the learning—especially the exercises—with a colleague. A colleague's different perspective can stimulate ideas about alternatives and tradcoffs and will help in testing the plausibility of solutions.

In the classroom the book may be used as a core text, as one of several texts, or as a supplement to other works. All or parts of the exercises may be used, or the basic procedures may be applied to the instructor's own case materials. For workshops, in-service training sessions, and other short courses, the contents will be used more selectively.

Whatever the mode of study, readers will find the book very useful for helping them solve problems on the job. They can review the chapters or sections that deal with the problem at hand and use the exercises to work through the appropriate procedures.

We should point out that in general we pay more attention to budgeting than to fiscal management, but we discuss in detail cost analysis methods relevant to both. Similarly, we focus far more on *expenditures* than on *revenues*. These emphases follow from our assessment of the kinds of problems agency administrators most frequently encounter and also of the availability or paucity of other literature. If equal emphasis were given to all these matters, this book would be twice as long or half as thorough.

Further, we have chosen to simplify the exposition of all basic procedures by treating them largely as applied to single-source funding on a single, annual cycle. The far more onerous demands of multisource funding on scrambled budget cycles can be dealt with only after mastering the basic procedures; once these have been learned, they can be applied directly to more complicated patterns.

This book is directed at *program managers*, not financial managers. A number of accounting guides have also been developed specifically for not-for-profit organizations, and some are cited in the text and the bibliography. We try never to violate accounting principles and have taken pains to point out their relevance and ways to integrate and cooperate with accounting departments to get additional information specifically important for program management.

Many readers may also want to learn more about "grantsmanship." We acknowledge its importance but consider it only obliquely related to this book, because we believe that basic budgeting skills ought to be developed *before* beginning efforts to locate and obtain funding.

Countless guides offer information about how to seek out and select potential sources from available resource pools, and how to approach them for funds. (Among the best of these is Virginia White's *Grants, Grants, Grants. . . .* [1975].) Others concentrate only on techniques for obtaining funds, and some of them briefly raise a few of the topics in this book. Still other guides concentrate only on particular steps in the process, such as proposal writing. (An excellent standard reference for both subjects is Mary Hall's *Developing Skill in Proposal Writing* [1977].) Typically, however, these guides stop at the point of submission of the funding application.

We believe an emphasis on tactics can be more misleading than not, and have several concerns about the risks unwittingly taken by persons or agencies who rely exclusively on narrow views of fund procurement. The requirements today for obtaining funds have risen dramatically since the 1960s and 1970s, the competition is much stiffer, and the perils of being misguided are far more severe.

We argue throughout the book that budgeting demands

attention to matters of genuine substance: program goals and designs; commitments to clients, staff, and community groups; and efficient, effective use of resources during program operations. Keen awareness of such matters, and others as well, is crucial *before* search and procurement efforts, while some competence in planning and conducting service programs is essential if the funds are to be properly and wisely spent. We do not believe it possible to prepare and submit a reasonable and acceptable funding proposal without looking and planning further ahead. In our view the receipt of a funding award is only the end of the beginning.

Budgeting for Not-for-Profit Organizations

1

A RATIONAL VIEW OF BUDGETING

ADMINISTRATORS IN not-for-profit organizations must struggle with the uncertainties that go hand in hand with dependence on economic conditions and public support. The need for funds is perennial, and drastic reductions in public funding force not-for-profit organizations into heroic efforts to survive. Even in good economic circumstances older programs face stiff competition from newer programs that may be addressing different needs or the same needs in more innovative ways. New programs, in competition from the established ones, have to prove they deserve a share of the money pie. As public policies change from time to time, funds are shifted to reflect new priorities. Thus, regardless of the total amount of public funds available, any given program faces an uncertain future.

In the past funders—including government units—were often bewildered by the barrage of requests for money: Problems and needs could be defined, but how could they tell which programs would do best at solving them? By now, however, funders have amassed plenty of experience, especially with social programs. They have learned that many programs prove unable to accomplish what is hoped for, expected, or sometimes promised. Funders are now more knowledgeable and selective, have higher expectations of demonstrable results, and set more rigorous standards for obtaining funds and accounting for them.

Most administrative staff in not-for-profit organizations, on the other hand, receive little or no formal training in financial matters. The occasional brief training workshop may increase rather than lessen their sense of frustration. In the good old days of the 1960s on-the-job learning by trial and error was perhaps possible; honest mistakes and innocent confusion were better tolerated. Now, however, administrators' responsibilities have become more complex, and organizations can ill afford the risks of on-the-job learning. Even if the organization has an excellent backup accounting staff, program managers are expected to show leadership and take responsibility for critical decisions about money (resources) and management. They are supposed to know what resources are needed, how to make the best use of them for achieving program objectives, and how to account for them.

Further, until recently acquiring and accounting for money were often viewed in the not-for-profit sector as unwelcome distractions from an organization's efforts at providing good services. External demands for more detail and accountability often seemed arbitrary, without rhyme or reason, and the logic behind them was rarely explained or understood. The demands came from different sources: governing boards, standard-setting bodies, concerned citizens' groups, and, of course, funders. Service providers today have come to recognize that accountability demands and procedures are here to stay and that they must comply with them.

We are convinced that there is a far more productive and advantageous way for service providers to view the whole accountability issue. The view we propose is the keystone of this book. Put simply, it is this:

- Dollars always represent resources.
- Resources are used to provide services to clients and to maintain the organization.
- The more the organization knows about where and how it uses its resources, the better service job it can do.
- The required procedures can usually be converted into vital information about resource consumption.

- Planning and decision-making for program services can be greatly enhanced by more accurate knowledge of resource use.

In sum, we are saying that the procedures associated with accountability can be valuable tools *for* the program manager and the organization; they can contribute to better program planning, allocation of resources, and delivery of services.

It is possible to pick up information about how to deal with nitty-gritty budget and reporting details—in fact, most reference and guideline materials deal largely with these aspects. But nowhere is it possible to learn, in a unified presentation, how resource planning, management, analysis, and overall program objectives and results are critically interdependent or to learn how to oversee successfully the real-life workings of this interdependence.

That is the purpose of this book. We have a few basic goals: to help administrative persons in not-for-profit organizations (1) understand how to think about the budgeting process as a tool for accomplishing program objectives; (2) learn how to use accountability requirements as vehicles for enhancing program operations; and (3) know how to tie together and apply key procedures of resource management for achieving major objectives.

The "state of the art" in financial management is developing rapidly—but unevenly—among states, communities, agencies, and professionals. It is not at all unusual to find some agencies using certain very sophisticated systems (with, for example, computerized processing of financial data and service statistics) while simultaneously relying on quite elementary cost analysis methods that have elsewhere been superseded by more advanced procedures. It is equally common to observe the sudden adoption of a new budgeting method by a governmental jurisdiction or a funder, which in turn requires prompt shifts at the recipient agencies. Zero base or performance budgeting, for example, may be suddenly adopted—usually in part—and it becomes necessary for all recipients to learn and apply the new method immediately. We believe that the chief elements of familiar procedures are incorporated in all the more recent approaches and that much of current knowledge and practice can be applied directly to the newer techniques. When one knows what constitute basic budget and cost facts and how to collect and assemble them, they can be organized and adapted to meet many different requirements. That is why we concentrate on fundamental principles and skills.

We focus on the most important processes in budget development, fiscal management, and cost analysis currently in general use in the not-for-profit sector. These processes involve planning, assigning, managing, and accounting for the resources needed for program operations. They impose on administrative personnel a number of repetitive tasks and involve established procedures that are always inextricably tied to program planning and management tasks. Planning programs means, in part, determining the amount of needed resources and acquiring them; carrying out program operations means using resources in deliberate ways to achieve program objectives; managing program operations refers, in part, to prudent and orderly ways of using whatever resources are available. Budgeting and financial management are thus always linked to programming, and throughout this book we try to clarify their interconnections.

The chapters in the book follow the progression of these processes before, during, and after the fiscal year. A more complete description of their contents is given at the end of Chapter 2. Here we shall briefly summarize the sequence of topics covered.

In Chapter 2 we review the ways that budgeting is carried out in contemporary agencies and programs: what it is, who does it, its interdependence with program planning, and how it fits into the annual fiscal cycle.

In Chapter 3 we detail the steps, tasks, and procedures associated with planning, estimating, developing, and submitting a complete, fully documented budget proposal. In Chapter 4 we introduce our illustrative service program and present the first set of exercises, here dealing with budget development and submission. In succeeding chapters we follow the same pattern: each set of exercises deals with the principal topics and procedures discussed in the preceding text.

In Chapters 5 and 6 we focus on prospectively allocating the budget resources among the planned program activities.

We discuss cost and responsibility centers, production and support centers, and explain the allocation process step by step.

Chapter 7 considers expense/revenue management procedures and problems and offers practical ways to obtain general fiscal information and to monitor and manage resources.

In Chapter 8 we go through the end-of-year cost analysis procedures, explaining input/throughput/output measures and service unit costing.

Chapter 9 traces out the steps involved in allocating and distributing a program's support costs among its production activities so that full service unit costs can be determined.

In Chapter 10 we review the entire year's program and fiscal experiences and relate them to planning for continuation budgeting. We explore the ramifications of generating additional revenues, including fees, charges, and purchase-of-service contracts, and the problems of decremental budgeting.

Because of the diversity of agencies, programs, practices, legal and fiduciary requirements, funders, and so on, we cannot hope to address all conceivable variations. But we have sought to reflect this diversity and extend the book's applicability in several important ways. First, the *principles* of conventional budget and financial practices are stressed as much as the training in their techniques. Therefore, the rationale of each major procedure is thoroughly detailed, along with its pragmatic application. Comprehension of the procedures in their fundamental terms is emphasized so that they can be effectively used under widely varying circumstances.

Second, we cite some of the more significant procedural variations in current use. Differences in these procedures are often more apparent than real and generally relate to specialized forms, terms, limitations, and the like. The basic reasoning, however, is almost invariably the same, and similar procedures are almost universally applied. Only the numbers and other details are really different.

Third, we use case problems and other materials—all carefully extracted or recomposed from contemporary situations—to show readers how the procedures are applied under varying conditions and how to recognize the underlying connections between all aspects of any program. We point out the opportunities as well as the requirements and pitfalls common to all.

We have chosen throughout to explain the mainly rational and pragmatic aspects of budgeting and fiscal management, though we recognize that other crucial dimensions and elements, such as the ethical, are quite legitimate objects for study. We also emphasize the many points at which choices must be made and illustrate the variety of factors involved in choosing one or another course, including personal values and agency commitments. Administrators must also be guided by good judgment and the legitimate interests of agencies, and—most important—dedicated to optimizing the transfer of program resources to the intended beneficiaries, the clients. These commitments represent a value orientation and may be seen as sources of bias in our writing. But we believe that values do and must play a part in budgeting and related tasks and that these necessarily involve dilemmas and conflicts. Nevertheless, contending values can benefit from rational examination and may then yield to modification and compromise.

Budgeting tasks are too commonly regarded as annoying exercises in applied arithmetic, with most of the real meaning squeezed out in favor of endless numbers. They seem loaded down with arbitrary rules and other formal trappings, including undecipherable documents. Many people working in the not-for-profit sector also believe that the "real" decisions are political, based on influence, connections, and behind-the-scenes maneuvers. The political aspects of governmental budgeting and the effects of power differences on the allocation of resources have been explored by Wildavsky (1974) and others. Those writers have successfully documented their arguments, and we have no quarrel with the validity of their findings. Yet none argues that *only* power and political maneuvering are sufficient to obtain funds, and none denies that numerous rational steps are also necessary. Even with the crassest exercise of political power—short of outright corruption—monies must still be counted, revenues and expenditures must be recorded and reported, and commitments must be honored or defaulted.

We strongly believe that what you do with the money is more important than how you get it. Because of this stance, it may sometimes seem to readers that we accept and approve all the rules, regulations, limitations, and so on imposed by funders and other external groups. We contend that these demands are a fact of life, that agencies generally have limited power to change them and therefore should learn to apply them constructively to serve their *own* interests and objectives.

Our pragmatic stance leads us to emphasize the *procedural* means by which values or ends can be pursued within the context of actual agency tasks and operations. Without confusing ends with means or substituting one for the other, we try to guide administrative personnel to practical ways of implementing their objectives. Rather than pleading any special arguments or theoretical schemes, we prefer to test and prove the adequacy of these procedures by the results they show. In given situations individuals will have different priorities and may wish to optimize different values and objectives. For that reason, we try to offer ways by which such differences can be identified and examined, as well as ways to scrutinize the connections between means—our procedures or others'—and these differing ends before choices are made.

The most obvious manifestation of the rationalistic view of fiscal duties in general is the attention we give to the calculational aspects of these tasks. Although all calculations taken together—however sophisticated or extended—cannot resolve the critical decisions that must be faced in the real world, without mastery of fundamental calculational skills one can neither perform the required procedures nor comprehend the results obtained by others assigned to perform them. Therefore, we approach the various kinds of calculational tasks in several related ways.

We draw attention to one of the most striking recent developments in the not-for-profit sector: the *quantification* of many elements of plans and operations, cases, services, staff activities, and so on. Information about resources and their consumption must now be given in quantified terms, and standard techniques have been established for ordering and reporting such data. To obtain the quantified information, *arithmetical* techniques must be applied for reports and for obtaining totals, averages, rates, ratios, and the like. All sorts of information must be analyzed using several calculational methods to clarify relationships, to explain implications, and to justify resource consumption. We begin to apply certain of these methods in Chapter 3 and continue to expand on them thereafter. The mathematical steps we use are no more difficult than long division, although the sequences of steps and their application to seemingly complex combinations of financial and other data may sometimes make them seem more difficult than they really are. *All* procedures can be handled by ordinary hand calculators or office machines, as they usually are in most small and medium-size organizations.

A few points should be emphasized about the illustrative service program whose budget and fiscal tasks and problems are faced and solved by readers in the exercise sections. For all readers, the most important fact about this agency is that it gives *service to clients*. Thus its budget, its functions, and its problems are readily translatable into terms pertinent to any not-for-profit agency giving any kind of service to any kind of clients. Particulars may differ among programs or agencies, but the budget categories and major items will be much the same for all. All agencies will have costs for personnel, fringe benefits, supplies, equipment, communication, and travel. A particular agency will have a few idiosyncratic categories, but that does not invalidate the universal applicability of the illustrative budget. Likewise, although agencies' services differ in name and content, they all exist to give something to some kind of client, hence their services are intrinsically the same as those of the illustrative program. So, for example, readers should have no difficulty translating its intake, referral, and counseling services into admissions, contraception counseling, and public information; into site inspections, institutional sanitation, and waste management; into testing, classroom instruction, and on-the-job training; into rehearsals, performances, and community education; or into drop-in activities, organized groups, and community outreach activities.

The series of exercise problems included in Chapters 4 through 9 are carefully constructed to help readers "learn by doing." Each set of exercise steps raises program, management, and budgeting issues, and readers cannot resolve one apart from or at the sacrifice of the others.

The steps are aimed at expanding the varied skills needed by present-day administrators. Therefore, in each chapter readers are asked to address some or all of the following:

- Calculations and analyses of fiscal data
- Judgments and choices for budgets and program activities
- Implications and consequences of decisions
- Interpretation and justification of decisions and choices
- Documentation of fiscal and other information in accord with standard practices
- Remedies to problems and proposals for changes

The exercises call for solutions in which the main procedures are applied to the illustrative program's activities and budget. The reader is cast in the role of a participating administrative staff member who must try to solve the problems with no more information than is typically available to such personnel. These problems reflect the uncertainties, the dilemmas, the assumptions, and the ambiguities of the real world. Desirable ways to approach sound solutions are addressed in each set of exercises. These solutions are intended as *examples* of well-reasoned—not unique—responses to problems. They try to optimize the possibilities, based on all the facts of the situation *as known*, which would include, in addition to the actual budget information, the objectives of the program, the rights and duties of staff, the community environment, and so on. Readers can thus explore with us the ramifications and cause-and-effect relationships involved in making the fiscal decisions.

Our observations of prevailing agency practices and our teaching experiences with the material in the book indicate that both the procedures and the calculational methods needed to implement them can be readily learned and applied. A few basic ideas must be understood or learned, but there are no abstract theories to contend with, no arcane techniques to be mastered. The subject matters directly pertain to those regularly addressed in the normal course of agency affairs. Readers who work their way through the materials should quickly become desensitized to apprehensions about either "complicated" materials or calculational techniques. At the very least, readers should never again feel intimidated by multicolumn, multiline fiscal data. At the very best, they will understand that paying attention to procedural and calculational matters makes even clearer the importance of making choices and exercising judgment when performing fiscal tasks.

2

BUDGETING PROCESSES

The Fiduciary Role

AT THE OUTSET we must distinguish the fiduciary role of an agency from the service programs it carries out. In all states it is the *agency*, as a corporate and legal body existing under relevant statutes, that must seek, obtain, expend, and account for funds to support its service programs. The support provided by outside sources—generally regardless of the form in which it is given—is allocated *to* the agency but *for* particular service programs. (Here we follow common practice and use the terms "services," "programs," and "service programs" interchangeably.) Programs rarely denote actual departments of agencies, but they may often represent important operating components within them. The agency itself, often referred to as the "parent" agency (or organization), remains wholly accountable for all funds, as well as for the overall management of its service programs.

People, sometimes confused about these distinctions, think that the service programs themselves receive funds directly from outside sources and are then accountable for them. Managers of programs are, of course, accountable to their agency superiors, but programs are not, as such, incorporated under state laws. They cannot independently

11

receive and spend money; they are not employers of record; they do not report directly to taxing authorities; and so on. Agencies do serve in all these capacities and therefore must be chartered under state laws, must obtain status corresponding to certain federal provisions (especially those pertaining to tax exemption), and must remain fully responsible for all financial and other activities performed for or by their service components. The implications of such considerations will become further apparent at various points throughout the book.

The pattern may seem to vary in some situations. When the service programs are themselves actual operating units of government, especially at the local or municipal level, and the funds they receive are allocated from local revenues by municipal legislative processes, then the agency and the program *appear* to be one and the same. But even here we must recognize that municipal departments are generally only operating components of a city government, and it is the city government, not the department, that serves as the legal and fiduciary entity and performs all the parent agency functions.

We also find many service programs that are supported by funds from two or more independent sources. Since outside support is almost always provided for *particular* services or clients, when two or more fund awards are made, they are typically designated for only parts of a program or for some of its clients. In this case the program, itself a unit within a larger organization, comprises two or more subprograms, each drawing support from separate accounts for specific or limited purposes. These situations involve what is known as *multisource funding*, and perhaps even *scrambled budget cycles*, both of which are largely outside the scope of this book. But the basic principle remains the same: The *agency*—not the program—is the fiduciary entity to which the funds are awarded and it is responsible for them.

In still another situation we find very small agencies that offer one service and receive all their support from a single source, perhaps a community fund or foundation. Only in these conditions are the agency and the program one and the same. However, once the agency moves to obtain supplemental funds from a second source for additional services the distinction applies. The agency becomes the fiduciary and administrative entity, and both parts of its operations become the service programs.

What Is Budgeting?

Total budgeting, as we view it throughout the book, comprises at least seven major processes: planning, estimating, managing and coordinating, assessing, reporting and accounting, and projecting.[1] Each process is bound up with the others, has significant time perspectives, and involves a variety of procedures that, together, produce a distinctive process for each.

Planning and estimating are essential for defining and specifying *all* the resources the organization needs to carry out both its general and its concrete objectives over a particular time period. The budget documents express these resource requirements, as determined by the planning and estimating processes, in specific dollar amounts for specific activities for a specific time period.

Managing and coordinating are essential for ensuring that the plans, as expressed in the budget documents, are being carried out. These processes go on over the entire fiscal period.

Assessing and reporting/accounting are essential for retrospective understanding of the *actual* uses of the resources. Projecting is necessary for developing future plans based on the retrospective information.

Together, these budgeting processes enable the organization to determine the resource needs for each aspect of its program objectives; to think through and adjust each to the others; to reassemble the parts into a rational, well-thought-out whole; to maintain control over the use of the resources; and to know and be able to explain how the resources were actually consumed. Thus every objective the organization expects to accomplish and every resource it needs and uses

---

[1] It must be clearly understood that in our context the terms used to define these areas (planning, etc.) refer almost entirely to activities involving *resources*. They should not be confused with similar terminology used to describe other administrative activities (personnel management, client relations, and so on).

to meet its objectives are tied together and expressed through the budgeting processes.

With these definitions in mind, we shall first establish the connections between budgeting and programming. Second, we shall describe the tasks, responsibilities, and participants associated with carrying out budgeting processes and suggest more fruitful ways to handle these tasks. Third, we shall examine the basic yearly cycle of activities within which the budgeting processes revolve and around which the following chapters are structured.

Budgeting and Programming

THE CONVENTIONAL VIEW:
DISJUNCTURES AND PERCEIVED DIFFERENCES

For a variety of reasons, budgeting and programming activities have become separated in contemporary agencies. As a result it is widely believed that they represent different lines of effort that are often competing and frequently antithetical. The following conditions exemplify some important reasons for these unfortunate consequences:

- Divisions of labor and structure within agencies result in separate units, with different personnel working in either one or the other area, having limited interchange and understanding little of each other's work and its significance.

- The specialization in background, experience, and particularly in training of professional personnel in the respective areas that underscores these divisions. For example, in many human service agencies the accounting and service staff pursue different, established career lines.

- Differences in the daily routines, tasks, problems, and so on tend to segregate staff assigned to program services from those assigned to fiscal duties. The *things* these groups work on and think about seem quite different, and their terminology and rhetoric have often been mutually unintelligible. Program personnel focus on interactions with clients, fiscal personnel focus on numbers—but both must contend with endless forms!

Other conditions also heighten and help to exaggerate these perceptions of dissonance:

- Mounting retrenchment pressures result in declining and still more precarious support for service programs. These harsh realities pervade the climates of all agencies, and segmented staff groups are pressed toward more severe choices and actions, which are often interpreted as confirmations of existing mutual suspicions. Thus, protagonists of supposedly competing areas come to see themselves and each other in more extreme terms: as "realists" or "people who care," as "hatchetmen" or "victims." Such views are further exaggerated when political discourse at the national level seems to pit fiscal "responsibility" against service programs.

- Higher-level administrators, too, are frequently sequestered and communicate little to subordinates; they sometimes even stress the differences between staff groups.

Understandably, then, members of each staff group develop strong *perceptions* about dissonances in meaning between their work and that of the other group. Notions easily crystallize about the radical, if not antithetical, differences in their respective jobs.

THE CONTRASTING VIEW:
ALLOYS OF THE SAME COIN

We assert that both budgeting and programming, and thus both fiscal and program management, are alloys of a single coin and that the decisions and actions that characterize each parallel and complement those of the other. Despite the conditions and perceptions just described, the following arguments support our view:

- Budgeting and programming are always joined at the upper and highest levels of authority (director, executive staff, board).

- All major and many less important budget or program decisions unify or reconcile choices about *which* programs will receive *what* resources, thus bringing about compromises among competing demands and priorities and channeling scarce resources accordingly.

- Every decision of consequence for either budget or program typically has comparable import for the other.

- Many of the newer budgeting approaches actually combine budget and program matters: In functional budgeting and in performance and zero base budgeting, the forms, projections, decisions, and reports link or fuse them so they cannot be disentangled.

- These interconnections are facilitated by modern information systems that enable the rapid *merging* of data and permit syntheses between estimates, analyses, and reports pertaining to both areas.

In a highly bureaucratized and professionalized society it is far easier to separate otherwise relatable lines of work than to integrate them, so that separation is more likely to occur. We believe there is a kind of compelling validity, which experienced managers and administrators understand, in arguing that *every* major budget or program decision has import for the other and that it is perilous to ignore this reality. Why and how this is so, and how the two sides can be better integrated are matters that now deserve our attention.

TIME PERSPECTIVES

In the simplest terms, budgeting and program planning are distinctly *prospective* activities, undertaken *prior* to a fiscal and program year; whereas financial management and program management distinctly go on *throughout* the year. In temporal terms, at least, both kinds of activities parallel each other, adopt the same time frames, and adhere to the same fiscal year.

The neat distinction between prior planning and ongoing

management is necessarily arbitrary. Planning seldom ends with the start of the fiscal year; unexpected developments usually force the recasting or updating of earlier programs, plans, and budgets. When adjustments must be made in either area, we may regard them as management actions taken to accommodate unfolding experiences (changes in case volume or in market costs, for example). But when crises occur in either area, the extensive replanning required cannot be regarded merely as ongoing management. For this reason, some agencies have developed "rolling budgets" (Anthony, 1974) by which they periodically recast and update all forward fiscal and program projections. These procedures may well require almost as much effort as was initially invested in budget and program planning, making it readily apparent that planning is not restricted to a time prior to the fiscal year.

Program planning must precede budgeting in at least one respect: It is impossible to develop an adequately detailed budget without a documented program design or plan. Until the main aspects, the scope, and the volume of the program have been defined—at least within reasonable ranges—resource requirements cannot be estimated. However, two variations on this chicken-and-egg situation are often found in real life. One occurs when a budget ceiling is established before program plans have been completed, and a concrete program has to be planned within this ceiling. The other—far more common—occurs when those responsible for budgeting find large gaps in the program plans and must fall back on rough estimates for such portions of the budget. Let us consider some examples of both situations.

When federal and state funders send out Request for Proposal (RFP) announcements, they frequently declare a ceiling for each award.[2] This also happens when a legislature authorizes the support of new programs in locales where none exist, and the funding agency can decide on a formula for distributing these funds. Agencies are encouraged to develop their own program plans within general guidelines,

---

[2]To avoid confusion, we use "award" generically to denote any authorization of resources from a funder. Terminology varies (e.g. from government-to-department allocations to purchase-of-service contracts), but the federal government now uses the term "award," and specific terms are not at issue here.

but the maximum, and sometimes the minimum, levels of financial support will already have been set.[3]

More often, however, the planning problem lies within the agency. During the budgeting process, for example, elements of the program plan are found to have been overlooked or inadequately specified. In such cases cost estimating can proceed only by using rough "ball park" figures, and then with great risk. Of course, discovery of these gaps can bring about a recasting of program plans, and then the two efforts can continue in tandem far more efficiently.

PARALLELS AND AFFINITIES

Operations represent the main production processes of service programs and consist of the staff activity and patterns through which service (production) objectives are achieved. These processes are as diverse as making adoption placements, delivering home nursing care, providing job counseling, providing residential care, carrying on a summer baseball schedule, sustaining a professional organization, or giving legal services. Staff who carry out these program activities are the main-line operatives. Except in the smallest agencies, their roles are different from those of the support and administrative staff.

The activities and roles of staff must be distinguished from the *planning* and *managing* of the program operations. Within agencies the systems of program planning and management and of budgeting and fiscal management focus on *resources* and their *utilization* to support activities that achieve program objectives. In larger agencies and in state and local governments, personnel and responsibilities for these systems may be assigned to two different "structures," one that organizes and controls program operations (through the establishment of program units) and one that organizes and controls fiscal activities (through the establishment of "responsibility centers"). The prevail-

---

[3]Political or other criteria often determine these formulas and funding ranges, and the results may have little to do with rational program criteria.

ing separation of these two lines of managerial activities increases disjunctures and hinders coordination. We believe that important bases exist on which to improve coordination and cooperation between the two "structures." Thus it is our intent to help persons who perform administrative tasks better understand the nature of the relations between programming and budgeting, so they can perform their tasks in ways that are beneficial to both areas—and thus enhance program accomplishments.

Despite the obvious differences in things the two administrative groups *do* each day (maintain ledgers versus confer about client waiting lists), the *decisions* they must make reflect important commonalities and affinities. First, the logic and reasons behind the decisions are increasingly parallel. Second, much of each group's work addresses the same basic issues, and both talk about many of the same matters or problems, which mainly have to do with resource deployment and conservation for a given program. Third, the language used by each is becoming increasingly the same, with growing reliance on *quantification*, although the fiscal area is currently stronger in this regard.

Until recently program planning was not systematically analyzed or written about and lacked general conventions to guide either the process or the documentation of plans. However, there is some evidence that at least the documents, if not the processes for their preparation, are now becoming more orderly, more rational, and more standardized. Many funders now require standard outlines for explaining program plans, and most of the forms ask for basically similar information despite superficial differences. These mandatory outlines stimulate, or even necessitate, certain steps in prior reasoning and preparation, as well as in documentation. A variety of guides are now available to assist planners in preparing such outlines.

As part of the same mandatory outlines and guides, government funding agencies and several national associations (e.g. United Way of America, Child Welfare League of America) have also developed uniform definitions and measures for various elements of program plans, just as they had done earlier for budgeting. Thus, definitions of cases, staff full-time equivalents (FTEs), child care days, contact hours, and various other measures of efforts have gained wide currency. These new terms have shaped the thinking of program planners and have also affected the kinds of documentation required. The introduction of codified, quantitative elements into program planning has a significance beyond the movement toward uniformity; most of these standardized terms have direct equivalents in budgeting and are thus powerful means for fostering parallel decisionmaking and collaboration.

RECIPROCAL RELATIONS

Along with the parallel decisions and activities, each area interacts with the other, and decisions that determine principal elements for one also define boundaries for the other. Thus, when the *kind* and *scope* of a program are determined, the main budget costs are at least outlined, and a floor and a ceiling for the total budget may also be defined. Similarly, when a budget total is determined *a priori* or subtotals are set for major object costs (e.g. personnel), this directly influences—if only by restrictions—the kinds and scope of the services. Reciprocity occurs in these conditions, because resources (kinds and levels) are at issue in either set of decisions and because resources are crucial to both.

Next, each major decision made in either area tends to have compelling consequences for the other. A decision to change the scale of a program or to alter significantly its main activities directly affects the budget. Conversely, as everyone can understand, a decision to reduce the budget total or funds allocated to certain items directly affects program plans or operations. It cannot be the same service program if its budget is cut in half or if it must function with a decrease in its primary personnel.

Reciprocity not only occurs during the planning stages but remains a critical factor during the whole fiscal period. In fact, one could say that good operational management, from both the budget and the program views, results from mutual understanding of the interplay between program and budget decisions. Naturally, each area will sometimes have to make concessions. For example, the fiscal manager may at some time during the year inform the program manager that one or more services is headed for financial trouble. Depending on the relationship, the fiscal manager may or may not recommend alternative solutions, and the program manager may or may not be guided by those recommendations. In a well-run agency, however, the problems will be discussed back and forth in an attempt to reach mutually satisfactory solutions. Neither area can operate independently, even though one may occasionally be able to impose its will on the other. Who has the final word is often less important than the occurrence and quality of the dialogue itself.

Changes in *procedures* or methods in either area will have direct effect on the other. For example, in performance and zero base budgeting, the use of workload indicators and cost analyses focused on staff activities will have important implications for both areas. Introducing (or imposing) more efficient operational procedures or new productivity standards will have direct implications for both, regardless of how or why they came about. Either change alters the ratios of resource consumption to outputs, and the ramifications of such changes will affect persons, activities, things, and costs. In performance and zero base budgeting, which use both workload indicators and output measures, the different reporting and analysis experiences will alter both accounting and program practices.

Finally, the lack of reciprocity can have serious consequences for the *cumulative* results of program activities, especially as agencies shift toward contract funding. A program with highly successful service results may not secure continued funding if its budget was overspent because of slipshod accounting practices. Excellent use of resources does not equal excellent accounting. Again, a program with meticulous spending and accounting may not be re-funded if it does not achieve its primary service objectives. The way resources are consumed may not always be the main issue; program ineffectiveness can be due to many other factors, including faulty program design or ineffectual implementation of services.

Who Does Budgeting?

We have asserted earlier that a wide assortment of professional positions are involved in some way, at some level, in the budgeting and management processes. Almost every professional (and board member in a private agency) is likely to be engaged in them at some time.

However, only the top person in the administrative position (whatever the title) has special formal authority over fiscal matters, including budgets. We know of no exceptions to the rule that senior officials must "sign off" before budgets, financial reports, and similar documents can be confirmed internally or communicated outside the agency or governmental unit. Therefore, regardless of the organization's size or the chief administrator's title, that person assumes ultimate fiscal responsibility. We realize that this authority may often be only nominally exercised, with other staff making most of the actual decisions and certifying the final documents for official signature. But experienced executives know it can be perilous—for themselves and their organizations—not to scrutinize everything they sign. We also recognize that in most private agencies the executive submits financial materials for review and final action to a board of directors, which may or may not actively participate in developing them, and that for governmental units the review and final action move up the hierarchy.

The size of an organization and the degrees of specialization within it perhaps account for some of the main differences in how these tasks are assigned and performed. Thus, as has already been discussed, medium to large agencies are very likely to have accounting sections that usually play an important part in these tasks, far beyond that played by bookkeepers in smaller organizations. However, wide variations also exist among agencies of the same size, as well as among those providing the same kinds of services. These variations are found even among district and local offices within the same centralized state agency, where local administrators are apt to engage in or assign budgeting and fiscal management responsibilities differently. We have closely observed a variety of agencies and have received reports about many others, and we can neither explain these differences nor offer more than general suggestions for ways to integrate the basic processes more efficiently and effectively. These realities underlie our deliberate aim of directing this book toward persons in all kinds of roles in the organization, because we are convinced that sooner or later, just about all agency personnel will find themselves involved in these activities.

It may be helpful to sketch out some of the main patterns we have noted and to comment briefly on each. First, in centralized organizations the top administrator and selected assistants or deputies sometimes perform all the main budgeting tasks except for "keeping the books" and may also be very active in fiscal management. This pattern may be highly efficient, assuming they have both the expertise and the time to handle these duties along with other responsibilities. But it tends to exclude others—program managers, for example—from key phases of the processes to which they could make valuable contributions, and it deprives these others of information that could have critical bearing on primary program activities.

A second pattern illustrates an opposite administrative style and is often found in small agencies: The executive recruits almost everyone to assist during critical "budget times." Some may handle cost estimation, others may write program descriptions, and still others may do many of the calculations, allocations by functions, and so forth. A similar pattern can sometimes be found in larger organizations that have a deliberate policy of involving many staff members in budgeting and fiscal management. Here, however, the pattern of participation is likely to show a more careful use of staff abilities and special knowledge of agency operations. In either case, new "in-house" expertise may emerge as individual staff members develop and perhaps demonstrate unusual abilities in some phases of budgeting. They may then be increasingly assigned to fiscal duties, which can eventually lead to special assignments or promotions.

Elsewhere, agency or program heads put together *ad hoc* work groups; members are drawn from various parts of the organization, and each is assigned to different parts of planning and development. This mode is often common in times of crisis, but in some organizations it becomes an annual routine. This pattern, with its temporary and shifting composition of work groups, impedes the retention and buildup of shared expertise.

Finally, in some agencies outside people are recruited or hired for budgeting and other fiscal duties. Agencies of various sizes under private auspices often call on selected board members for guidance or help and may deliberately recruit board members with accounting, management, or business experience. These and other agencies may also contract for accounting firms, budgeting consultants, or fundraising experts to handle some of these tasks.

Our basic stance toward budgeting and program planning argues in favor of approaches that seek broad within-agency participation in all these processes. We have several aims in mind: the enhancement of services by unifying program and fiscal perspectives and management, the development of staff knowledge and skill in both areas, and the improved quality of decisions from more open and collaborative administrative patterns. The fundamental interests of agencies are ill served when administrators make no attempt to upgrade the budgeting competencies of their professional personnel, given their lack of systematic training in these areas.

The Fiscal Year

All programming and budgeting processes are tied to an annual time frame or cycle that parallels the rhythm of governmental appropriations and funding, on which many are heavily dependent. The annual cycle has become so well institutionalized that all agencies, regardless of sponsorship, typically base their forward, current, and retrospective operations on some form of the yearly pattern.

An extended series of stages and steps customarily occurs over the course of the program and fiscal year: Plans and decisions are completed; operations are carried out; and reviews, reports, and audits follow. These recurring sequences of activities are necessary to procure financial resources, to expend them in support of program objectives, and to account for their use. The repetitive cycle does not always coincide with the calendar year (the *federal* fiscal year runs from October 1 through September 30), but the basic program and fiscal period is almost always twelve months long and is referred to as the Fiscal Year (FY). Particular projects within agencies may sometimes last for shorter or longer periods, but they too conform to the basic fiscal year pattern. In contemporary society most organizations and businesses—including the profit sector, unions, and the IRS—carry out, or at least think about, their affairs and transactions in similar annual terms.

The fiscal year serves additional useful purposes. First, since the national and most state governments operate on an annual cycle, revenue-generating enactments and fund appropriations generally follow a similar schedule. Second, the regularity and frequency of appropriation processes presumably allow the legislative and executive branches to exercise their policymaking authority through annual budgeting, which can be attuned to changing conditions, priorities, and interests.

Third, the budgeting, appropriation, and allocation processes occur before the fact, and later review is necessary to determine how funds were actually spent. This oversight and control authority is strengthened when both revenues and expenditures must be accounted for on a regular yearly basis. Units of government are subject to a tighter rein when they must report annually about how they allocated and used their funds. Annual accounting has been institutionalized across the nation for *all* organizations and for other entities empowered to act as fiduciaries under federal and state laws.

The annual cycle, therefore, establishes a powerful, universal rhythm for the *policymaking, control,* and *accounting* functions. For both public and private service organizations a year is generally taken as the basic time span for mandating new or continuing programs, for regularly formulating and reviewing policies, and for accounting for the receipt and expenditure of resources. Synchronization is achieved through the annual cycle: The organization's internal activities are meshed with the *schedule* of external legal and fiscal requirements.

In these conditions a strong connection exists—or should exist—between program and fiscal endeavors. The annual tempo of continuation funding (that is, yearly reapplication for outside support) forces agencies to reconsider their program operations at regular intervals. As cost containment and retrenchment pressures increase, the yearly cycle structures efforts to absorb cuts, to improve the quality of results, and to compete for future fiscal support. For all agencies, in all circumstances, therefore, the annual cycle affects program planning, operations, and replanning.

Some administrators overlook the usefulness of the interlocked review, reporting, and reapplication tasks. Such periodic responsibilities keep the organization attuned to various external events and to situations that might otherwise be slighted or ignored. They help assure accountability, thus underscoring the public character of the organization; further, an annual renewal legitimizes and justifies the organization's practices and accomplishments. Burdensome as they may be, the yearly obligations serve to reassert the needs of the organization's constituencies and the support of its efforts by the broader public.

An inevitable *a*synchronization can occur when projects or programs span more or less than the twelve-month period or when the agency's yearly calendar does not coincide with that of its funders. Such problems are exacerbated when an agency receives funds from two or more sources that do not have identical annual cycles. Then budget cycle tasks must be scheduled to fit the different funding cycles.

The Budget Cycle

The *full* series of activities associated with the program/fiscal year must occur over a much longer period: Some must be carried out well before the start of the actual fiscal year, others occur during it, and still others after the year is over. We refer to this extended sequence as the *budget cycle.* Complete budget cycle activities overlap more than one year, but all are critically related to the operations of a single program/fiscal year. The concrete steps that constitute a given agency's actual budget cycle vary in keeping with its structure, service programs, traditions, and so on, as well as in response to the requirements of the funding sources. The cycle's features, however, are very similar among agencies and typically include the following essential activities:

Program and budget planning
Needs assessment and feasibility study
Program planning
Cost estimating
Budget development

Funds procurement
  Budget request submission
  Negotiation with funder
  Rebudgeting and resubmission
  Award and acceptance

Fiscal management
  Designation of cost and responsibility centers
  Internal funds allocation and rebudgeting
  Establishment of restricted accounts
  Financial transactions, recording, and accounting
  Operations monitoring and reporting
  Cost control and containment

Performance assessment, financial reports, audits
  End-of-year (EOY) financial statements
  Financial audit
  Performance audit
  Cost analysis

Recycle
  Program replanning
  Continuation budgeting
  Cost-finding and rate-setting

THE BUDGET CALENDAR

It should be abundantly clear by now that agencies need to set up *calendars* for scheduling dates and time frames for preparing, reviewing, deciding, and submitting the detailed materials required for all the tasks on the budget cycle list. The calendar should specify due dates for beginning and completing each task and should also indicate to which persons which tasks are assigned. A single person may be given primary responsibility for particular activities, but the collaboration and help of other staff will undoubtedly be needed. Everyone's assignments should be specified and scheduled in the calendar.

The basic agency or program/fiscal year dates, not the program's operational dates, should determine the calendar. Budgeting steps are tied to the fiscal year, while program operations may follow quite a different annual rhythm, perhaps adjusted to seasons (e.g. educational or recreational programs, musical or theatrical events). But the fiscal year is usually defined by the funding body, which commonly follows either the calendar year (January 1 to December 31) or the federal cycle (October 1 to September 30). A budget calendar should be developed for each *program* in an agency for which an account must be designated since a program's FY may well differ from the agency's own FY.

The Book Format and the Budget Cycle

Because the budget cycle activities occur so universally in the not-for-profit sector, we have organized the central chapters in this book around the comprehensive sets of procedures needed at key points during the extended cycle. We present the sets of procedures most fundamental to contemporary agencies and most frequently mandated by funders. The chronology of the basic cycle itself provides a rational order for the presentation and application of these procedures. We start, then, more or less at the beginning of the budgeting process—*before* the start of an actual fiscal year but *after* a program's conception and initial planning—and move through the procedures as they must be successively employed.

The many stages and steps listed above can be collapsed into three general phases, each with a distinctive time perspective: *preparation, execution,* and *assessment.*[4] The correspondence between these phases and the budget cycle list should be obvious. Policymaking is especially critical in the preparation phase, control in the execution phase, and accountability in the assessment phase. Although each phase is characterized by a dominant function or set of activities, the tasks are not restricted to single phases. In fact, elements of all phases recur *throughout* every cycle.

Program planning, budgeting, and negotiations with funders are the primary activities in the preparation phase, and the time perspective is largely *prospective* or forward.

---

[4] Lee and Johnson (1983) offer four categories—preparation, approval, execution, and audit—which include most, but not all, of the essential activities on our budget cycle list.

Service objectives and plans must be developed, and the needed resources must be concretely identified. Because these endeavors usually occur long before the service activities begin—sometimes up to eighteen months ahead—the main budgeting procedures consist of estimating the costs of these future activities. As we shall see, obtaining reliable estimates of future market costs in times of cost volatility presents many difficulties. But the more profound uncertainties and risks in estimating future costs stem from indeterminant program plans and from trying to predict behaviors and events related to service delivery. Along with preparing plans and estimates, the organization and the funding sources must interact and integrate the planning with changing expectations, requirements, funding levels, and the like. The preparation phase concludes with the submission of a final program and budget proposal acceptable to the funder, followed, it is to be hoped, by an award of funds to conduct the projected program.

In Chapter 3 we focus on concrete steps, for both new and ongoing programs, in developing plans, estimating costs, and documenting proposed budgets. (Appendix C details some of the specific personnel measures underlying these basic budgeting procedures.) In Chapter 5 we examine a major additional planning and budgeting task increasingly imposed by funders: allocating awarded funds according to the expected service *functions* of the program. In Chapters 3 through 6 we are still concentrating on the future, since program operations have not yet begun. The final tasks are increasingly important, because more often than not funds are awarded at different—usually lower—levels from those requested, which necessitates important program and budget modifications. These readjustment steps should properly be considered part of the preparatory phase.

The second main phase, execution, occurs as service operations are actually carried out and funds are spent. This phase starts and ends with the fiscal year (or project period), because expenditures can be made only within the dates specified in the fund award. The time perspective is thus largely *current*, focusing on immediate and balance-of-the-year activities. The chief tasks include fiscal and program management, oversight of actual operations, and financial transactions. Almost all fund awards are *contractual*, so management is concerned primarily with maintaining activities and expending funds in conformity with the terms of the award or contract. During this phase efforts are concentrated on overseeing and recording both program and expenditure actions and decisions. The future intrudes into this phase as program managers must continually estimate year-end balances and anticipate possible audit problems. Increasingly, as financial support has eroded in the not-for-profit sector, agencies must engage in cost containment and retrenchment, which means a struggle to absorb reductions, offset escalating costs, and remain within budgeted totals. In Chapter 7 we deal with the more significant procedures and problems in fiscal management: controllable and uncontrollable costs, recordkeeping systems, and some common problems in monitoring expenses. Simple yet comprehensive ways of projecting future expenditures are described in detail, and parallel revenue issues are also included.

The third main phase of the budget cycle is assessment. This nominally begins the day after the end of the fiscal year and lasts until final accounting and auditing obligations have been met. The time perspective is *retrospective,* as the focus is on past endeavors, completed financial transactions ("historical data"), and program results. Primary tasks include preparing and submitting summary financial and program reports in accord with award agreements or accounting conventions, *and* cooperating in an outside audit if this becomes necessary. Because, under various state and federal regulations, outside audits may be conducted at any time over a period of years, this phase may be extended almost indefinitely. In Chapters 8 and 9 we concentrate on retrospective cost analyses, service unit costing, and distribution of support costs. We present lists of typical initial and final reporting and accountability requirements in Appendix A.

The agency is as concerned as the funder in drawing on cumulative and recent information—financial, programmatic, and other—as bases for its forward planning. For such planning, procedures must be developed for rapid reporting and analysis of current and balance-of-the-year data of all kinds. It would be erroneous, however, to believe that such reporting and analysis during a given fiscal year are useful only for planning directed at the next year. Most agencies recognize the value of prompt, systematic cost and program analyses for optimizing *current* operations, for updating balance-of-the-year plans, and for long-range forecasts. The cost analysis procedures dealt with in Chapters 8 and 9 are framed and applied with both purposes in mind. The retrospective analysis thus leads directly to the steps appropriate for developing continuation program and budget plans.

Programs usually continue over several cycles and carry on repetitive processes despite periodic changes, as distinguished from projects that typically have a one-time-only existence. Whenever a program extends over two or more fiscal years, the agency must deal with the special issues of overlapping cycles and must engage in additional procedures, which deserve examination. The necessity to plan for and seek continuation funding beyond a current fiscal year compels the agency to begin preparatory work on the next year's program and budget proposals while in the midst of executing current operations. Overlaps involving several calendar years are portrayed in Figure 2–1.

The whole issue of continuation budgeting is examined in Chapter 10. All the material in prior chapters is related to contemporary and emerging approaches—for example, cost containment, rates, fees, and charges. We include also the

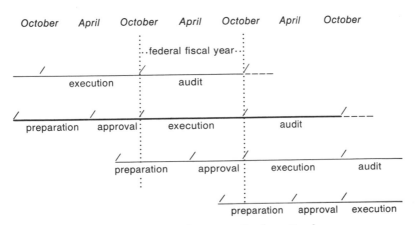

Figure 2–1.   Overlapping Budget Cycles

Modified from Robert D. Lee, Jr., and Ronald W. Johnson, *Public Budgeting Systems*, 3d ed. (Baltimore: University Park Press, 1983), p. 60.

various problems and effects of retrenchment as the budget cycle completes one turn and begins another.

The very nature of the not-for-profit sector makes it certain that new ways will be sought to systematize, define, and analyze an organization's activities and achievements, as well as its cost requirements. Because we do not yet know—and may never know—how to compute the exact value of the delivery and benefit of such services, as we can with the manufacture and sale of hammers and nails, we must expect and be prepared for ever changing procedures and requirements in the quest for more precise information.

3

BUDGET DEVELOPMENT AND SUBMISSION

THE SPECIFIC STEPS TAKEN by agencies as they plan, prepare, and submit program and budget applications for funder review have endless variations, but the fundamental processes and tasks are much the same no matter what differences exist among agencies, funders, and programs. The greatest difference in planning and preparations occurs between new and continuing programs. With continuing programs, the agency already has experience, information, and established practices and arrangements, all of which are directly relevant to succeeding preparations. For new programs, however, all work must proceed from the ground up. Comprehensive budgeting is the term sometimes used to refer to such preparations, because *every* feature of the proposed program and budget must be carefully planned, explained, and costed.

Planning a budget for a new program and approaching a new funder probably offer the best insights into the tasks and issues of budget development. But to use such an example throughout this chapter would complicate the discussion. Therefore, we try here to achieve a balance so that the presentation of the main procedures in budget development and the methods for applying them are useful and pertinent for both new and continuing programs. We do, however, attend to some of the special budget development problems for a new program in the exercises in Chapter 4.

Four separate sets of matters must be addressed and eventually coordinated in working up a budget.

1. The kinds and levels of resources required to continue an ongoing program or to implement a program plan
2. The mandates, requirements, and prohibitions imposed on program plans and budget development by parent agencies, funders, and statutory enactments and regulations
3. The conventions, classifications, and standardized terms by which each resource is generally denoted, and the types of market cost information that must be obtained and presented about each
4. The series of steps and procedures needed for thinking through all these matters, assembling necessary information, and gradually formulating (and eventually submitting) the budget proposals and materials

Our presentation would be immeasurably simpler if we could deal with each of these matters in turn, explaining the principal elements of each and their relevance to budget development, then passing on to the next. Each topic does have its own terms of reference, but each becomes tightly intertwined with the others in the actual process of planning a budget, and the particular ways they impinge on each other are of overriding importance for the task before us.

Perhaps our problem can be illustrated by analogy. Suppose you have accepted an assignment from a small committee to draft a report for submission by the group to a large number of people who will be attending a conference. To prepare the report you must gather together several sets of materials for review: reference works from the library, a newspaper backfile, documents previously issued by the committee, the conference agenda and outline for reports, and some special information you yourself have developed for inclusion. You might prefer to go over the outline guide and then to place the materials on your work table one set at a time. You review and take notes on each set before proceeding to the next, until you have gone over everything and are ready to start writing. You might even attempt to put the report together in this sequential fashion. If the subject is at all complex, however, you are likely to find yourself moving back and forth between the source materials, drafting parts of sections, relocating certain items for more careful review, seeking advice from others on the committee, and perhaps contacting the conference planners for clarification of their expectations. Your work is likely to move in some circular manner, with approximations and starts and stops as you gradually absorb the facts and begin to shape ideas that allow you to start writing a text that can be finally put together as a draft report for the committee.

This is more or less the way budget development typically proceeds for agencies and their staffs. Aspects of the several sets of matters cannot be fully understood or encompassed all at once and must be returned to—probably more than once—in the course of the work.

For these reasons we have chosen to present only selected elements in each set of the topics in a sequential order, returning to address still other aspects or to delve more deeply into some topics, very much in the way such work unfolds in agencies. And to ease the reading of this material, some of the more technical facets have been put into appendixes for reference.

Determining Resource Needs

Cost estimating is a term used to refer to so many steps in budget development that it can be misleading. We prefer to restrict it to only those steps involving actual *dollar* estimates. The final budget to be submitted must, indeed, present dollar figures for each major type of resource and for all of them added together (the "bottom line"). But before we can arrive at these detailed and concrete figures, three questions must be definitively answered:

- *What* resources are needed for this program?
- What *levels* of each resource are needed?
- What will each unit or total of each resource actually *cost?*

These questions are deceptively simple, but at least they offer a guide for the *order* of steps we must take. It is pointless to ask how much a particular resource will cost until we have decided that the program actually requires it and how many units are needed. Are one or two program aides needed? How much office space must be obtained? How many miles of local travel will staff need to perform their out-of-office duties? What specialized things does *this* program require that are not consumed in other kinds of programs? And so on.

Before addressing the factors that bear on resolution of these questions, and methodical ways of generating answers to them, it may help to note the existence of certain universal resource relations among service programs that affect budget planning. These relations are intuitively grasped by most persons in these organizations, and when deliberately recognized they can offer efficient modes of problem solving. Almost all service programs rely primarily on *personnel* with various kinds of competencies and other desired characteristics; and they will receive *employee benefits* of various kinds, and be subject to *payroll taxes*. Personnel require some kinds of *space* or physical facilities where they can carry out program operations, which invariably entails furnishings and utilities to make the space usable. Personnel also consume a variety of *materials* while performing their duties, which are also sometimes used by or given to the clients or beneficiaries of the program. This calls for supplies and the other wherewithal customarily associated with each kind of program. Finally, programs often require *supporting services* or assistance by a parent agency, all of which are included (if possible) within what are generally known as the *indirect costs* or overhead expenses. All the resources may be sought and obtained entirely through a single budget presented to a single funder; they may be obtained from several funders; or they may be obtained partially from the parent agency or by fundraising efforts.

This series of requirements can be seen as a definite series of *demand relations* between resources, beginning with personnel. Programs differ greatly in the not-for-profit sector, but these kinds of resources and the demand relations among them are almost universal. Effective use of personnel—the key resource—necessitates provision of benefits, and then of space, materials, and so on, down the list of essentials. Thus, those who prepare budgets often begin with personnel and proceed in the order of these demand relations, a sensible, logical order of progression. Before any budget costs can be specified, however, both the program and imposed or mandated requirements must be thoroughly reviewed and taken into account. We shall now consider those matters.

PROGRAM REQUIREMENTS

Budget planning must start with knowledge of the resource requirements set by the design of the particular service program. A program plan can be considered fully developed and specified only if it includes enough concrete, detailed information to derive reliable answers to the first two of the three basic questions listed above.

What should we expect to find, then, in the documentation of a good program plan? For budgeting purposes, this material has to provide reliable answers to our first question by identifying clearly the most essential *types* of resources required to conduct the core activities of the program. In labor-intensive service programs this means specification of the most critical *kinds of staff competencies* needed; that is, the particular skills, expertise, and the like. It should also detail any other *distinctive* nonpersonnel resources necessary for program operations, such as delivery vans for a meals-on-wheels program or training equipment for a vocational program for the handicapped. With this information concretely stated, it becomes possible to make reasonable inferences about the supplemental and support resources customarily needed, such as standard office space and materials.

These sets of information about resource requirements allow the second basic question (the *level* needed for each resource) to be at least addressed: *how many* training specialists, library aides, or foster parents; and how many delivery vans, audio-visual setups, or prosthetic devices. These issues usually depend on the intended size or scope of the program and its case volume or service delivery projections. Again, reasonable inferences can be made if sufficient information is presented in the program statement, but those who do budgeting should not be forced to guess at such matters. And, as we shall see, they often become central to budget reduction steps when desired funding does not become available.

At the present state of the art, unfortunately, program planning and documentation are extremely variable and seldom yield adequate details about the kinds of information we have cited. Except where persons skilled in budgeting have been active participants in program development, we have yet to read or even hear of a program design statement that has clearly specified all the elements essential to answer the first two questions. Careful reading of most program designs or plans is likely to lead to one of three results. First, one can usually trace the need for standard, traditional resources, such as certain operational staff, space, and supplies. Second, one may learn about at least one type of resource for implementing this program that is not ordinarily found in others, perhaps an unusual kind of expertise, some item of specialized equipment, or distinctive space requirements. Third, one will probably discover that the program statement offers sketchy guides to most other resource requirements but obscures their precise determination even when all reasonable inferences are made. A word of caution about reasonable inferences: All those made by persons responsible for budget development should be carefully identified as such and then reviewed by program planning and management staff to ensure that resource estimations based on them are valid.

Service program plans can be deceptive for the financial planner in other ways as well. For example, if they outline a program of a kind with which the budgeter is quite familiar, there is a tendency to believe that much more is known about its particular resource requirements than may actually be true. If the plan presents many highly factual elements, and especially if these are presented in quantitative terms (e.g. number of expected clientele and their characteristics), the resource requirements may be presumed to be equally determinate. But a common sort of program often contains uncommon features, and in any event budgeting must denote the *specific* resource needs for a program's unique location in time and space. Quantitative specificity about the features of a program may or may not be accompanied by equal determinacy about its resource elements.

The sooner a program's resource requirements are recognized in the planning process and the sooner persons responsible for budgeting become actively involved, the more efficient the process, because fewer steps will have to be retraced. Planning is also stimulated by the factual questions typically raised from the budgeting perspective. These help to reveal gaps and anomalies in designs and to clarify otherwise murky features of the plan. Even in conditions of optimal collaboration, however, many issues arise in both the program planning and the budgeting processes that compel reciprocal changes or adjustments in each. These include, but are not limited to, the unavoidable likelihood of having to reduce or change the scale of program operations to accommodate a different level of funding or having to modify program plans at the given level of funding. For example, the funder may impose new requirements at the same dollar level, or new state regulations may require agencies to perform additional activities (perhaps in hiring or reporting) without additional dollars. Any developments that affect agency or program operations usually have resource, and therefore budget, implications and necessitate changes—sometimes at five minutes to midnight.

EXTERNAL DEMANDS AND CONSTRAINTS

Neither program planning nor budgeting proceeds in a vacuum. At this point we shall describe some of the demands and constraints imposed on these processes and identify their main sources and their main effects. The parent agency, the funder, and governmental statutes and regulations are the three primary sources. Demands and constraints vary in details, depending to some extent on the nature of the program, but they are universally present and applicable. We shall briefly consider each source and certain of its typical impositions.

The Parent Agency.   All service programs are conducted by formal organizations that are established and function under relevant state or federal statutes. The policies and capabilities of the parent agency provide the foundation and context for all program planning and operations within it, and no program can be undertaken contrary to agency directives. The priorities and objectives, and even the reputation, of the parent agency are powerful influences on program design, but other factors associated with the agency usually have a more direct impact on budgeting itself.

Lacking parent agency willingness and ability, the planning and budgeting essential for programs cannot be carried forward. The agency's administrative, financial, and other critical "support" capabilities are required to develop and conduct any of these programs. New agencies encounter formidable problems in attempting to mobilize sufficient expertise and in-house capacities to meet these basic requisites. Very few programs are wholly self-contained (even when "fully funded"), and even long-established organizations might find it difficult to demonstrate that they could meet every requirement associated with new programs: access to potential clientele, adequate program monitoring and reporting systems, specially designed physical facilities, or ability to attract and retain certain technical personnel. It is not uncommon for funding to be denied to agencies because they have no prior experience in conducting particular services, because they lack adequate information processing or cost analysis systems, or because of inadequate patterns of collaboration with other local agencies and community groups. Any or all of these may be valid requisites for conducting a program, and the positive aspects of such funder requirements should be thoughtfully weighed.

Many features of agencies' policies, practices, and requirements may also be seen as direct, *a priori* standards or mandates imposed on program planning and budgeting. Prevailing arrangements of agencies frequently determine such matters as these:

- Personnel position hierarchies and salary rates
- Employee benefit packages
- Staff workload and other performance standards
- Space utilization standards
- Cost factors for indirect, administrative, and support services
- Reimbursement rates for staff travel and other expenses
- Client fee or payment schedules
- Definitions of case and staff activity measures

Arbitrary determination of such matters at least eases

some steps in the planning and budgeting process. Both funders and agencies require that program budgets conform to existing policies, practices, standards, and rates *unless* they are inappropriate or inapplicable to a given program—for which both special authority and special explanation then become necessary. Problems arise, however, when prevailing agency arrangements are at variance or in conflict with the requirements of a new funding source. In such cases, those responsible for planning and budgeting must search for ways to accommodate agency and funder demands or must seek adjustments by one or both to achieve a reconciliation. Although it should not be assumed that either party will remain intransigent, planners are well advised to seek accommodations that do not call for policy changes.

The Funder. Parent agencies' preestablished arrangements have their corollaries in a variety of predetermined funder constraints. Conventional wisdom has it that funders are more capricious, more inflexible, and less reasonable than agencies. But this perhaps reflects myopia and ignores similar assessments of agencies by their clientele. It also overlooks the pressures or control on the funding bodies themselves by many outside influences that may impose their own prohibitions and demands, including mandates to apportion fund allocations according to various arbitrary formulas.[1]

Examples of prevailing kinds of funder requirements and constraints include:

- Dollar ceilings on program support
- Form and duration of funding (e.g. three-year grant) and method of payment
- Program and budget application forms, formats, and documentation
- Program component and performance demands (e.g. evaluation, multiagency collaboration)
- Allowable and unallowable line-item costs

---

[1] Still other statutory and legal requirements may be stated *by* funders, but their sources are governmental; these are discussed in the next section.

- Cost factors for indirect, administrative, and support expenses
- Unit costing, reimbursement rates, and similar cost standards
- Program activity and financial reporting procedures

Applicant agencies learn to inquire about requirements and restraints *before* undertaking the intensive work of preparing and submitting a program and budget proposal, for they may be unwilling or unable to conform to a given funder's terms.

Many funders, especially those at the state and federal levels, publish their requirements and similar basic facts and distribute them for solicited and unsolicited proposals. Typically known as *guidelines*, these often include (sometimes in "program announcement" communications) information about current funding areas, priorities and predetermined dollar amounts to be awarded among the areas, funding ceilings per award, program component requirements, and so on. Notices about such publications by federal agencies, and the guidelines themselves, regularly appear in the *Federal Register*, which in most communities is available in some library. State-level agencies in most parts of the nation follow similar practices, and private sector funders (e.g. community funds, foundations) usually can provide comparable information.

Funding bodies also indicate where additional information may be obtained. Interested organizations can request formal application and other materials and receive a packet usually including full guidelines and detailed instructions about application procedures; program and budget documentation outlines and forms; application and review schedules, procedures, and criteria; and the name and office of funder representatives to whom completed applications should be sent and from whom still more information and assistance can be obtained. The summary lists given in Appendix A, "Initial and Final Documentation Requirements," outlines many common stipulations.

Funder application materials have many elements that bear directly on program and budget preparation steps and decisions, and all should be read carefully. Inexperienced staff sometimes invest considerable time and effort in developing materials, only to discover that a prospective funder imposes some obligation that is unacceptable to the agency—a fact that could have been learned at the outset. Some funders generate what seems to be an overabundance of detailed information and instructions (in cost schedules and manuals of various kinds), and understanding all of them may be tedious and time-consuming.[2] But it is wise to obtain *advance* notice from the prospective funder about as many matters as possible that bear on the planning, initiation, and conduct of programs (and all of their fiscal aspects). Prior notice can avoid later misunderstandings and conflicts. It can also help planners to detour around impasses before it is too late to change course (for example, knowing ahead of time all the program and fiscal reporting demands for the entire fiscal period).

As we regularly point out, final grant or award approval notices assume contractual status, and the agency falls subject to *all* the requirements declared in prior materials, as well as all those codified in the small print of the *stipulations* and the *general and special conditions* attached to the actual awards. Funders are sometimes willing to modify or relieve certain requirements if the applicant has good reasons that can be explained and justified, and if agreements are negotiated in advance.

Government Statutes and Regulations.   Federal, state, and local governments put forward a plethora of ever changing requirements and prohibitions that pertain to agencies and impinge on their programs. They may flow from any level or branch of government. As we have noted, some of them may be declared by the funder with or without citation of their ultimate governmental source. For example, agencies are subject to federal Affirmative Action requirements, to state licensure and liability regulations, and to municipal zoning and fire codes, as enacted by legislatures, promulgated by executive branch officials, or interpreted by the courts.

It is helpful to distinguish between demands imposed on *all* entities operating within a government's jurisdiction, in-

[2]Funder materials may reference still other documents that define requirements that must be adhered to by all organizations, such as Office of Management and Budget (OMB) Circulars.

cluding profit-sector corporations, and those imposed on agencies or programs that function only in designated service spheres, such as hospitals or residential shelters. Many obligations apply to almost every corporate entity in the nation, others to every one empowered to function within a particular local jurisdiction. These obligations presumably embody the basic principles and standards for engaging in a legally organized activity; they exist for the protection and wellbeing of all citizens as well as of all such enterprises. Not-for-profit agencies should not be exempt from such universal obligations (beyond their tax exemptions).

For many spheres of service programs, however, special requirements and prohibitions apply because of the nature of their activities. We can appreciate the reasons for the external demands that afford protection to hospital patients. We should be able to appreciate as well the validity of various kinds of regulations that apply to programs serving minors or other vulnerable populations, to those providing residential care, to educational or vocational programs preparing persons for standard credentials, and to those engaging in research involving human subjects (e.g. the human subjects review requirements and restraints in research).

Some of the demands pertain specifically to *financial* activities and accountability (e.g. annual audits); others pertain specifically to *employers* (e.g. affirmative action); and still others pertain only to *program* activities and responsibilities (e.g. open eligibility or access for the handicapped). Established agencies usually are knowledgeable about governmental requirements applicable on any basis and have systematic methods for keeping themselves updated about changes. National and local associations of agencies often inform their members about such matters. New agencies, however, may find it very difficult to learn about all their obligations and the constraints on their autonomy. They should seek advice energetically and early and, if in doubt, consult an attorney.

Not all the pertinent statutes and regulations are specifically cited in funder award notices, but the agency has a clear-cut responsibility to understand *all* legal and other requirements. Whenever an agency expands its *kinds* of services, therefore, it should extensively investigate any and all new and different requirements that must be met. Most states have statutes that protect ("hold harmless") governmental personnel acting in good faith, but there are few such protections for governmental agencies as such, and even fewer for nongovernmental agencies or their personnel.

Estimating Market Costs

The relevance of many of the factors just discussed for basic questions of resource determination can be summarized in a simple diagram. It indicates how the principal influences on budget development impinge on specific questions of estimation. Further, immediately under each question it shows the concrete budget detail and documentation elements that result as facts and figures are generated.

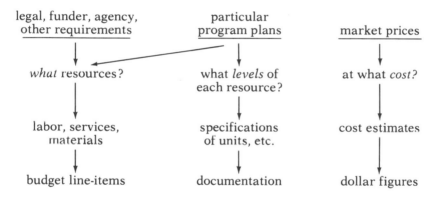

Standardized budget information terms are widely used in the not-for-profit sector, and we use most of the terms and definitions in the United Way UWAACS classification system (United Way of America, 1975), which is generally accepted across the nation. In this system each type of resource is classified as an expense under an appropriate "object" label and code and is then inserted on a particular *numbered line-item* on funders' budget forms. Rather than interrupt our discussion here to explain these terms, the reader should turn to Appendix B, where the items are listed and exemplified.

Let us assume that for a hypothetical program the first two questions—resource types and levels—have been generally but not yet precisely determined. We now wish to gain more precision while seeking concrete market cost information about three kinds of line-items for a program: certain staff positions, an office desk, and office space for one work station. How do we proceed to determine both precise specifications and actual market costs? At this point we shall simply ask about the *current* prices of these items and set aside the issue of the period for which future cost data are needed.

The entire cost estimation process discussed in this section is as appropriate and valuable for continuing programs as it is for new ones. The steps in the process force a regular reevaluation of needs, uses, alternatives, and relationships between budget and program—important in the best of times, but critical in times of cost containment, retrenchment, and new demands.

Item Specifications.   The search for price information will immediately clarify the need to detail particular items more precisely and will help us to do so. Assuming that we need to estimate the cost of one secretarial position, we must decide what qualifications are necessary for what kinds of task assignments. The parent agency undoubtedly already employs such personnel and has current position descriptions, qualifications, and salary rates. But reliance on these begs the questions under discussion, so we shall search out information elsewhere. Efficient inquiries can be directed at three sources in the community: local employment offices, local business or other employers, and a service program comparable to our own. Each source also employs secretaries and can easily provide relevant information. While inquiring, we are likely to learn that the position qualifications must be more precisely defined and that different kinds of competencies are available at different salary costs. What words-per-minute typing skill is really needed? What specialized equipment will the secretary be expected to use? What contact with the public is involved in the job? Is prior experience necessary? Each of these and other aspects must be determined with some reasonable certitude to satisfy program needs and to obtain concrete cost information.

COST ESTIMATION FORM

BUDGET LINE NUMBER	UWAACS CODE NUMBER	OBJECT LABEL or NAME	OBJECT SPECIFICATION	$ PER UNIT	NUMBER UNITS	TOTAL COST
Example: 4	8106	Pencil sharpener	Elec. pencil sharpener for stand. size pencils. 4" x 7" x 4"; steel cutter; auto pencil stop; lrg shavings receptacle; 4 colors; 2 yr grntee. Perf. Manf. Co. Mdl # 34-C-78 Source: M/M Off. Supplies, 4/15/8X	$26.50	2	$53

Once these matters are settled, the several sources of information can provide the more limited salary dollar costs we are seeking.

If we rely mainly on the parent agency for costing information, it would be important to consider how this program's needs fit into prevailing personnel and other standards to assure both effective and economical resource use.

All the information obtained by these and other search procedures should be entered on a *Cost Estimation Form* and retained for reference. (A model of such a form is reproduced here.) Details entered on the form will provide quick verification of figures in final budgeting steps, information about cost ranges if cutbacks become necessary, and backup details for documentation if figures are challenged.[3]

Similar steps can be followed in obtaining cost estimates for an office desk. Let us assume the desk is for the secretary. When we make inquiries at two or more office furniture suppliers, we will learn that secretarial and other desks come in different sizes, materials, and levels of quality and cost. Decisions will have to be made about each of these features, and knowing about the alternatives helps us ensure that our choices fit operational needs, in this instance a desk suited for the secretary's specific tasks. Newspaper ads and the phone directory can direct us to discount houses and used furniture stores for perhaps even "better buys." Again, all this information should be retained on worksheet forms.

Now we turn to estimating space costs, probably to find a more complicated set of issues and options. Preliminary contacts with realtors and rental agencies will provide information useful for deciding about the *kinds* and *amounts* of space needed for personnel and program operations, the *locations* where such space is currently available within the community, and the various *bases* or terms for space rentals. Visits to one or two possible premises will reveal the layout, the partitions, and so on.

The effect of differing space arrangements and locations on operation, performance, and comfort may well make choices and decisions about space seem singularly difficult. The risks, dollars, and long-run consequences involved

---

[3]Such detailed object specifications and cost estimates also contribute materially to explicating and justifying the line-items, as will be discussed later.

would seem to call for special caution, and much time and energy may therefore have to be spent consulting back and forth between landlord, agency, program head, funder, and others. But this complexity should not mislead us: Essentially the same cost estimating elements and procedures are involved here as for all other resources, and the estimating form is equally useful.

We are now ready to deal with another source of uncertainty: estimating market costs for periods up to eighteen months in advance. Initial cost figures are often developed well before an actual program fiscal year begins; this adds twelve more months to the planning time frame. Persons experienced in budgeting frequently update all resource cost estimates—or all of major importance—shortly before the final request budget is submitted, as we shall discuss later. Inflationary conditions will force planners to look for compensating cost *reductions* to remain within a budget ceiling. Tracking price changes and balancing increases with cutbacks are equally useful precautions in many other phases of budgeting and fiscal management.

These approaches represent forms of *contingency planning:* preparing deliberate plans to adjust to likely but unpredictable developments. Even if most prices are expected to move upward, the rises will occur unevenly among different items or resources. To discern these trends, information about recent and anticipated price changes should be collected during the initial cost estimating. Suppliers and large employers are more sensitive to price fluctuations and can often provide some guidance about expected changes for particular items. This information should also be entered on the forms, and the search for lower-cost alternatives can be concentrated on those objects for which predicted increases seem most problematic. For example, effort should not be wasted trying to anticipate the pattern of airfare increases for programs calling for little staff travel, whereas a good deal of effort should be given to vehicle purchase prices, leasing, repair, maintenance, and resale costs for programs that transport clients. By these means reservoirs of information are obtained and used from the outset to note cost range *possibilities,* including ideas about possible future cuts in costs or numbers of units.

A careful contingency approach can prepare one for the

readjustments that will undoubtedly occur before submitting the final request budget, for absorbing further reductions if the funder declares a lower support ceiling, and for coping with cost shifts during actual program operations. The first two of these possibilities will receive more attention later in this chapter (the last is discussed in Chapter 7).

If detailed cost estimating and contingency planning as outlined here seem too demanding, and if the uncertainties seem to preclude firm estimates, planners may be inclined to rely mainly on "ball park" figures and rough estimates. Recourse to rough estimates may be necessary for a given item or resource requirement, but it is inadvisable for most budget items, and certainly for the entire document. Nor is it advisable to inflate the request budget figure by some percentage on the presumption that all funders routinely cut budgets by approximately that amount. Most funders are sophisticated about budgeting matters and many employ experienced fiscal analysts to review and assess applications. Even more serious are the perils of living with a "fudged" budget and then attempting to explain the myriad departures from it and from the program plans.

Funders understand the difficulties of estimating the costs of a program for forward periods, especially during inflationary times, and particularly when new or greater modified programs are at issue. They prefer that applicants clarify specific, significant uncertainties about the program and distinguish between them and the problems of predicting future market costs. These two kinds of uncertainties should never be confused. The term "best estimate" should be used only to identify those cost estimations where the applicant has secured all reasonable information about current and forward market costs and has calculated and explained them as precisely as possible.[4] These and other components of the stated program plans (e.g. intended services, number of clientele) and budget information can then be offered as "good faith" declarations and so stated. It is very risky, however, to invoke either "best estimate" or "good

---

[4]Items labeled "Miscellaneous" or "Contingency" are rarely found on funder forms. Where they do appear they are typically given narrow definition and limited use. They are not intended as catchall lines to absorb market cost and other uncertainties.

faith" language when the reasons for the uncertainty cannot be explained. Presenting specious data and making spurious claims are improbable ways to build trusting relationships between an agency and its funders.

Variability and Uncertainty

This chapter would be expanded enormously if we were to attempt to offer thorough explanations with full illustrations of the entire budget development process.[5] Each program plan is unique—however similar to others of the same general kind it may appear—and requires a particular set and level of resources to implement its activities. Although the *types* of important resources are generally common, they are mustered in an infinite variety of mixes, limited only by the ingenuity of program planners and by imposed requirements. Furthermore, since each program's funding and local market costs are also unique, we can do no more than point to general kinds of variability.

The indefiniteness of most program plans has already been cited as a primary source of uncertainty in budget development, but this should not be confused with uncertainties in cost estimating proper. We have emphasized that step-by-step efforts to obtain cost estimations usually stimulate clarification of vague designs, while funding ceilings and other external demands force resolutions of dilemmas about plans.

We realize that persons with little experience in program planning and management may also have difficulty comprehending how various features of a program design point to or denote specific resources for which object cost estimates must be sought. One guide for those facing these fundamental difficulties is offered by the *series of demand relations* already mentioned. Novices are encouraged to pace through those resource connections repeatedly, trying them out for several kinds of programs until they grasp their rationale and usefulness. Planners should also seek out

---

[5]This chapter is also limited to development of a line-item budget; we have postponed the subject of functional budgeting until Chapter 5 to avoid too much complexity here. Line-items must always be included in functional budgets, of course.

other agencies and persons with experience in these matters, not to receive answers, but to get suggestions, explanations about their own procedures, and information about others' prior experiences (usually gained the hard way and well recalled). Once a new program is under way and actual operational and cost information is available, it can be directly invested in the continuous efforts to plan ahead.

Some who prepare budgets for new programs find it helpful to rely *initially* on various rules of thumb that have some general currency. For example, they may use lists of the presumed minimum basic square footage, furniture, and equipment needed for each work station, or analogous standards for the sleeping area and furniture for each child in a typical care facility. Reliance on these general standards or package lists may ease some of the *preliminary* work, assuming they have some rough validity and provided they are suitably modified to fit the particular program. Guides to these standards or lists are sometimes available from national associations of agencies, are set forth in state licensing regulations, or are shared among units of associated local funding organizations.

"Cost factor" guides are also used for developing preliminary cost estimations. For example, costs of employee benefits may be summarized as a factor representing a certain percentage of total salary costs and calculated as such in the initial stages. Obviously, these figures must be reexamined and modified before submitting the final request budget so they will accurately reflect current and projected benefits of the actual staff roster for *this* proposed budget. In certain sectors other factors are used to estimate the costs of ordinary office supplies, but careful double checking is necessary given the escalating costs of paper, postage, reproduction, and so on.

- A simple time-saving formula can be used when the same cost factor must be applied to a line-item base in repetitive calculations, as with fringe or indirect percentages.

- The cost factor is converted to its decimal form, then added to 1.00, and the line-item base figure is *multiplied* by the new 1.XXX factor. Thus, a fringe benefit rate of 18.8 percent converts to .188, which, when added to

1.00, equals 1.188. If this factor is used to multiply a revised Personnel line-item subtotal of $42,780, it yields the new Personnel-plus-Fringe subtotal of $50,823, which can then be added quickly with other line-item figures to produce a new working total.

- The 1.XXX figure can be used repeatedly as changes are made in Personnel subtotals, and also quickly shows how the Personnel-plus-Fringe subtotal is affected by each change in staff dollars.

	Usual Calculation Steps	*Short Method*
Personnel subtotal	$42,780	$42,780
Fringe (@ 18.8% of Personnel)	x .188	x 1.188
	8,042.60	50,822.64
Personnel + Fringe =	42,780 8,043 (rounded)	
Subtotal	$50,823	$50,823 (rounded)

Two special types of line-items deserve brief explanations: Indirect/Overhead costs and Match/Contributed funds.

Provision for Indirect or Overhead costs (the terms are used synonymously here) is common for most programs. Because programs are conducted by agencies engaged in other ongoing activities, they usually share in the agency's central support services or draw on its basic resources and capabilities in various ways. As we have noted, the parent agency handles personnel matters, may provide auditing and legal services, has some kind of bookkeeping and accounting system, and so on. If each program duplicated these basic provisions, it would be needlessly expensive and would also attenuate the parent agency's oversight responsibilities. Much of the agency's support is provided in very concrete ways to each program, such as centralized accounting services, but is seldom given directly to the program's clientele. Some agency support, however, is less tangible, such as its membership in national accrediting bodies.

Although the resources and services we are discussing are used by all programs within the parent agency, each benefits to a different extent. An externally funded program cannot directly pay for this assistance in the same way it does for market resources, because the agency is not in the business of "selling" its services. For these reasons each program's proper share of its agency's support services cannot be cost estimated in the same line-item format used for all other "direct" resources. Therefore, a different principle must be invoked: acknowledgement of the burden to the agency of necessary and defensible costs for each program that are not represented by the line-items that constitute total direct costs.

Funders approve different mechanisms to serve this principle. In the simplest method a cost factor is declared, by which indirect costs are calculated as a *fixed percentage* of either total direct costs or of certain line-item subtotals (for example, Personnel-plus-Fringe). This arrangement greatly simplifies the cost estimating task but has the effect of putting a ceiling on indirect costs, which may seem disadvantageous to some agencies. Another method requires specifying and costing out every element the agency wishes to include in its indirect cost request, using negotiated or audited recent cost experience from the agency's own files. This is obviously a more demanding procedure but is more precise than a fixed cost factor.

Regardless of how indirect costs are determined by funders, most of them increasingly expect that all indirect elements will be specified and subject to possible audit; that all will represent allowable costs (e.g. external support for agency fundraising is usually prohibited); and that the subtotal for these costs will not exceed some fixed level.[6]

Funder requirements for matching or contributed funds do not denote a different type of expenditure but are provisions for *cost sharing* support of the program by the parent agency. Numerous kinds of federal and state funding for local programs (private or governmental) are contingent on the agency's generation of some proportion of matching

[6] Federal guidelines and regulations covering indirect costs for nonprofit organizations are described in OMB Circular A-122 (July 8, 1980); for state and local governments, they are described in OMB Circular A-87, Part X (January 28, 1981).

monies or contributions directly from its own assets or from other local sources. This matching or contributed support is typically set at a percentage of the grand total costs for a program. Sometimes the percentage must be increased during successive years of funding. For example, a private agency may be awarded a grant provided it can generate 20 percent of the total program costs during the first fiscal year, 35 percent during the second, and 50 percent thereafter. The agency is usually prohibited from diverting other federal (or state) monies to meet this requirement. Even more stringent requirements may be imposed, but the principle remains the same: The parent agency is obligated to share in program support by generating some proportion of total program costs from other local sources. This arrangement is intended to encourage local support from the outset and gradually to shift responsibility from the original funder. "Hard" matching funds refers to the provision of actual dollars, while "soft" matching support can be provided "in kind" through contributions of resources other than dollars. Use of volunteers, assignment of agency staff paid from other local funds, and provision of space or vehicles are examples of in-kind matching of contributed funds. Audits are customarily conducted to assure the outside funder that these stated obligations were, in fact, met as promised.

Resource Priorities and Balances

At some point a set of preliminary cost estimations will be in hand for all resources. Most often the total dollar cost (the "bottom line") will exceed the stated or expected funding ceiling, so reductions must be made. At this stage a few items may be cut back or deleted entirely because they are considered extravagant. However, we do not recommend immediately aiming at reducing the full amount through a line-by-line and element-by-element review.[7] Still worse would be an across-the-board reduction of every line by the same

[7]"Element" here means particular objects/costs *within* numbered lines of the budget form. Each numbered line often incorporates two or more elements; these are sometimes grouped and referred to as subcategories or subitems.

dollar or percentage figure. At this juncture in the budgeting process we have just come out of the woods, so to speak, and do not fully understand what all the preliminary figures represent. Therefore, the line-by-line approach is too piecemeal (and we will lose our way back among the trees), and the across-the-board approach is mindless and mechanical.

We recommend instead that budget planners step back and review their preliminary work in terms of a priority schema that can guide reductions rationally and coherently—resulting in a logical budget focused on the objectives of the program.

For this important purpose the entire set of preliminary line-item costs should be ordered by a schema into at least three main partitions. This ordering allows costs to be prioritized in terms of their *immediacy in transferring benefits to clients.* To the *first* partition should be assigned all item costs defined as representing the *most immediate* and *most direct benefits* this specific program is intended to provide to its clients. Intended benefits vary, of course, among programs, so priority assignments of costs must be relative to their desired mix of resources. For a library, these would be books, periodicals, and other materials for readers or learners, *plus* librarians to aid patrons in using the books, and so on. For a crisis hot-line program, the most immediate benefits presumably are represented by capable persons available to offer direct voice help, counsel, or support, *plus* the costs of adequate telephone communications. For a job-training program, the most immediate and direct benefits are provided through instructors and the instructional equipment and materials used in the educational process itself.

Many other resources are necessary to implement any kind of program, but they are not directly transferred to the clients. To the *third* partition should be assigned all item costs for maintaining the program services that are *most distant* from the point of transference to clients. Indirect/-Overhead costs obviously belong in this distant subset: They represent various costs associated with support of a program but not given to clients, or even visible to them under most circumstances. Standard office equipment also belongs here, but X-ray equipment in a medical diagnostic center would belong in the first partition. Let us use office equipment to explore the logic of this schema. Typewriters are used by secetaries to prepare client forms, file items, and for correspondence, as well as for reports and materials for the program as a whole. Most of these tasks are generated by line staff out of *their* direct contact with clients. Line staff, secretaries, and typewriters (and thence paper and file cabinets) are all necessary for service programs but *in a descending order of cruciality*. It is the efforts of the line staff in a service organization that have the most immediate benefit for clients; without these activities there would be little for the secretaries to do. Office equipment costs allow vital agency activities to be conducted more rapidly and efficiently, but by themselves they are of no value to clients. They may be bypassed during periods of extreme urgency or unused during power shortages, for example, while service continues. Secretaries represent a more significant program resource (because of the direct contact some have with clients and the variety of other program operations they help perform), but they have less immediate significance for clients than do line staff.

To the second or middle partition, then, are assigned all item costs that are *proximate* in their transfer of benefits to clients, midway between the distant and the immediate partitions. We suggest assigning secretarial and similar support costs here, some but not all of ordinary consumable supplies and reproduction, and, for many programs, travel costs except those needed for clients or on behalf of particular clients, and so on.[8] After all line costs have been assigned to their appropriate partitions, all subtotals should be calculated and also computed as percentages of the total budget. The path to take for making important budget cuts should now become clear: *to increase the proportion of total costs assigned to the immediate partition.* This is done by focusing initial reduction efforts on the third, or distant, partition and then, to a lesser extent, on the second. Each cut in costs in the third (or second) partition necessarily increases the *proportion* retained for the first partition. Of

---

[8]Costs within line-items usually must be broken down for the schema: *Portions* of travel, communications, consumable supplies, and other costs often should be assigned to different partitions.

course, cuts are usually necessary in all partitions, but the aim is to enhance—or at least not to decrease—the percentage in the immediate one.

Let us now look at an illustration of budget modification using a schema for a hypothetical youth summer camp (Table 3–1). Several things about this example deserve our attention. We note that the preliminary grand total was cut by $7,017 or 8 percent (all figures will be rounded), which is rather modest, so we do not expect to find any dramatic changes. Now note the partition subtotals at the bottom: It is interesting that the proximate resources subtotal was cut by a not insignificant amount, yet the percentage of costs in this partition remained almost the same between the two budgets. Immediate resources rose very slightly from 32 percent of the preliminary budget to 33 percent of the final budget, whereas distant resources declined from 31 to 29 percent. Decrements or increments in absolute sums or raw dollars do not necessarily alter the *proportions* that subtotals of costs—or costs of particular items—represent within larger total amounts. The key to understanding the pattern of cuts in this example is given on the last line at the bottom. Here each partition's percentage of the *total reductions* is shown, and it is obvious that they will reflect the priorities we advocate: 47 percent was taken from distant resources, but only 16 percent from immediate ones.

A few other aspects of Table 3–1 are worth review. Readers may not understand what all summarized item costs mean for a camp or may not agree with their assignments among the partitions in this example. But these assignments adhere in a general way to our explanation of the partitions, and they were not altered between the two budgets. Perhaps more important in this context, a review of the specific item figures reveals that not all items were reduced, even in the distant partition; nor were they reduced by the same dollar (or percentage) amounts within or between partitions. For example, it appears that property taxes and insurance could not be cut at all—a likely situation for most organizations. Equipment, maintenance, and grounds upkeep were all reduced, the first by a considerable amount, following a pattern common to many not-for-profit organizations during hard times. Office, grounds, and recreational supplies were all cut, but the latter least. Costs

TABLE 3–1.   Sample Schema: Resource Priorities for a Summer Youth Camp

Distant Resources	Proximate Resources	Immediate Resources	TOTALS
PR & camper recruitment $3,000 $2,900	office supplies $3,100 $2,700	counseling/activities staff + benefits $18,750 $18,000	
staff recruitment $2,000 $1,900	laundry $800 $720	food/meals $4,680 $4,500	
insurances $1,980 --ok	vehicle maint. $900 $800	first aid/medical supplies + services $987 $990	
equipment (office/grounds) $2,700 $1,600	grounds upkeep $3,210 $3,000	recreational supplies and equipment $4,000 $3,800	
property taxes $2,100 --ok	admin. & support staff + benefits $20,000 $18,500		
building repairs $1,500 $1,200	utilities $3,400 $3,300		
mortgage payments, capital improvements $3,900 $3,600	loc. travel/transp. $1,000 $890		
ACA membership + accred. $500 --ok	pre-season training counselors $1,850 $1,750		
parent agency indirect costs $9,950 $8,560			TOTALS
prelim $ 27,630 prelim % 30.6	prelim $ 34,260 prelim % 37.9	prelim $ 28,417 prelim % 31.5	$90,307
final $ 24,340 final % 29.2	final $ 31,660 final % 38.0	final $ 27,290 final % 32.8	$83,290 - 7,017 - 7.8%
% of total reduction: 46.9	% of total reduction: 37.1	% of total reduction: 16.1	100%

59

of counselor/activity staff were cut very little, and medical costs were not cut at all, but parent agency indirect costs and camp administrative support staff costs were both considerably reduced.

This limited example demonstrates that application of the resource priorities schema entails differential reductions both *between* the partitions and *among* all the cost items. Regardless of the priority we might like to assign certain types of costs, each must be addressed with careful regard to its own logic and to market realities. The budget *reduction* process, then, follows procedures we have recommended for budget *development*, with item-by-item attention within a larger framework of priorities and preferences.

Partition Schema

Distant Costs	Proximate Costs	Immediate Costs
cost items	cost items	cost items
.	.	.
.	.	.
.	.	.
subtotals	subtotals	subtotals
percentage	percentage	percentage

direction of resource priority

LO -------------------------- > -------------------------- > -------------------------- > HI

direction of reduction emphasis

HI < -------------------------- < -------------------------- < -------------------------- LO

What is the validity of this approach to budget priorities, balances, and cost reductions? In merely practical terms it provides a more focused and guided method of cost cutting, even if every item is eventually reduced in some measure, and it helps avoid a helter-skelter or mechanical approach. The three partitions closely parallel the series of resource demand relations: A program's most critical resources are generally those listed in the first, or immediate partition, whereas those in the proximate and distant partitions are needed to *support* service endeavors and can be justified only in their supplementary roles. The schema is also a valuable tool for assessing and improving a program's cost effectiveness, because it gives priority to resources and costs most closely linked to program results. All other things being equal, one generally gets "more action for the dollar" from immediate than from distant costs. The schema, therefore, embodies the value preferences of most funders: emphasis on benefits transferred to clients over support and other costs, however important they may be.

Application of some kind of priority schema will almost certainly be made by the funder when assessing new and resubmitted support requests. A funder's fiscal analyst can easily compare an initial line-item budget request with a later one having a lower ceiling to discover the *nature and direction* of the agency's cost changes. The grand total and line-by-line subtotals are already known for both budgets; the question is what these totals *mean* in terms of altered resource balances. Funders may also use such a schema for comparing and evaluating competing funding requests for the same kind of program, because resource priorities can thus be seen relatively despite differences in specific items, local market costs, and the like.

We recommend that agencies apply the schema as a guide to achieving an optimal cost-effective and well-balanced budget, and certainly when they must impose cost reductions. The schema is secondarily useful for *interyear* budget comparisons: for identifying drifts in resource balances (gradual shifts toward proportionately greater distant or proximate costs), for detailing more cogently the effects of price inflation across many line-items, and for supplementing other cost analysis procedures.

The assignments across the partitions are, of course, largely a matter of judgment, especially for those item costs at their boundaries, and we can offer no invariant rules for such assignments. But item costs should be *consistently* assigned to the same partitions, or else valid intrayear and interyear comparisons are not possible. Discussions with the funder about classification of certain types of item costs may help to develop mutual understanding about which resource costs should have highest priority and why—even though the funder probably uses a different schema (and different terms) for reviewing and assessing budget requests. Thus, for example, an agency may need better justifications for why it considers certain program costs as immediate if this assessment is not shared by the funder. The funder's skepticism about some priorities may stimulate reconsideration of the relative importance the agency has given to certain of these. Applicant agencies tend to consider *all* proposed costs important and necessary, but they cannot all be equally so, and stringent pressures for cost containment should stimulate more critical reexamination of budget priorities and of the relation of resources to benefits.

Priority or partition assignments should fit those generally prevalent within given sectors of service, or interagency comparisons will be meaningless. When looking across sectors, we can quickly appreciate that total occupancy costs and their priorities assume very different meanings for residential programs and for standard office space. Recreational or play materials for a summer camp or a nursery school cannot be assigned the same priority as consumable office supplies in another kind of program.

More often than not the programs cited in this book are labor-intensive. That means staff constitute the primary resource both in importance to the service activities and in proportion to total budget costs. But this should not obscure the special requirements and costs for programs that rely heavily on additional kinds of resources, which may match or exceed the personnel costs.

Residential and housing programs of all kinds depend on staff, but they also require a large allocation of resources for physical facilities. Still other kinds of programs rely heavily on man/machine technologies (health care, testing laboratories, and computer services) that call for quite different resource mixes. Similarly, libraries and museums must allocate a large share of their costs to acquiring and caring for books and collections. Such differing valid resources bases underscore the need for comparisons to be made *within* sectors of similar programs; comparisons across sectors should be undertaken only with such variations in mind.

We want to caution budget planners about certain kinds of costs that funders usually regard with concern and skepticism. In our experience the following are sensitive items that may invite funder challenge:

- Staff conference travel and related costs
- Outside consultants and subcontracts
- Memberships in associations, professional libraries
- High levels of indirect and support costs

Budget planners should exercise great prudence in estimating such costs and should provide careful justification for any of them.

Trimming the Budget

We now address a common task: trimming a preliminary budget down to a funder's declared or implied ceiling, while also seeking improvements in earlier work to assure the best possible program and budget proposal. A series of orderly steps must be taken to achieve these aims; they usually overlap but are set out sequentially here. Those doing the trimming should take notes continuously during the process to facilitate whatever backtracking is necessary.

The first step has already been mentioned: reviewing or correcting line-item cost estimates known to be only rough approximations or dubious for other reasons. These adjustments are as likely to be upward as downward, but they should be made before going further. Second, all item costs should be given priorities according to a partition schema, and the implications of the resulting partition cost proportions should be assessed. Are the percentages of costs in the immediate category the highest that can be achieved, and are they the lowest in the distant category? Can these proportions be well defended against funder skepticism or challenge? What dilemmas in assigning item costs (or portions of each) to one or another partition offer insights into the reliability of the estimations themselves or into the rationales for including these amounts in the total budget and program plan?

Although *every* item and cost estimation will be reexamined and possibly modified, the logic of the schema emphasizes seeking reductions first from the distant and last from the immediate, or working from left to right. A series of item-by-item questions, alternatives, and possibilities will emerge from this process, and notes on these should be retained for later review.

The third step calls for recalculating the partition subtotals and the budget total (applying all mandatory cost factors as appropriate: fringe percentages, indirect costs, and so forth) to discover any discrepancies that remain to be addressed by further cuts. At this point it is important to observe in which directions the cost proportions within the schema have shifted. Ideally the shifts will have been toward immediate costs, but this may not be the case.

It now becomes necessary to return to the notes and cost estimation forms to strive for substitutions and other economies. In this phase of cost cutting we are not yet facing significant changes in the character or scope of the service program; we are considering changes only in the level of resources to support it. Among the first things that can be dispensed with are preferred but not essential items—perhaps some equipment that would be nice to have. Sometimes essential or highly desired items can be deferred until another year, but deferring expenditures does not always solve a problem. For example, basic equipment that is not maintained can suddenly break down and cause critical problems; interruptions in regularly acquiring new resources (such as training materials or word-processing equipment) can create serious lags that must sooner or later be overcome. Many organizations may defer truly necessary expenditures, like building repairs, which later must be undertaken at higher cost. Perhaps the *number of units* of a given item can be cut down without sacrificing the resource entirely; for example, reducing the number of file cabinets, the space footage, the days of outside consultant service, or perhaps the secretarial/staff ratio. The budget is being trimmed, not hacked; it will be leaner but not eviscerated. For numerous items the initial estimation efforts should have produced less costly alternatives, and this information will have been retained on the forms. It is usually possible, for example, to substitute a used typewriter for a new one, a cheaper office copier, or less attractive stationery. Downgrading staff positions is also an example of this kind of saving, but it is to be undertaken only with great care. It may be done by retaining the same basic position duties but reducing the salary rate if the agency permits, or by reclassifying the position at the next lower level. Both actions will, of course, result in less experienced or less skilled personnel.

These several kinds of cuts are known as *cost efficiencies*, whereby the same level of results is sought through less expensive means.

All these methods, particularly those involving personnel, presumably affect program operations, but such economies do not *ipso facto* change its basic character, scope, quality, or level of achievement. If we assume—as most people seem to—that modest dollar increments can *enhance* a continuing program without fundamentally changing it, we should also assume that *modest decrements* in support reduce enhancement without doing violence to the program. This, obviously, is true only up to a point, depending on *which* items are decremented. Not every alternative for enhancing or decrementing a program by $1,000 would have equal consequences for its character or quality. In making wise choices about such cuts, therefore, we must seek to minimize the adverse effects on goals, commitments, and clientele.

Cutting Deeper

When this phase of budget trimming is finished, it may well be necessary to consider further reductions of a magnitude that do necessitate important program changes. If the targeted total of cutbacks was not reached by trimming, the next step involves difficult decisions of a different sort. It is now necessary to review the program plans in their entirety, together with the information developed when program operations were translated into resource requirements. This review will probably yield still other plan elements that were initially overestimated or previously noted as desirable but not truly necessary. The budget corollaries of the design elements can now be altered to gain further savings.

In a time of declining resources, however, it will more often become necessary to go farther and deeper and begin replanning to reduce the scope, volume, domain, or quality of the planned services. At earlier steps in the reduction process minor modifications may have been made, intentionally or unwittingly, in limited *aspects* of program operations (e.g. attendance at fewer or no professional conferences, or slight reductions in total weekly hours of clinic service). But we are now considering significant program changes, for example, deleting one component of a multipronged service, curtailing rigorous evaluation activities, reducing the program's outreach services, substantially decreasing the numbers of clients to be served, or other painful changes of comparable import. "Cutting into the bone" becomes necessary when all procedural means of cost reduction have failed to bring costs under the award ceiling. Clearly such changes cannot be weighed merely, or even mainly, from a budgetary perspective. They involve critical issues of program design, objectives and policies, agency and funder mandates, and commitments to clientele. It would be beneficial at this point if such possibilities had been entertained during earlier program planning so that some implications of each had at least been thought about and could be recalled now. In any event, the task is a matter of listing as many feasible program modifications as possible, then assessing each from both a valuational and a fiscal perspective until it becomes possible to pursue two of them more intensively.[9] We suggest that novices begin by examining only *two* major program changes to sharpen their insights into the valuational and policy issues, as well as to take advantage of comparative savings that might be generated. As often as not experienced planners move toward a mix of two, three, or more program cutbacks to minimize the adverse effects of implementing only one.

Let us imagine a program designed to serve clients widely dispersed through a city and its environs. Faced with a substantial reduction in funding, one alternative might be to limit the service area to the municipal boundaries; another might be to circumscribe the clientele by more stringent eligibility requirements without changing the service area; and a third might be to narrow the program's planned spectrum of services without changing either boundaries or eligibility. Each of these changes will have quite different consequences for some or many of the intended

---

[9] Another logical route is to try to conceive of *alternative programmatic procedures* that can meet the same goals and mandates within the budget ceiling. Doing this in a thoroughgoing way is very difficult, although alternative elements may find their way into these program modifications. Such efforts are directed at increasing program *cost effectiveness* and may sometimes be required of fiscal and program planners.

clientele, and each would call for a different mix of resources and therefore of costs.

Assuming that previous program design, budgeting information, and work notes have been retained, it should not be too difficult to identify the particular line-items that must be reduced to implement each selected program modification. If all goes well, the sum of the reductions will bring the total budget within the declared ceiling, and a final choice can be made among the alternatives—or a final mixture of changes can be adopted. If all does not go well, further reductions must be sought. Tedious as it may be, *all* items and their costs must now be reviewed and recalculated to ensure overall accuracy and integrity. Again, certain costs not directly implicated in the program modifications are indirectly affected (employee benefits, indirect costs, volume purchases) and cannot be overlooked.

For much of the period to the late 1970s the effects of decisions involved in imposing reductions of these kinds on continuing programs were not severe, however frustrating. Even then, however, a funder's refusal to support a new program or a carefully planned expansion or an agency's sudden loss of previously reliable support created major crises and forced full-scale reviews. But those were not everyday occurrences. Budgeting generally proceeded in a climate of optimism, and reductions frequently took the form of a slower rate for annual increments. By the early 1980s, however, as sources of funding started to shrink, the situation changed drastically. Continuing programs began their struggle with sharp cutbacks, and every new program faced the likelihood of demands for large reductions, if lucky enough to be funded at all.

The language describing these circumstances and describing the necessary accommodations to them has changed to reflect the different scale of problems, of decision dilemmas, and of budget strategies. *Retrenchment budgeting, downsizing* of program, *termination* support, and other phrases indicate the seriousness of these conditions in some sectors. Although this book is addressed to prudent budgeting, not crisis survival, all the practices we recommend become even more important as the risks increase. The steps we have just set forth are necessary for achieving "normal" reductions and are approximations of procedures applicable under far more critical conditions. As should already be clear, the essence of our argument is that budget building and budget cutting must be rigorously linked to program planning, and at key junctures in these processes one must move from fiscal calculations back to program decisions before further steps can proceed coherently.

A strong argument was made in Chapter 2 for close collaboration between program and budget planning staff. It should now be apparent that significant final program changes made at the last minute by budget staff working alone will almost inevitably result in unintentional dislocations and infringements of interagency agreements or commitments to clients, as the budget gets balanced in good but erring faith.

The series of successive approximations we recommend fulfill several requisites. Specific item cost estimations are reviewed more than once, and their reliability is thus better assured. The demand relations among resources have been retraced to avert accidental omissions or needless extravagence. Perhaps most important, some deliberate order of resource priorities has been explicitly connected with program requirements and objectives and readjusted in the process of effecting successive budget reductions.

All this work bears additional rewards at subsequent points in the larger budget cycle. The final submitted budget (and supporting documentation) will be far more coherent and defensible, and funder questions or challenges will be more easily handled. Should additional reductions be necessary, enough is known about possible alternatives to avoid hasty cuts. And during the actual fiscal period, as expenditure experiences inevitably depart from plans and expectations, cost containment and contingency management will be made easier by the thorough groundwork laid during the preparatory period.

Budget Documentation

We now turn to the remaining steps needed before submitting a final budget to the funder. We have already referred to the packet of forms and other materials furnished by the funder that applicants should keep in mind through all the preparatory work. Documentation requirements will always vary among funders, so applicants must be alert to different definitions, varied backup evidence, unique methods of calculating or reporting program and budget information, and so on. Whatever the requirements, they are all arbitrary and must be fulfilled exactly as requested and complete in every detail.

The kinds of information and documentation generally required by funders are listed in Appendix A. A glance at the lists indicates that much more must be submitted than a statement of the program plan and a line-item budget. We shall set aside the list pertaining to the parent or sponsoring agency and move directly to the section that deals with the programs themselves.

The program or project section of the list in Appendix A has two main parts, preceded by a summary of the program proposal, often in the form of a one-page facesheet. The first main part consists of a *program description* or plan —sometimes called a Program Narrative—where a succinct summary of the proposed program or project is given, often following a required outline. Typically included are text sections describing evidence of the problem or need, program rationale and goals, characteristics of the intended clients or beneficiaries, nature and scope of the effort or services, expected results, plan of procedure, time schedule, and so forth. All this information must be stated in clear and straightforward terms so that the funder can reach a preliminary judgment about the merits of the application. Equally important, this text must also present a readily understandable foundation for the budget and related information given in the fiscal part of the application. The budget part should hold no surprises for one who has carefully read the program description text.[10]

We are more concerned with the second main part of the application, where all the requested fiscal information is presented together with related or supplementary details. More often than not specific forms are issued by the funder, and all figures and text must be inserted properly into these

[10] Discussions and examples of program description materials are offered in White (1975), pp. 225–43, and Hall (1977).

forms (with attachments as appropriate). Because page or word limits may be imposed for every part of the application, all text should be concise, well-organized, and easy to understand.

The fiscal part concentrates on budgetary information and is sometimes called the Budget Narrative. It almost always includes a mandatory summary form for presenting fiscal data, colloquially called the "budget summary," and a staffing table. It may also call for various other kinds of related data or measures, such as client fee or charge schedules, unit costs, and so on. Once the final budget cost estimations have been developed according to the procedures described in this chapter, work then focuses on the *text* that must accompany and clarify the budget summary itself. *Assuming that the Program Narrative has been clearly and adequately presented,* the budget text section bears two burdens: first, *explication* of the line-item (and other) fiscal details that are entered on the budget forms and, second, *justification* of all elements in the budget request. It is desirable and usually possible to weave these two strands together in the actual text, although they address different aspects of the requested items. The funder needs to be informed about the details of each cost element (explication) and about why each is needed (justification). The order of information may vary among applications, but the kind of information will match that cited here.

Budget Explication.   In this part of the application explanations are given for each and all costs of line-items and their elements. Sometimes only one kind of object is entered on a single line of the budget, but usually there are two or more kinds of objects, perhaps with subtotals, which must be dealt with separately. Recall how much detail has presumably been collected on the cost estimation form about each object now presented in the budget request. The funder must receive some but not all of this information to gain an understanding of cost elements, line-items, requested amounts, and the proposal as a whole. Even when the funder approves the program proposal and most of the requested budget, certain item costs may be disapproved solely on the grounds that they are insufficiently explained or justified.

Explications are usually given by following the order of line-items on the budget summary. For each line-item and its cost elements, certain basic information is typically requested: *One*, the standard name of the item with sufficient specification to clarify the kind of object (e.g. kind and size of desk, kind of travel costs); *two*, the number of units of each object (e.g. 4.25 FTEs [full-time equivalents] of outreach workers, 25 reams of paper, 1,230 miles of intracity travel); and *three*, the cost per unit and the sum of these costs (e.g. 5 office chairs @ $50 per chair: 5 x 50 = $250). We can again see the value of obtaining precise cost information and retaining it throughout. Examples of typical explication text are given in the illustrative materials in Chapter 4. If the application form permits, it is often desirable to include item justification text immediately after explication to avoid flipping back and forth through the application.

When submitting applications to funders with whom one has had no previous experience, it is hard to know how much detail or what level of detail should be given as explication. Our experience indicates that funders increasingly expect an abundance of detailed text and cost information, so it is advisable to overdo when in doubt. In general, funders expect a sufficient amount and level of detail to understand what is being requested and why. They are less able to comprehend unusual or extraordinary kinds and amounts of costs, so more explanatory details have to be provided for these. But what is unusual or extraordinary? It includes those items rarely encountered in most projects, highly specialized in nature or content (whether personnel or equipment), or infrequently requested for *this* type of program. Funders are well informed about most office supplies, normal modes of travel, and common professional positions. Recall also the listing of items about which many funders are skeptical: It is safer to provide full explication and justification text for such costs.

Detailed information about personnel costs usually must be given on separate forms supplementing the personnel line on the budget summary; fringe benefit costs may also have to be separately broken out. Appendix C, "Personnel Measures and Fringe Benefits," identifies and discusses many of the elements pertinent to this whole critical topic.

Budget Justification.   In this part of the application *reasons* are given for some or all the requested line-items (and their cost elements) in terms of their particular relevance or indispensability to the proposed program. The need for every line-item and cost element may seem self-evident to applicants, but skeptical outsiders may not so easily grasp the reasoning involved. This text must address reasons not only for an item or an element's inclusion in the budget but also for the number, quality, and basic cost of units. For example, the role of a program's counselors may have been clearly set forth in the Program Narrative, but that text did not make clear why the *number* of counselors (aides, supervisors) is really needed, or why these persons must be hired at the salary levels stated. Justification statements tie together the budget (and its explication) and the program description and rationale and, again, will be easier if anticipated in preparing the Program Narrative.

As pointed out in Chapter 2, administrative tasks and responsibilities are assigned and managed in widely varying patterns. Thus in many organizations a number of people will be assigned to prepare different parts, or parts of parts, of the funding proposal. This seems to make sense because the full documentation packet can so readily be subdivided and parceled out. This way of proceeding is fine *if at least one person* has full responsibility for collecting all the parts; for checking that they are accurate, sufficient, and valid; for filling in the gaps; and for ensuring that they fit together. Whatever administrative arrangements are decided upon, the final documentation packet for the funder must present an explicit, clear-cut image of the program *as a whole*. This means that all the materials must be consistent and integrated.

Despite the hectic scramble usually associated with preparing these documents, we urge administrators to leave enough time to be able to stand back, review the whole packet, and ask themselves:

- Is the program description concise and comprehensive, or is it full of ambiguities and jargon, signifying little?
- Does it focus on the primary purposes of the program, or are they buried under pages of verbiage?

- Does it portray expected accomplishments realistically, or does it make global promises?
- Does the budget accurately reflect the program plans, or are there gaps and redundancies?
- Have the calculations been checked and rechecked, or has accuracy been assumed?
- Are all stated requirements satisfied and included in the packet, or are there still loose ends to be attended to?

When all such questions can be answered satisfactorily, the document packet is ready to receive final agency approval.

Submission to the Funder

After the entire application packet has been prepared, it must be submitted as a formal request by the agency in its capacity as fiduciary; that is, as the organization to which funds will be awarded. The proper authority of the agency must be exercised in reviewing, approving, signing, and forwarding the application document. A fund award is legally binding when approved and signed by officials of both parties, and thus is contractual. Allocations within state or local governments do not involve contracts as such, but they do require adherence to proper legal procedure and mandates. We have presumed that senior agency officials (and members of governing boards or commissions where these exist) have approved the program and budget development effort, as discussed throughout this chapter, and have had continuous knowledge of its progress. In many agencies such senior persons will themselves have participated in key steps of this work. In larger organizations they will have authorized these efforts but become directly involved only to deal with critical decisions, and at the end to give formal approval to the application. Obviously this would not be the time to discover that certain features of the proposed program and budget are at variance with agency policy or intention. We have also presumed in this chapter that some interactions have occurred between the agency and the funder—including notice of a lower award ceiling in midstream—so the final package should not create a crisis within the agency or an impasse between it and the prospective funder.

The end of the beginning is reached when the responsible agency official signs the application and forwards it to the funder, then awaits the outcome of the funding review process.

4

THE ILLUSTRATIVE PROGRAM AND EXERCISES

Introduction to the Exercises

THE FOLLOWING INSTRUCTIONS give the essential information you need to work out all the exercises in the book. They are intended as guidelines to help you understand the general ground rules that apply to the problems and their solutions.

We emphasize at the start that *there are no tricks or gimmicks in any exercise.* We try never to deceive or confuse the reader; every effort has been made to present the information, the tasks, and the procedures in understandable terms. These exercises have been put to the test many times in workshops and classes and with people at widely differing levels of knowledge and experience. Readers with ample experience may wish to pick and choose among the steps.

Often you may believe that to solve a problem you need more concrete information than appears to have been given. At such times, we suggest two complementary approaches. (1) Reread all the information you have, keeping in mind the problem confronting you. This may well include details about the program from previous chapters. (2) If concrete information still eludes you, make reasonable assumptions based on the facts you do have. More facts may be available than are obvious at first, and certainly sufficient information is always given to make logical, reasonable assumptions. You may well wish for more data—but then so do most administrators most of the time.

The exercises simulate the kinds of tasks and standard practices found in the majority of agencies and programs. They follow the sequential and cumulative mode of the book. Since the exercises deal throughout with one program, the solutions to the set of exercises in one chapter serve as the basis for the material given in those following. The exercises span a broad range of necessary administrative problem-solving skills: comprehending basic information; calculating, handling, and analyzing a variety of data in a variety of ways; making estimates, judgments, and choices about program and budget matters; clarifying, interpreting, and justifying decisions; documenting fiscal and related facts; and proposing remedies, changes, and successive actions.

Each set of exercises will have its own introduction in which the situation at the illustrative program is brought up to date, the main tasks and problems are outlined, and some general advice and cautions are offered. Additional text is often given to point out the implications of various solutions for a problem. We suggest that you read through all the exercise steps in a chapter *before* starting to solve any of them so that the relationships and reciprocal effects between the problems (and their solutions) are well understood.

Each exercise presents a specific problem to be addressed and resolved through a set of detailed steps. For certain steps—especially those consisting entirely of calculations—only one result or answer is correct. Most of the time, however, there is no "unique" (that is, one and only one) solution. Alternative solutions are not only possible, they are to be expected. The task then consists in *optimizing* the solution in relation to the overall issues raised by the steps, rather than searching for a single "right" solution that does not exist. Optimization means more than accurate and prudent handling of fiscal resources or adherence to agency or funder requirements, although it never means less than that. It also means maintaining or improving the quality of program services with attention to the implications of fiscal issues and decisions on staffing, performance assessment, external relations, service delivery, relations with clients, and so on. These considerations should play a large part in all your problem-solving.

Calculation errors are a common hazard, and a pocket calculator is invaluable for the exercises. Most people heavily involved in budgeting prefer a printout calculator, but this is not essential for these exercises.

A Note About Budget Forms. Agencies typically use different, but compatible, forms for different fiscal purposes; even similar agencies tend not to use identical forms unless they are imposed by a funder. Administrators thus must become familiar with a variety of fiscal reporting forms. We introduce in the exercise section of this chapter a budget form for the illustrative program that is the first in a series of forms. Our forms have been simplified and generally standardized, but important features of each are varied to fit the specific purposes of a set of exercises. However, all the forms include the *same line-item labels and numbers.* To facilitate work on the exercises, we purposely use fewer line-item categories and subcategories (elements) than may be common in most organizations. In general, the categories and labels we use are congruent with those in many kinds of agencies and governmental units, and readers familiar with other forms should have no difficulty understanding ours. If a line-item has a special definition, it will be explained on the line itself or in a note at the bottom of the form. (A complete listing of customary line-item categories and elements is given in Appendix B.) Several features of our forms will differ between chapters: The captions will indicate the particular fiscal period and purpose, and the columns will have different headings from chapter to chapter, but all accord with common usage.

Introduction to the Illustrative Program

Beginning in the next section and through Chapter 10 we follow the progression of budget cycle processes and procedures through the medium of an illustrative exemplary program, which is established within a larger parent agency. All the exercises in the book are cast around the fiscal tasks and responsibilities of this program. Readers are asked to translate the explanatory information given in each chapter into solutions of this program's real-life problems. As the program moves through the budget cycle, readers work on the authentic tasks faced by administrative staff at that particular time in the cycle.

We have designed a program that deals with a serious issue. As should be clear to readers from our numerous examples in the text, this program's underlying fiscal burdens and problems (as well as their solutions) are deliberately representative of those faced in the not-for-profit sector. We urge readers associated with other types of programs—or with similar ones having a different clientele—to become thoroughly familiar with this one. We are convinced that most of the *kinds* of budget and fiscal problems, all the procedures used to solve them, and the general kinds of judgments called for are generic in the not-for-profit sector. Idiosyncratic differences can be better handled when the fundamental issues are fully understood. In fact, even those acquainted with comparable programs will be introduced to demanding new situations and considerations.

We adhere to several important, unchanging prescripts throughout the fiscal history of the illustrative program as it is unfolded below and in succeeding chapters.

1. The amount of information given simulates reality. Everyone in administration faces unknown factors, ambiguities, dilemmas, and imponderables. So does the coordinator of this program. For example, some of the job titles in the illustrative program are purposely vague, because job descriptions are frequently not specifically defined for these types of jobs in small and medium-size programs and agencies or are outdated in larger organizations. Thus readers will have to think about the most productive ways to use these staff members, what their main and secondary duties should be, and the presumptive staff skills implied by the salary rates. The facts on which to make such judgments and decisions are either included in the background and evolving information, can be logically deduced, or must be simply estimated, as in real life.

2. The program's objectives and responsibilities are consistent all the way through. Its basic purposes at the start of the program do not change, but in later phases some activities may be modified in the light of experience.

3. To simplify mastery of the procedures, the entire cost of this program is supported by a single funder. The funder's

behavior is typical and representative, so a specific identity is irrelevant. The procedures can be applied to multisource funding (and scrambled cycles) only after they are fully understood; the single funder approach helps us clarify the rationales and techniques for the procedures.

4. The various phases of the budget cycle are exemplified at *different points* during the program's operation. That is, to cover major fiscal events, we will be involved with the program as it develops and reduces its first full year's budget, during its start-up phase, halfway through a fiscal year, at the end of that fiscal year, and as it plans for the next year. Thus the fiscal history is *sequential and cumulative*—as we "drop in" at crucial points. This plan also allows us to deal with the use of cost analysis procedures in forward program and budget planning.

Let us now get acquainted with the illustrative program as you the reader begin your new job as a member of the administrative staff.

Program Case Description
Johnson Youth Center—Community Youth Services

COMMUNITY, AGENCY, AND PROGRAM BACKGROUND

The Johnson Youth Center is located in Johnsonville (about 120,000 people), one of several cities in the county. Johnsonville has a few large factories and a number of smaller manufacturing and service-related industries. The surrounding area is mainly agricultural, and the county boasts a diversified economy.

Johnson Youth Center (JYC), a nonsectarian private agency, provides *residential* services for male youth aged thirteen through sixteen. Some of these youngsters, whose troubles include family problems, behavioral difficulties, and delinquency, have been adjudicated and sent to the Center by the county juvenile court. On the average, thirty boys are in residence at all times through the year, and no other such residential facilities are available in this part of the county.

The center employs a total staff of thirty-five. Its revenues for this year are derived from a variety of sources, including the United Way, purchase-of-service contracts, contributions, private fees, and a modest endowment.

For the past few years both the juvenile court judge and community leaders have expressed concern about Johnsonville's lack of *non*residential services for youth—both male and female—having behavioral problems in school, in the community, or at home. The county seat has long had a Community Mental Health Center (CMHC) that provides nonresidential services, but the county seat is more than 45 miles away, and the CMHC has not been able to extend its activities to other parts of the county.

About nine months ago Judge Parker of the Juvenile Court, after informal talks with various community leaders, approached a prospective funder who showed definite interest in the idea of such a program and indicated possible participation at a "reasonable level" (direct quote). The Judge then requested the Johnson Youth Center (JYC) Board of Directors, in collaboration with community groups, to begin developing plans for a program that could offer nonresidential services for youngsters not receiving help with their problems. The Judge stressed the need to relieve the court, which was seriously overloaded, but also affirmed his (and the community's) view that most of the youth experiencing or demonstrating difficulties could and should be "diverted" from the juvenile justice system, and that they might well be served through other resources already existing in this community. Youths' difficulties could be resolved by engaging the assistance of a wide variety of local groups, agencies, schools, employers, and, of course, the families.

The Board agreed in general with the Judge that such youth can often be better served in a nonresidential setting and, further, that JYC had at least as much competence as any other agency to develop this new alternative program. The Board was also aware that Judge Parker wielded considerable influence and that he indirectly controlled much of the Center's purchase-of-service funds.

The Board, therefore, organized a Planning Committee, which included interested people from diverse community groups, and assigned the JYC Executive Director to coordinate and guide the committee's efforts. The Board empowered the committee to document the need for such a program ("needs assessment") and then to start drawing up plans for a program that would operate under the aegis of the JYC agency. The committee charged the Director to begin work immediately with some JYC staff to formulate specific objectives for the new program, define its scope and activities, survey community resources, set up an organizational plan, and make initial budget estimates. The Planning Committee met regularly with the Director to review the emerging plans and to contribute its own ideas, recommendations, and criticisms.

At an early stage in the planning the committee, the Board, and Judge Parker agreed that the public should be able to distinguish clearly between the new program and the existing residential services at JYC. It was decided that the new program should have a different name—*Community Youth Services (CYS)*—a separate staff, a separate location, and a separate fund account. In addition, it was decided that although all CYS operations would be separately identified, the program would be entirely subject to the policies of the JYC Board, with the JYC Director maintaining executive authority.

After four months' work, the Planning Committee had prepared the needs assessment, mapped out an overall program plan, and developed a preliminary budget for the CYS program. The JYC Board, the Judge, a representative of the prospective funder, and some community leaders were then invited to a meeting for a full-scale presentation of the committee's plans. Various parts had been previewed by individuals from the Board and the community, and the Judge had been apprised of the plan's general features. At this review session the planning group thus hoped for general agreement and approval of its plans and a decision about the next steps to be taken.

At the meeting the Director at JYC, who was asked to be spokesperson for the Planning Committee, first briefly outlined the charge given to the committee and the rationale and objectives for the new program, and then moved directly to the results of their efforts, as follows:

The Community Youth Services (CYS) program will provide services to a variety of male and female youth in the 12–16 age range who are exhibiting or experiencing difficulties that might eventually bring them before the juvenile court. Since the major sources of referrals and petitions to the court are currently the police, schools, families, and social agencies—in that order—it has been assumed that the new program will draw its clients from the same sources. However, to maintain its goal of "diversion," CYS must attempt to have its services used *before* any formal court proceedings have begun. In line with Judge Parker's directive, CYS—to avoid even a semblance of coercion—will not accept any youth for whom a *formal* petition or charge has already been filed with the court. Youth will also be able to seek CYS services on their own initiative, but regardless of who requests the services, these will be given only when, and for as long as, a youth—with parental consent—voluntarily agrees to participate. As a corollary objective, CYS will actively seek broad community understanding and ongoing community collaboration in implementing its activities.

The planners found that experienced observers are convinced that problem situations frequently call for little or no direct formal organizational action. For example, when unfounded complaints or charges are made against a youth; or when the problem is trivial; or when formal intervention may only complicate a simple resolution of the problem. The CYS program is to be based on the belief that in most other situations a youth's difficulties can be adequately handled by discriminating use of existing community resources and opportunities—including help from families and neighbors, schools, social agencies, churches, voluntary associations, private employers, etc. An early and continuing effort must be made by CYS to identify these resources, to mobilize their interest and cooperation, and to facilitate youths' access to them.

Therefore, the new CYS program will concentrate on four major activities (see the flowchart below) [Figure 4–1]:

- *Screening* all potential clients and *Intake* for those accepted
- *Referral* out to other community resources for the less demanding cases
- *Consultation/Referral* for clients with more complicated needs requiring collaborative services between CYS and the referral sources
- *Counseling* for those few clients for whom no other assistance is available

During the discussion of these program plans, the review

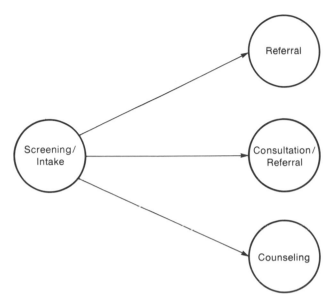

Figure 4–1.   CYS Program Activities

group agreed, on the whole, that the CYS activities as outlined met the general objectives that had been intended. Further, the reviewers concluded that only with experience
could it be decided whether the program should concentrate
on diverting and actively referring clients, or on coordination of services and youth advocacy, or on more counseling—or whether it should maintain a mix of all these. They
therefore decided not to make definite long-range decisions
yet, to accept the proposed mix of activities, and to recommend that this question be reconsidered after a year's experience with the new program.

The JYC Director assured the group that the CYS program staff would systematically collect several kinds of
basic information from the outset. Accurate files on clients
would be developed, time logs would be used to record staff
activities, and reliable records of all fiscal transactions
would be maintained. All these files would be linked in ways
that would permit monitoring and reporting of activities, so
that service data and comparative costs would be available
for assessing services and reaching sound decisions about
the future directions for CYS.

As soon as the reviewers reached consensus on the program plans, copies of the line-item Preliminary Request Budget were handed out. At this point the atmosphere in the room became more charged as everyone sensed that all would depend on the reaction of the prospective funder's representative (seated next to Judge Parker), who had not joined in the previous discussion. The Director stressed that it had not been possible to determine or confirm every jot and tittle of the Preliminary Budget before them, but the Planning Committee believed that it had done a good job given the time pressures and the uncertainties characteristic of a new program.

Selected portions of the Budget Narrative were also handed out to illustrate how the committee had estimated some of the line-item categories; the Director pointed out that the number and type of personnel were based on an estimated total of about 1,150 clients for the year. (Major items in this Preliminary Budget will be analyzed in the following exercise section.)

After the review group had studied the documents and people had a chance to ask some questions and make some comments, all eyes turned to the prospective funder's representative. He began by complimenting the planning group on their efforts to be as specific as possible and then stated that he had two serious reservations about the budget as a whole.

First and foremost the total amount requested was higher than he was prepared to recommend to the organization he represented. He was impressed by the program plan and was ready to recommend support for the package if the total budget were reduced by at least $63,000. At the same time his organization would expect the contribution from JYC to be continued at approximately the same level shown in the Preliminary Budget.

Second, he was convinced that it was not really possible—and not wise—to plan a budget for a full year's operations starting from the first day the CYS began its program. At the most practical level, how could CYS hire and prepare a full staff ready to go to work on Day One? He believed it would be more sensible to plan and budget for an initial startup period during which staff could be hired and trained, relations with community organizations could be developed and cemented, and certain kinds of costs—like those for one-time-only expenditures—could be segregated from ongoing operational expenses. A followup twelve-month budget would then delineate a fully operational program.

Therefore, he believed his organization would be prepared to support the CYS program under the following conditions.

- Using the basic information already gathered, the JYC Board, as the fiduciary body, should develop *new fully documented budgets* for a two-part CYS implementation and funding plan to span sixteen months.
- Part 1 would consist of an initial four-month budget incorporating the concerns and matters he had just indicated; and Part 2 of a full fiscal year budget starting at the fifth month with the program in place and all staff on board, but at a maximum of $292,430.

The funder's representative emphasized that the preparation of a two-part application proposal would have several advantages: It would clarify planning to distinguish between the CYS initiation phase and the period when it should be able to commence full services; it would identify program activities and costs that should be quite different during the startup phase; and it would mean that the first full fiscal year of program and expenditure experience could serve as a more reliable guide to future CYS planning and costing because startup activities would not be mixed up in it.

Sensing the group's hesitancy to respond, Judge Parker expressed the gathering's great appreciation to the funder's representative for his positive response and constructive suggestions. He then informally "moved" that the JYC Director be authorized to begin implementing the representative's proposals with the help of a staff team and with the continuing cooperation of the Planning Committee. The Judge further recommended that within one month the committee's revised budgets be submitted through the Director to the JYC Board for approval. He was sure this was possible because so much of the preliminary effort would be useful as the plans and budgets became honed and refined.

The group gratefully endorsed the Judge's "motion" and

set a date, one month hence, at which time the JYC Board would report on its approved new full-year budget and the four-month startup budget. With that the meeting adjourned.

Exercise Problems

You, the reader, now begin your new role at CYS. It is assumed, here and in succeeding exercise sections, that you are a member of a larger administrative group and that many fiscal activities and decisions are handled by others in the group. Therefore, you will actually participate—as in the real world—in only some tasks and efforts at CYS. Often you will be directly informed about the results of others' work; sometimes you may learn about them obliquely; and at other times you will find out by inference or deduction.

In this exercise, you first take part in some of the tasks of the Cutback (twelve-month) Budget team; later in this section you will join the Startup (four-month) Budget team. For the first team, you are mainly responsible for working on some of the backup details it needs to make sound decisions about reductions. Thus your initial tasks focus on ways of using basic techniques for manipulating and distilling essential fiscal data.

Introduction to Exercise Steps

Several members of the newly appointed Cutback Budget team had not been part of the Preliminary Request Budget group, and they were urged to prepare for their first meeting by studying the notes of the Planning Committee, the entire line-item Preliminary Request Budget (see p. 87), and the accompanying Budget Narrative (excerpts on pp. 89–92).

At the first Cutback Budget team meeting the JYC Director reviewed the planning and rationale of the Preliminary Budget, provided background information, and answered questions. Many of the questions raised by the team focused on the line-items not dealt with in the Budget Narrative excerpts. The full discussion is summarized here.

JOHNSON YOUTH CENTER

Program Community Youth Services

For Internal Use Only

PRELIMINARY REQUEST BUDGET

Line Item		Requested Budget Col. 1	Contributed Budget Col. 2	Comments on Line-Items Col. 3
Personnel	FTEs			
1a. Prog. Coordinator	1.00	25,900		
1b. Screening Sup'or	1.00	22,260		
1c. Intake Worker	1.00	18,400		
1d. Liaison Workers	4.00	71,400		See Budget Narrative
1e. Counselors	2.50	41,310		
1f. Secretaries	2.00	22,000		
1g. Bookkeeper	.25	3,000		
	11.75			
1. Total Sal/Wages		204,270		
2. Employee Benefits & Payroll Taxes		40,854		At JYC rate of 20% of Sal/Wages
3. Professional Fees		11,110		See Budget Narrative
4. Supplies, Communications, & Reproduction		10,452		See Budget Narrative
5. Occupancy: Rent Renovation		15,000 2,500		1,775 square feet at $8.45 per sq. ft.
6. Travel: Local Conference		2,620 3,225		See Budget Narrative
7. Equipment		4,480	8,400	See Note A Below
8. Assistance to Clients: Vendor Charges Financial Aid		3,500 3,200		See Budget Narrative
9. TOTAL DIRECT COSTS		301,211	8,400	
10. Overhead/Indirect		54,218		At prevailing JYC rate of 18% of TDC
11. GRAND TOTAL		355,429	8,400	

Special Note:

    A. Includes funds for one-time-only purchases; Contributed Funds from JYC for basic office furniture, etc.

PRELIMINARY BUDGET REVIEW

1. The *types and range* of positions in the *Personnel* category were derived from both the general and specific objectives for CYS as enunciated by the Planning Committee. The *number of positions and the FTEs* were based on an

early estimate of approximately 1,150 youths for the first year of operations. The *salary rates* parallel those for approximately comparable positions at JYC—but at the higher end of the range for each—and at several other local agencies. As indicated earlier, this practice justifiably allows for some flexibility in a preliminary budget when specific individuals at specific grade levels and salaries are unknown. Excessive "padding" is not the issue here—merely cautious estimates in the face of many unknowns.

2. *Employee Benefits and Payroll Taxes* were based on the same *percentage* factor of total Salaries/Wages used at JYC.

3. *Occupancy* costs represent the actual price for a preferred location among several acceptable alternatives: 1,775 square feet at $8.45 per square foot—a moderate per square foot cost in this locality. The price includes heat, electricity, and water. The amount of square footage requested was based on the type and number of planned personnel, the number of expected clients, and the nature of the staff/client interactions.

4. *Equipment* consists of the costs of renting a copying machine and the purchases of a mimeograph, typewriters, and other office equipment. All standard office furniture was included in the JYC *Contributed Funds*, which, as noted earlier, represent cost-sharing support by the parent agency.

5. *Special Assistance to Clients* contains two subcategories. *Vendor Charges* relates to certain special aid that may be deemed essential for selected clients to advance their opportunities for employment or to correct minor physical problems; for example, to attend brief training sessions or short remedial courses, corrective dental or medical procedures, eyeglasses, and so on. The funds in *Financial Aid* are to be expended for specific short-term work experiences for a few clients, sometimes at CYS itself; or to underwrite temporarily a portion of an employer's hourly wages to enable the client to demonstrate capability in that job.

6. *Overhead/Indirect* costs were based on a formula of *18 percent* of Total Direct Costs. This percentage conforms with what is allowed by other funders of the JYC agency. The exact formula allowed by the actual funder was not known at the time.

By the end of the meeting the group was fully aware of the nonspecific status of some of the line-item costs in the Preliminary Request Budget. Clearly, the Revised Budget team would have to pin down and firmly fix many of the dollar figures.

Narrative Excerpts—Preliminary Budget

PERSONNEL

1a. Program Coordinator   1.00 FTE $25,900 annual salary

Explication.[11]

The Program Coordinator will assume overall administrative management of CYS under the general direction of the JYC Director and subject to the policies of the JYC Board of Directors. The duties of the Coordinator will include: leadership and direction in the final planning and initial implementation of the CYS program; recruitment, selection, performance assessment, retention, and termination of CYS staff; interpretation of the CYS program to community agencies and groups and to the general public; development of collaborative relations with appropriate service organizations, youth referral sources, the Juvenile Court, and other local groups; direction and coordination of all CYS operations and personnel, maintenance of program quality, and assessment of results; management of CYS resources, maintenance of necessary files and reporting procedures, and cooperation with JYC central services staff; responsibility for periodic reports on all aspects of the CYS program to the JYC Director and Board, and to the funder.

Qualifications: Master's degree in social work or equivalent professional degree; at least three years' experience in programs serving youth; and demonstrated administrative skills.

Justification.

As a responsibility center, CYS must have at least one person with full administrative authority. Given its small size and its close ties to JYC, it was considered sufficient to vest all such authority in the Program Coordinator position.

[11]The words "explication" and "justification" are included here for demonstration only; they are often not used in an application.

PROFESSIONAL FEES

A total of $11,110 is requested for consultants to be expended as follows:

1. *Explication.*

A total of $4,900 for advisers during the first few months of the new program. Some of these consultants will be specialists in program and organizational development, others in legal and juvenile justice affairs, and probably still others in behavior theory. This will permit the Coordinator to engage skilled resources in the community to aid in the major tasks and problems in developing and launching CYS.

2. *Explication.*

A total of $6,210 for special and technical consultants needed as the program becomes fully operative. Such consultants might include experts in behavioral techniques, counseling, learning disabilities, delinquency, etc.

Justification.

To make the program's efforts successful within the first year, it will be necessary to call on additional advice from persons with particular skills. The staff of CYS, while sufficient for ongoing tasks, will gain greater competency from the expertise of knowledgeable, recognized specialists, who will advise on individual cases and program plans.

All consultants will be paid at the $175 per day *maximum* rate (per JYC regulations). Prior approval of the Program Coordinator will be obtained for each consultant. The $11,110 provides the equivalent of almost 64 work days at $175 per day for the fiscal year.

SUPPLIES, COMMUNICATIONS, AND REPRODUCTION

This category includes all office supplies; postage and telephone charges; and reproduction of reports, forms, and documents. Total cost $10,452.

A. *Office Supplies.* Supplies for routine office operations are estimated and budgeted as follows:

1. Paper supplies (pads, folders, envelopes, etc.)	$724
2. Standard office supplies (ribbons, pencils, etc.)	394
3. Subscriptions to important journals—16 at $22 each	352
4. Reproduction supplies (stencils, mimeo ink, etc.)	556
5. Paper collator	250
6. Four printout calculators @ $65	260
	$2,536

B. *Office Furnishings.* (bookcases, chairs, etc.) $850
C. *Postage.* Calculated at 30 items per day at 20¢
   each = $6 per day x 5-day week = $30 per week x
   52 weeks. $1,560
D. *Telephone.* Estimated at $275 per month (for 4
   lines) x 12 months = $3,300. Installation and
   equipment charges = $1,340. $4,640
E. *Reproduction.*
   1. Letterheads
      a. Stationary estimated at $45 per 1,000 x
         10,000 sheets $450
      b. Imprinted envelopes at $30 per 1,000 x
         10,000   300
   2. Duplicating paper at $5.80 per 500 sheets x
      10,000 sheets   116
                                                                   $866

Summary: A . $2,536
          B .   850
          C .   1,560
          D .   4,640
          E .   866

   Total $10,452

TRAVEL

Projected costs (total $5,845) for all activities in this category are based on the following:
1. Intercity costs are estimated according to prevailing air fares.
2. Intracity costs adhere to the mileage reimbursement rate currently used by JYC (21¢ per mile).
3. Prior permission for conference attendance will be obtained from the JYC Director for each trip.
4. Per diem at conferences conform with JYC guidelines.
The requested funds will be used as follows:

A. *Local Travel* ($2,620).

Mileage costs for intracity and county travel were determined at 21¢ per mile, conforming to JYC current reimbursement rates. It is estimated that all staff members, except the Intake Worker and secretaries, will have to drive to various points in the city and its environs for a variety of reasons: arranging school and agency placements, meetings with parents in their own homes, attending selected staff meetings at JYC, informational and public relations meetings with a variety of local officials, transporting clients to appointments or job opportunities, etc. The sum requested is less than the purchase and operating cost of a vehicle for

CYS. The budget figures reflect the best estimate of 48 miles per day x 5-day week = 240 miles per week x 52 weeks = 12,480 x 21¢ per mile = $2,620.

B. *Conferences* ($1,945).

Professional conferences can immeasurably enhance the skills of staff, especially for a newly developed service program. Therefore, a broad selection of such meetings is included in this request. All trips are based on current RT airfare rates.

Program Coordinator	
Atlanta: National Association of Social Workers	$275
Los Angeles: Diversion Program Directors Association	450
Screening Supervisor	
Houston: American Psychological Association	275
Washington, D.C.: Council of School Social Workers	275
Liaison Workers (2 persons on trip)	
New York City: training session by Criminal Justice Institute @$200	400
Counselors (2 persons on trip)	
Nashville: behavioral modification training session @$135	270
	Total: $1,945

C. *Additional Conference Travel Costs* ($320).

1. Included in this category are costs to and from airports in the home city and in the destination city while attending conferences. These are based on current actual prices for home city/airport travel, and on estimated averages to/from airports in destination cities (@$16 RT, making a total of $32 per trip per person. Thus, as explained above, 8 out-of-state trips x $32 = $256).

2. Also included are taxi fares to/from hotel while attending conferences. These are estimated at $8 per conference. Thus, 8 trips x $8 = $64.

Total: $320

D. *Per Diem (Subsistence) at Conferences* ($960).

Costs here are based on $60 per diem. For each of the conferences listed above, it is planned that staff (1 or 2 persons, as stated) will attend for two days. 16 conference days x $60 = $960.

Total: $960

Exercise Steps: Part I

The team decides that it must come to grips with the whole issue of Personnel before any other budget cutbacks can be considered. It is therefore agreed that *you* will decode the following vital information and will distribute it to the team before its next meeting in two days. (Note to Reader: working out these exercise steps will help anchor the material discussed at length in Chapter 3. By actually doing the tasks, the techniques and explanations can be better understood.)

The concrete information you will produce is absolutely essential, because the cutback group must be able to get behind the summarized totals in the Preliminary Budget when deciding whether to cut part of an FTE, decrease a salary rate, change a position grade, and the like. Actually, your work retraces some of the processes that went into the development of the preliminary totals; unfortunately and typically, however, those backup data were either misplaced or lost. Administrative staff must often create their own backup worksheets to disentangle certain fiscal information and to make new calculations. Usually the process involves first transferring pertinent summary data to the worksheet, then separating out the underlying needed details, and, lastly, summarizing the new data on reporting forms, as needed. Worksheets and the backup data to support them should always be retained; it is amazing how often some piece of that information turns out to be critically important at a later time.

Step 1. Complete the following detailed chart *for each position line* shown in the Personnel line-item in the Preliminary Budget. (Occasionally, as in this chart, we give some portion of the correct figures to serve as both a check and a guide.)

Step 1A. Transfer all the summarized Personnel information in the Preliminary Budget to Columns 1, 2, and 3.

Step 1B. In Column 4, enter the *annual salary rate for 1.00 FTE* for each position line, rounding to the nearest dollar. You must use the *average* for those lines showing *more* than 1.00 FTE since no individual rates are known at

TABLE 4–1.   Detailed Personnel Chart (From Preliminary Budget)

Title (Col. 1)	Salary Subtotal (Col. 2)	FTEs (Col. 3)	Average Annual Salary Rate Per FTE (Col. 4)	Average Monthly Salary Rate Per FTE (Col. 5)	Total Work/Months Per Position (Col. 6)
1a. Pr. Coord.	25,900	1.00	25,900	2158.33	12
1b. Scr. Super	22260	1.00	22260	1855	12
1c. IW	18400	1	18400	1533	12
1d. Liaison Workers	$71,400	4.00	$17,850	$1,487.50	48.00
1e. Counselors	41310	2.50	16524	1377	30
1f. Secretary	22000	2	11000	916.66	48
1g. Bookkeeper	3,000	.25	12,000	1,000	3
Totals			n.a.	n.a.	

this time; for any line showing *less* than 1.00 FTE, give the equivalent full-time rate for that position.

Step 1C. In Column 5, fill in the *monthly salary rate for 1.00 FTE* for each position line. Again, you must use averages for those lines showing more than 1.00 FTE, and the equivalent full-time rate for any line showing less than 1.00 FTE. Do not overlook the importance of the *cents* in a monthly (or weekly) salary rate.

Step 1D. In Column 6, report the *total work/months* of service for *the actual FTEs* on each position line in Column 3 of the Preliminary Budget (see the exemplary exhibits in Appendix C). It is simple to check your results in Col. 6; first, multiply the total FTEs in Col. 3 by 12; then add your total work/months in Col. 6. If they are not the same, you have made a mistake and should recheck your Col. 6 figures.

Step 2. Calculate the *ratio* of secretarial FTEs to the subtotal of *all other* FTEs in the Preliminary Budget. Refer to Appendix C for a full explanation of ratios and their significance.

Step 3. Review the Preliminary Budget Narrative excerpts and decide on at least *two* budget *elements* given there that you would recommend as likely one-time-only (OTO) costs. Recall that a budget element refers to a single object (that is, thing, service, or material) within a line-item category.

Step 3A. For *either* of the OTO elements you selected,

determine its precise specifications and obtain its actual market price in your locality from *two* reliable sources.

Step 3B. Using the column headings on a facsimile of the Cost Estimation Form given in Chapter 3, fill out work sheets with this detailed cost and other information.

Step 3C. Give *four* reasons why (justification) this element should properly be purchased in the CYS startup period.

Step 4. Create a job description (explication) for the particular position you, *the reader*, currently hold in your real-life employment. Tie the duties to specific objectives of your program; do not refer to any general guidelines that may be issued officially by your organization. Then ask a co-worker to review your explication.

The Revised Cutback Budget

Upon completion of these tasks, you are reassigned to the Startup Budget team, which, within a short time, receives the completed Revised twelve-month Budget. This has been reviewed, modified, approved by the JYC Director and Board, and then accepted in principle by the funding organization. The Revised Line-Item Budget and the accompanying explanation—both *for internal use only*—are reproduced here. Both documents will serve as planning bases for the startup phase at CYS.

REVISED BUDGET COMMENTARY

Personnel.

Every position was reassessed, focusing on the priority schema and on the type and level of essential skills, duties, and effort expected of the total staff complement and of each individual position within it. From this deliberate reevaluation, both the FTEs and the salary rates could be more definitively specified. (Remember that many of the salary rates in the Preliminary Budget had been purposely estimated at the upper end of the ranges.) The following summary chronicles the final decisions.

The Program Coordinator and the Screening Supervisor each remain at 1.00 FTE at lower, but still competitive, salary rates.

JOHNSON YOUTH CENTER   For Internal Use Only

Program Community Youth Services

REVISED 12-MONTH REQUEST BUDGET

Line Item		Requested Budget Col. 1	Contributed Budget Col. 2	Comments on Line-Items Col. 3
Personnel	FTEs			
1a. Prog. Coordinator	1.00	24,000		
1b. Screening Sup'or	1.00	21,000		Personnel reduced by
1c. Intake Worker	.80	14,720		1.65 FTEs
1d. Liaison Workers	3.30	57,750		
1e. Counselors	2.00	32,400		
1f. Secretaries	2.00	24,000		
	10.10			
1. Total Sal/Wages		173,870		
2. Employee Benefits & Payroll Taxes		34,774		Rate remains at 20% of Sal/Wages
3. Professional Fees		4,200		See text
4. Supplies, Communications, & Reproduction		6,500		One-time-only elements eliminated; standard supplies cut-back, costs refined
5. Occupancy: Rent Renovation		12,000 ---		Space reduced 20% Renovation eliminated
6. Travel: Local Conference		4,925 800		Increased over 85% Reduced approx. 75%
7. Equipment		3,000		One-time-only costs deleted
8. Assistance to Clients: Vendor Charges Financial Aid		3,600 3,800		Increased $100 Increased $600
9. TOTAL DIRECT COSTS		247,469		
10. Overhead/Indirect		44,544		Remains at 18%
11. GRAND TOTAL		292,013		

Special Note:

The Intake Worker position was reduced from full-time to .80 FTE; the salary remained the same. The team and the Director felt that the duties of this person seemed at this time to be sufficiently similar to those of the Screening Supervisor and the Secretaries to warrant a less than full-time position.

The role of the Liaison Workers vis-à-vis the Counselors evoked serious discussions about the entire program design and purpose. Their respective job responsibilities were more difficult to particularize, and it seemed that their tasks might well overlap or be interchangeable at various times. In addition, the reduced budget implied a slight decrease in the number of total cases that could be handled at CYS. It was finally agreed that CYS's in- and out-referral activities called for a lot of effort at achieving the support and involvement of the community, and that these activities—not intensive personal counseling—were to be emphasized. Therefore it was decided that while FTEs for both positions would be reduced, the larger number of FTEs and the higher salary rates for the Liaison Workers better reflected the importance and expected demands of their jobs. The fewer FTEs and lower salaries of the Counselors would reflect their more modest role in the service plan. It was agreed that more experience with the CYS program was needed before further distinctions could be made.

The Secretarial FTEs were kept at the same level, but the total salary allocated for these positions was slightly increased because higher competency might be required to absorb some of the reduction in the Intake Worker time.

The .25 FTE for a Bookkeeper in the Preliminary Budget was deleted entirely. Further inquiry indicated that a bookkeeper would merely duplicate services to be provided by JYC as part of the Overhead/Indirect costs. Overall budget and fiscal management would, however, still remain part of the Program Coordinator's duties.

Employee Benefits.

These remain at 20 percent of Salaries/Wages; the lower dollar costs reflect the reduction in total Personnel costs.

Professional Fees.

This line-item was drastically cut for several reasons: (a) Most of whatever consulting is needed by CYS should properly occur during the startup phase; (b) the Preliminary Budget team underestimated the abilities expected of the professional staff; (c) such resource persons should be sought in the community at little or no cost; and (d) the funder—like most others—cast a jaundiced eye on the use of many consultants.

In addition to specific cuts in nonpersonnel costs, most other reductions in these categories were predicated on the inseparability of such costs from the number and activities of personnel. Thus, fewer staff members (and fewer cases) need fewer support resources.

Equipment and Supplies.

The cutback team made some critical assumptions about a variety of elements in these categories that it believed could and should appropriately be purchased during the startup phase. These elements ranged from mimeograph machine and telephone installation to letterhead stationery. Since the funder had specifically noted that one-time-only costs should be separated out from the twelve-month budget and assigned to the four-month budget, the team confined the costs in these two categories to ongoing, year-round expenses (monthly telephone and copying machine rental) and consumable supplies, and also obtained more precise cost information.

Travel.

This line-item also occasioned much discussion. The team immediately recognized that all funders look askance at conference travel and per diem. Since the value of conferences could be reckoned only in the most general terms, the total was quickly reduced. The Local Travel subcategory, however, stimulated serious debate about the execution of the program plan. If CYS were to emphasize clients' use of community resources and active community participation, it could well be that staff would have to make many local trips not only directly on behalf of or with clients, but also in search and maintenance of these community relations. Therefore, mileage expectations were recalculated, and the Local Travel budget was increased accordingly.

Occupancy.

The space requirements for CYS were reviewed in light of the smaller staff size, and arrangements were made to rent only part of the originally desired location. Renovation costs were deleted entirely; such costs should be included in the Startup Budget.

Assistance to Clients.

Both subitems in this category were moderately increased, although an internal memo was prepared for the JYC Board indicating that the team hoped additional community resources could be found in the future to support these activities.

Overhead/Indirect.

The team was notified at the start of its deliberations that this particular funder's Overhead rate was 18 percent of Total Direct Costs, which matched the prevailing rate at JYC used in the Preliminary Budget. Given the smaller total budget, the amount in this category was substantially reduced.

Grand Total.

The Revised Cutback Budget shows a 17 percent reduction from the Preliminary Budget and meets the funder's agreed-upon dollar ceiling.

• *Note to Readers:* To grasp thoroughly the effect of the budget reductions on CYS services, we recommend that you use the priority schema and apply the information both fiscal and programmatic—given in all the previous exercise steps. Comparing the Preliminary to the Revised Budget:

- Do the *percentages* of reductions in each partition reflect the priorities in the schema?
- Did the *immediate partition* receive the most protection?
- Were the reduction efforts focused on the distant and proximate partitions?
- Do you think the proportion allotted to the *immediate partition* should be improved? How could this be done?

The Startup Team: Tasks and Assignments

Now that the Revised (cutback) Budget has been approved in principle by the funder, we are ready to turn our attention to work on the startup budget and phase-in plan. This separate startup proposal is needed because program activities and costs during the first four months will differ markedly from those connected with full-scale CYS operations. In addition to rectifying and refining cost estimates, planning for the startup period should be directed toward facilitating an orderly and efficient launching of the new CYS program.

While you were busy with the Revised Budget team, the JYC Director met with the Startup team to review its assignment and to offer some specific suggestions about where and how to begin their tasks. Important parts of this information are paraphrased here and should be read carefully.

JYC PRE-STARTUP PREPARATIONS

The Director first listed the preparations that JYC as the parent agency and employer-of-record will have made even *before* the four-month period begins to assure that CYS gets off to a good start. A summary of these preparations is presented below, followed by a detailed report of the Director's important specific instructions. The Director intends to move on a number of preparatory steps so that the incoming CYS personnel can begin their duties with minimum loss of time when the first fiscal period begins. These preparations will be *completed before Day One of the startup period:*

1. Major policies and program directions for CYS will have been determined, but concrete expression of these must await development of a CYS manual of procedures.
2. The Director intends to have recruited and hired a well-qualified Program Coordinator (PC) and one Secretary to begin service on the first day of the startup period. The PC will thereafter be responsible for interviewing other job applicants and making hiring decisions. Basic job descriptions will have been written for all CYS positions and will have been published to recruit applicants for these jobs.
3. Through the earlier Planning Committee activities and word-of-mouth, key community agencies and groups will have some advance knowledge of the new program but will expect to receive concrete information and to be contacted directly to develop the collaborative arrangements appropriate to each. A descriptive brochure for general distribution will have been prepared and will be delivered during the first month.
4. A lease will be ready for signature to permit immediate occupancy of office space; some interior renovation will be necessary (e.g. some repainting, rewiring of lights).
5. Basic office *furniture* (JYC Contributed Funds in Startup Budget), but not equipment, will be ready for immediate installation in offices. Basic office *Equipment* will have been identified and plans for its early delivery, along with minimum basic office supplies, will be settled.
6. General outlines for administrative relations between JYC and CYS will have been developed to cover such matters as schedules for reporting to the JYC Director and Board, bookkeeping procedures and routines (to be handled by JYC staff), funder accountability, and reporting requirements and procedures. Copies of JYC policies and procedures will be given to the new PC and Screening Supervisor (SS), among others.

All the foregoing represent the kinds of preparatory activities likely to be undertaken by any parent agency for a new program it is launching. Some of these are specifically cited in the total budget application to the funder; others are efforts necessary to make the most efficient use of the four-month startup period, which could certainly not be done if JYC were to do nothing until after the PC was on board.

Instructions for Startup Planning

The Director emphasized that in addition to these preparations, many other tasks must be undertaken *during* the four-month startup period so that CYS can commence service activities. Numerous procedural matters need to be determined, the premises must be occupied and readied for clients, new staff must be hired and oriented to their duties, and concrete negotiations with community groups of all kinds must be undertaken. These are among the matters that your Startup team must address in fulfilling its planning assignments.

The Director concluded by laying out an orderly series of instructions to guide the team's work and your own thinking. You will not be expected to provide all the information and details expected of the team when you handle your own assignments, but you should know what is expected in completing program and budget plans.

First, to identify the primary tasks that must be completed in launching the CYS program: What are the main things that must be done, and what sets of activities will accomplish these? What should be done to prepare out-referral community resources to cooperate with CYS? And what about in-referral sources, including families and youths themselves? When should CYS begin accepting clients? Some things must be started before others, so there must be a staged sequence of activities.

Second, the division of duties among the CYS staff members must be considered: How do the position titles and salary rates suggest levels of skill and types of assignments for personnel? Who should be assigned to which activities? Which staff should be hired first, which should be hired next, and so on, through this period? All listed staff positions should be filled before the four-month period ends, and orientation of new staff must be completed so that service to clients can begin before the start of the twelve-month period. (The Director asks that you assume that qualified personnel will be available for employment when planned and, where this is not so, that appropriate adjustments will be made at the time.)

Finally, to prepare the concrete salary rate and personnel cost figures to implement your startup plan (according to the exercise steps below). These cost estimates must parallel the staff phase-in plans, using salary rates as determined under the approved Request Budget, and calculating actual salary dollars using work/month and equivalent FTE values.

Exercise Steps: Part II

After receiving its instructions from the Director, the team had one full work session together, during which it began concrete planning. Team members concentrated first on reviewing their instructions and making sure these, as well as the expectations for their final proposal, were thoroughly understood. (Note to Reader: You have not yet joined the team but will review the notes taken at this meeting.)

They then decided on a plan and procedure for reaching their objectives. First, they would spend some time working together on aspects of their assignment to become familiar with its main elements. Next, they would break up so each could work independently on preparing preliminary solutions to all parts of the assignment. They would then reassemble to review and assess their efforts, agree on a final solution incorporating the best features of their individual work, and then submit this collective proposal for the startup period.

They started together by developing a *partial* listing of various tasks to be undertaken or completed during the four-month period and assigned some of these to particular staff positions. Here is their partial listing; note that it is incomplete and unordered by any priority or time sequence:

- Contact civic groups, churches, neighborhood associations, and so on to interpret the new CYS program
- Train personnel to handle in-referral inquiries (Scr. Sup.)
- Finish ordering supplies (Sec.)
- List outside units and sources to be contacted for in- and out-referral purposes (PC)
- Occupy new office and assign staff work stations
- Identify vendors and consultants for specialized services (PC and Scr. Sup.)

- Begin establishing basic CYS office files and filing/reporting systems (PC and Sec.)
- Finish interviewing job applicants; select and hire for all positions (PC)
- Determine in- and out-referral criteria and procedures
- Contact and negotiate with outside units and sources about in- and out-referral collaboration
- Begin accepting and serving first clients

As this first work session ended, members gave themselves several assignments to be completed individually before their next team meeting. This is the point at which you join the startup work team—only a little late. These assignments are given below as exercise steps. As you proceed through these steps, you will be preparing your independent materials, just as other team members will be doing, and can look forward to sharing your results so that the entire team can then compose a single best set of proposals to submit to the JYC Director.

Step 5:

Step 5A. Complete the listing in Table 4–2 by entering the other tasks you believe must be undertaken or completed during the startup period. The dots indicate likely missing tasks; fill these in and add any others you wish. Note that you are expected to complete the monthly list of tasks separately for those items essentially intramural (involving only CYS staff) or essentially extramural (in association with representatives of other agencies or with JYC personnel). This rough division of tasks should help sensitize you to the different *kinds* of things to be done during the startup period.

TABLE 4–2. Ordered Listing of CYS Startup Tasks and Assignments *(dots indicate where information may be missing)*

	Intramural	Extramural
MONTH 1:	Develop detailed program operations plan (PC)	Develop comprehensive community relations plan (PC)
	Review and confirm final position descriptions (PC)	Begin contacts with priority groups and start mailing brochure (PC)

(Continued)

TABLE 4–2   (Continued)

	Intramural	Extramural
	Interview applicants, begin hiring staff (PC)	....
	Hire Screen Sup. and assign to major internal duties (PC)	Plan and begin selection of consultants (PC + SS)
	Initiate internal file systems (PC + SS + Sec.)	Begin community resources file (PC + SS + LW)
	Plan work station assignments (PC + SS + Sec.)	....
	Plan staff orientation/ training (PC + SS)	....
	Hire 1 Liaison Worker, orient (PC)	....
	....	....
	....	....
	....	....
MONTH 2:	Begin writing procedures manual, intake/referral criteria, etc. (PC + SS)	....
	....	Begin meetings, negotiations with in- and out-referral resources (SS + LW)
	Plan for and begin consultants (PC + LW)	....
	....	....
	....	....
	Hire 1 Counselor (PC) and orient (SS)	Select priority vendors (SS)
	....	....
	....	....
MONTH 3:	Hire Int. W (PC) and orient (SS)	Handle inquiries, etc. (SS + Sec.)
	....	....
	....	....
	....	....
	....	....
MONTH 4:	....	....
	....	....
	....	Begin client intake (SS + ?)
	....	....
	....	....
	....	....

Step 5B. Next, order each task list for each month according to which item should be started first, which second, and so on. You may also wish to schedule the tasks for approximate times within the month (e.g. first week, mid-month, or other). These orderings are not expected to be hard and fast; they are intended to clarify priorities and will be needed to plan the phasing-in of personnel.

Step 6. Now assign every task in both sets to one or more CYS staff positions (some will be performed by particular individuals, others will be shared duties). The Program Coordinator and Screening Supervisor will, of course, provide supervision to all other staff.

After you are certain that all major startup tasks have been identified, listed, ordered, and assigned, you may want to summarize these by CYS staff positions. This will help you reach decisions about when during the four-month period you would plan to hire each new staff person. Remember, you should work toward a "best case" or preferred schedule for staff hirings, realizing that this will necessarily be altered as the PC must make real-life adjustments to recruit the most capable personnel.

You are now ready to put together a phasing-in plan for all staff, using the ordered list of tasks you have prepared. The details of your plan should be recorded in the appropriate columns of the staffing table (Table 4–3) and will be shared with the team.

Step 7. Enter details about each position in the proper columns of the table. First, insert the work/month figures that record your decisions about when you would hire into each position. Note that correct information about the Program Coordinator has already been entered across all columns, and information about one Secretary has also been entered but only for Month 1. Enter column subtotals as you proceed.

For startup planning, you should assume that CYS can fill all positions with full-time staff except for those budgeted as part-time (the Intake Worker, for example). Staff can be hired at any point during a month, so that the entries may sometimes be less than 1.00 work/month—for example, .50 if a position is to be filled in the middle of a month, and .25 if hired for the last week of a month.

Because the JYC Director will have employed the new PC

TABLE 4–3.   Four-Month Staffing Table

	Month 1	Month 2	Month 3	Month 4	Total Work/ Months	FTES	Total Salaries
1a. Prog. Coord.	1	1	1	1	4	0.33	$8,000.00
1b. Scrn. Sup.	...	...	...	...	...	....	....
1c.	...	...	...	...	...	....	....
1d.	...	...	...	...	...	....	....
1e.	...	...	...	...	...	....	....
1f. Secretaries	1	...	...	...	...	....	....
Totals							

and a Secretary to begin their duties on the first day of the startup period, one work/month is the correct figure to insert on these position lines for Month 1. This figure, of course, is also inserted in each successive month to indicate the PC's full-time employment over the period. When the second Secretary position is filled, the work/month figures on that line must be increased accordingly.

For positions involving more than 1.00 FTE, work/month figures for successive employees should be summed in each column to show the cumulative work/months on those lines. Thus, if one Liaison Worker were hired at the beginning of Month 2, one work/month would be entered in that column; then, if a second Liaison Worker were hired in the middle of Month 2, the combined work/month figure would be 1.50 for Month 2; and the combined figure for Month 3 would then be 2.00, since both Liaison Workers would be on full time during that month.

When the chart is completed, we recommend that you stand back and take a second, objective look at your decisions. In other words, take on the role of those who will assess your efforts—in this case, the Startup team and the JYC Director. Let a little time elapse before taking this second look to gain some perspective on your first efforts.

Upon reexamination, you may well decide to change parts of the plan or correct some figures. Do not move into the next section until you reassess the entire phase-in plan, or you will lose most of the value of doing these exercises. (Note to Reader: Despite the ever present pressures on administrators, always try to leave some time for reflection and reassessment—and for rechecking and verification —before turning in a report on the results of major planning decisions.)

Self-Assessment Guidelines

We now present some important practical guidelines to use in evaluating the work you have just completed. The points we make, although seemingly specific to these exercises, represent various ways of thinking through the junctions between program objectives and resource use. In light of these guidelines, you may want to consider again how or if the elements in your plan should be modified.

A. Program Management. The PC will be unduly over-burdened if he or she must perform all program management and staff supervision duties. The CYS salary rate information shows that the Screening Supervisor will be a relatively senior person, and the position title specifically includes a supervisory function. Your plan should reflect the PC's intention to secure the services of a qualified person in this very important position at the earliest opportunity, preferably during the first month.

B. Sequence of Phasing In Other Positions. The need for prompt hiring of key persons has been repeatedly emphasized. Therefore, you should have asked if there are other key staff to be considered. In view of the community-oriented nature of the CYS program and the priority tasks in our month-by-month listings, we would expect a Liaison Worker to be added before anyone with primarily "internal" duties; that is, the Intake Worker or the Counselors. (This matter was also considered during the discussions of the Cutback Budget team, as noted in an earlier exercise section.) Job descriptions are not given for these positions, but their titles convey definite notions of appropriate tasks: "Liaison" must certainly involve activities with community groups, youth and their families, and sources that will refer clients to CYS as well as receive out-referrals. The PC cannot be expected to handle all these matters.

After one or both Liaison Workers are on board, either the Intake Worker or a Counselor should appear in your plan. Since the Screening Supervisor has already been hired and will join the Intake Worker in screening/intake duties, it might be preferable to engage a Counselor next. But keep in mind that the per month number of new hirings must also be controlled to avoid too many newcomers arriving at once, so hiring must be timed over several months.

C. Pace of Phasing In New Personnel. The new Request Budget provides for a total of 10.10 FTEs, which translates into at least eleven *individuals* to be engaged during the startup period, so that a full complement is on board on Day 1 of Month 5, as per the funder recommendation. If new employees were hired evenly across the four months, an average of 2.75 individuals would be phased in sometime during each month. No figure on your chart represents the per-month number of "new hires," but you can derive this by checking how many persons were added each month on each position line. Since staff should be phased in as promptly as is prudent, the number of new hires should be higher than the basic average during the early months and lower during the fourth and, probably, the third month. But only in the first or second month should there be as many as four new hires. If you have no new hires in any month or four new hires in any two months, you have planned to phase in too slowly or too rapidly. It would seem reasonable, therefore, that the last person will be employed not later than the middle of the fourth month. Recheck your figures to make certain you have met these conditions.

D. Completion of Phasing In and Beginning of Service to Clients. Client intake and service must begin during the startup period and should appear in your plan during the fourth month or, possibly, late in the third month. All positions must be filled not later than the middle of the fourth month, or there will be insufficient time to prepare the staff members hired last. Service could begin for some youth before all staff are on board, but at least one person in each position must have arrived earlier to be ready to handle even a few clients.

E. Support Staff Ratios. The Request Budget provides a secretary/staff ratio of 1:4.05 for the twelve-month period (8.10 nonsecretarial staff divided by 2.00 secretarial FTEs). Calculate the secretarial staff ratio for each of the four months under your plan, and then for the period as a whole. Because secretaries will offer essential assistance to other personnel and will perform numerous special duties during this period, the ratios should be better than the 1:4.05 for the twelve-month period (that is, the figure should never be as large as 4.05). Equally important, the ratio should be smallest during the first month—preferably close to 1:2—and then become larger gradually.

F. Verification of Salary Subtotals. Multiply the *unrounded* FTE subtotal for each position line by the annual salary rate for each, based on the figures in the Revised Budget (following the procedures used in Step 1B). The results should equal the position salary figures in Table 4–3. Dividing the salary amount on each line of your staffing table by the annual salary rate for each position should produce figures equaling your unrounded FTE subtotals.

Note that these verification procedures involve two rules that should be observed in all calculations and rechecking. First, *retain all decimal places* as you move through a "chain" of calculations; that is, when working toward a final figure or sum. Rounding at prior points throws off the final total. At the last *reporting* step in the chain, you should round as appropriate: to full dollars on budget summaries, to cents for paychecks, to two decimals for FTEs, work/months, and ratios. Second, calculations performed by multiplication can be checked through division, and vice versa.

G. Verification of Position Line Work/Month and FTE Figures. Divide the work/month subtotal for each position line by 12; the result should equal the FTE subtotal shown for each line. If this is how you originally obtained the FTE figures, multiply them by 12 and the result should equal the work/month subtotal for each line.

H. Verification of Total Work/Months and FTEs. The work/month and FTE totals for position lines should not exceed one-third of the FTE total given for each in the final Request Budget. If it does, your plan provides for a larger work force than permitted under the budget, since four months equals one-third of a calendar year. Divide each position line work/month subtotal by 12, multiply the result by 3; this result should be less than or equal to (but *not* greater than) that FTE subtotal shown on the Request Budget.

Keep in mind that there is no single best solution, but there may well be results that are incorrect or do not fulfill the requirements of your assignment. When you have settled on what you regard as an adequate and acceptable plan, you will be ready to rejoin the Startup team, to exchange ideas with other members, and to come to an agreement on a proposal to give to the JYC Director.

5

ALLOCATING PROGRAM RESOURCES

Functional Budgeting: What Is It?

Each of the various service programs carried out by an agency represents a complex set of activities aimed at specific objectives. Each has its own particular line-item resources to support these activities, which, taken together, constitute the services that lead to desired results for a given set of clients. Activities consume resources, and each program's distinctive activities determine the kinds and amounts of resources needed. The problem, then, becomes one of allocating *within* the program the resources that are needed to support all its essential activities. Within programs these sets of activities are commonly denoted by the term "functions."

Line-item budgeting does not explain for what program functions (categories or sets of activities) the line-items and their specific elements or objects will be used, or how the line-item elements or objects are to be allocated among categories. "Nonprofit organizations exist to carry out programs, not just to pay salaries or incur expenses. . . . [A] functional basis forces the organization to identify specific programs, and, equally important, to identify the cost of such programs" (AICPA, 1978). The functional format forces the

111

organization to budget resources according to the purposes and activities for which they are to be used.

Administrators readily understood the value of the functional budget for retrospectively analyzing how resources were used. However, the budget represents not only a plan of expected activities, it also "serves as a *target of performance.*" (Skigen and Snyder 1975; emphasis added). The usefulness and efficacy of the functional budget for planning and as a "target of performance" during all stages of program operations is only now beginning to be fully understood.

Prospectively allocating budget resources differentially among functions plays a critical role in program development and management, because the functional budget serves as a major tool in planning, deciding, implementing, and monitoring program operations.

Many federal and state funders require that a budget proposal be submitted in a functional as well as in a line-item format, but not all organizations appreciate its value, nor do they know how to deal with the complexities of functional budgeting. Differential allocation calls for a two-dimensional plan that discloses the use of *proportional* resources: *between* functions and *among* the line-items—all in relation to each other. Therefore, in this chapter we first address the bases for defining program functions, then we focus on clarifying the principles of resource allocation, and finally we detail the techniques for developing a rational prospective allocation plan. The uses of functional budgets in later stages of the budget cycle will be addressed, as appropriate, in other chapters.

A Note on Terminology.   We use certain terms in ways that may depart from meanings given them in one or another budget classification system. We do this partly because of ambiguities and differences in the literature of both cost accounting and human services, and partly to maintain consistency throughout the text and the exercises. For example, we use the terms "functions" and "categories or sets of activities" to designate the same thing: groups of identifiable activities, personnel, and material resources that can be clustered together and whose particular object costs can be specified. We reserve the word "program" to identify all functions taken together as they pertain to a designated set of objectives—as we have throughout this book.

The United Way (UWASIS) classification system has defined such terms in a descending hierarchy as follows: goals, service systems, services, programs, and activities (United Way of America, 1974). The meanings we assign to "program" and "functions" are closely allied to the last two definitions in this United Way series. However, for most of the literature in the field, it is important to consider the context in which terms are actually used, since each book or manual may adopt specialized meanings. (In United Way's own *Budgeting* manual, functional budgeting is applied to an agency's "program services" each of which is regarded as a separate program in this book.)

The Value of Differential Resource Allocation

The kind of thinking that went into developing the line-item budget (objectives—activities—resource needs) becomes further extended, and the relationships become more intertwined, when we move into differential allocation. Of course, we were keeping the planned activities in mind when we made decisions about line-items. But now we must make choices *between activities* and formulate definite intentions about how we will actually use the resources between and among these activities. *How* the program is carried out (operations) is inseparable from *why* the program is needed (purposes), from *what* is necessary to carry it out (resources), and from *which ways* it will be put into effect (implementation). Out of these deliberations we can solidify a comprehensive plan of total resource use for every aspect of the program.

Among the most critical of the critical matters we must decide about are the following:

- The nature of each and every set of activities (functions) in relation to major program objectives and to operational plans
- The nature of staff duties and responsibilities within and between functions
- The relative proportions of staff time and effort to be spent in each set of activities

- The expected flow of clients into and between functions
- The uses of nonpersonnel resources in relation to each and all functions
- The relative uses of total resources among the functions
- The resources directly consumed by clients within various functions

In other words, we must decide the planned uses of all resources in relation to each other and in relation to all the functions the organization intends to provide through program operations. Allocation not only reemphasizes the fusion between budget and objectives but also has powerful direct effects on implementation and on operations.

In this chapter we try to demonstrate that the definition of each program's functions and the allocation of resources among them are fundamentally a process of determining how the program will operate, how staff will perform their duties within it, and how clients will move (and be served) into and through it. By deciding how resources will be used relative to each other, we directly order their implementation and thus the course of operations.

Every function constitutes only a part of the whole and always must be viewed in relation to all the other functions that make up a program; therefore, constructing the budget around functions generates *unity of purpose*. Relations between functions are emphasized and barriers broken down precisely because no single function stands alone; it receives its share of the total program resources based only on its intended role relative to the role of each other function in fulfilling program purposes. Given a program's finite resources, the share allocated to each function must be balanced with the shares allocated to all other functions, or the operational plan cannot be carried out.

Cost and Responsibility Centers

Because every function represents a collection of costs, each is called a *cost center* (CC). CCs represent clusters of distinguishable activities that accrue costs, to which expenditures can be assigned, and for which ratios of resources to activities can be calculated and compared.

Within agencies the cost centers must bear a rational relation to the agency's structure, but they need not be identical with units shown on a formal table of organization.

Within programs CCs must be complementary and mutually exclusive. Sets of cognate activities may be combined into one cost center (e.g. Personnel/Payroll or Screening/Intake); and complex processes may be divided among several cost centers. However, it must be understood that CCs represent *activities*, not objects, and therefore line-items or restricted accounts are never cost centers.

One type of cost center, however, must be distinguished from the others. A *responsibility center* (RC), which is composed of a group of cost centers, is an administratively separate unit within an agency with a designated person in charge and particular resources allocated to it. It is not autonomous, but authority has been delegated to it to implement, manage, control, and account for the activities and the resource consumption of all the cost centers it encompasses. An RC is likely to be aligned with or identical to the administrative structure of the agency.

All responsibility centers are always also cost centers, but few cost centers are responsibility centers.

RCs range in size and level of resources from the smallest program in an organization to the organization itself: from the environmental health unit to the Public Health Department; from a summer camp to the YWCA; from the recreation department to the total city government; from the Bureau of the Census to the U.S. Department of Commerce. For purposes of this book, programs—including the illustrative Community Youth Services—are considered to be responsibility centers within their parent agencies, but in larger organizations two or more programs may be combined into a single responsibility center. *Cost centers are nested within responsibility centers;* responsibility centers, themselves, are often nested within larger responsibility centers. Figure 5–1 (p. 116) shows this nesting sequence.

A few more examples will clarify further the distinction between responsibility centers and other cost centers.

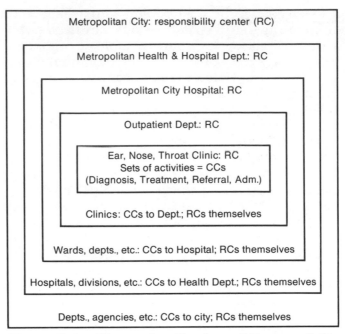

Figure 5–1. Illustrative Nesting of Responsibility Centers and Cost Centers

- The Department of Health is an RC within Prairie County Government, itself an RC. That means it

- Is administratively separate
- Has a designated person in charge (the Director)
- Is not autonomous from the county government
- Has been given budgetary and fiscal authority over its resources
- Fits the county's organizational chart
- Is also a cost center

- At the same time this RC (the Health Department) encompasses a variety of other cost centers, none of which is autonomous, but all of which represent clusters of distinguishable activities, accrue costs, can be assigned expenditures, and for which ratios of resources to services can be calculated. In this case the cost centers might include:[1]

Health education	Statistics/records
Maternal & child health	Administration
Environmental health	
Emergency services	

Another example:

- The Long Lake Summer Camp, sponsored by the Centerville Community House, is a responsibility center for the same reasons just outlined for the Health Department. It also encompasses various cost centers that represent clusters of activities that expend, accrue, and account for funds. It is itself, of course, a cost center within the Centerville agency. The following might represent the functions at Long Lake Camp:

Counseling	Food services
Waterfront/sports	Housekeeping/maintenance
Arts/music/drama	Management/general

Bear in mind that the funds for RCs and CCs may come from one or many sources, but only the functions—not the sources—can be cost and responsibility centers. Confusion sometimes arises because some funders may require that distinct cost (or even responsibility) centers be set up for operations supported by their funds, which would then be used only for specific functions, thereby fitting the principles for establishing CCs and RCs.

PRODUCTION AND SUPPORT COST CENTERS

The *kinds* of activities incorporated into a cost center must also be distinguished. This distinction is made on the basis

---

[1]Departments of Health typically include additional specialized functions and activities, but this listing is sufficient for our purposes.

of the function of a CC relative to the other CCs and to the endeavor as a whole. Two types of cost centers are generally recognized:

- *Production Centers* conduct service activities directly with and for clients or for the final products of a program. These outputs will, of course, vary with the character and goals of a program or agency. In some agencies production centers are called revenue centers.

- *Support Centers* provide services to all other centers, including the other support centers and the program as a whole—but *not* directly to clients. In some situations these are called nonrevenue centers.

Thus, in the previous example of the Department of Health, the health education, maternal and child health, environmental health, and emergency services each represent a *production center,* as do counseling, arts/music/drama, waterfront/sports, and food services at the summer camp.

In a day care center, the production centers might consist of child education and supervision, health service, food service, child development, and parent/community activities. In an art museum the production centers might be categorized as permanent acquisitions, special exhibits, art classes, and school services.

At the Health Department, statistics/records and administration represent support centers. They serve each other, all the production centers, and the department as a whole. At the summer camp, the SCs are housekeeping/maintenance and management/general. At the day care center the SCs might be administration, building/occupancy, and transportation, while at the art museum they might be membership, fundraising, security, and administration.

Criteria for Determining Cost Centers

Standards of Accounting and Financial Reporting (1974) recommends: "In defining its own service programs . . . an agency should attempt to confine its program service classifications to the major functional purposes it serves

and to those that exhibit practically distinguishable costs"
(p. 57).

A few basic criteria can be used to help an agency determine the kind and number of cost centers it should establish.
Most of these are distilled from the information already
discussed in this chapter, but a summarized list will
underscore their importance.

- Core functions must be represented (the summer camp could
  not leave out counseling or food services).
- Functions must fit actual activities (there could not be a
  fundraising CC if there were no fundraising activities).
- Functions must be congruent with operations (housekeeping
  and maintenance can be combined at the summer camp, but
  not housekeeping and waterfront/sports).
- Functions selected should aid in maintaining the unity of the
  program and organization (a county would usually avoid at-
  taching an unrelated function to its health department).
- The number and types of functions selected will depend on
  the *ability* of the accounting system to assign costs to each
  and the *burden* this places on that system.

The last criterion needs further explanation. The basic
reporting and accounting systems of the program (or agency) must be able to record and track expenditures of time
and money by the center (e.g. by staff time-logs, by purchase
orders, by case files). In midsize agencies too many centers
will put great demands on these systems; each increment in
the number of centers generates more costs in effort and
money, so selections will involve tradeoffs. Therefore,
although one should strive for the optimum number, in
general it is better to have too few CCs then too many.[2]

**A Rule of Thumb: Every program (RC) must have at least
one (usually two or more) production centers and ought to
have at least one support center.**

[2]Much more than the accounting system is involved in the monitoring of activities
and expenditures. Staff time/activity logs and basic information about clients,
their statuses within the program and services received, depend on other reporting
systems. The interconnections of these with the accounting system are discussed in
Chapter 8.

Major changes in program objectives, operations, or resources should generate rethinking about the cost centers. However, forecasts and retrospective comparisons will become more difficult if the functions are frequently or erratically shifted around among CCs. The reporting and accounting systems may already face serious problems if they have to account *to* several funders who are supporting portions of a single program (or only some clients within one program). Various coding techniques will have to be set up to track the clients, staff time, and dollars through the production and support centers. And in general, as we have noted, funders' requirements may shape the initial definition of centers and necessitate changes from time to time.

Administration or Management/General Cost Centers. At this point we should discuss *briefly* what activities make up a category called Administration or Management/General (the two names are often used interchangeably). It must be emphasized from the start that the administrative function comprises costs that can be attributed to operating the *program as a whole* and are not or cannot be attributed to other specific program functions. Just about every program carries out some support activities that fit into such a function, often referred to as the program management activities. Therefore, Management/General (or Administration) will typically encompass the following types of activities:

- Overall supervisory duties of the program manager or director
- Maintaining relations with the parent agency
- Developing contacts and arrangements with outside organizations
- Overseeing program budget and managing expenditures
- Developing internal program policies and procedures
- Preparing funding proposals
- Writing progress reports

From this list we can see that all of these activities relate directly to program operations, but to *overall aspects* of these and not to specific production functions. The cost of carrying out these important activities should properly be allocated, managed, and accounted for, which can best be done by accumulating them into a functional support center category.[3] All the programs we have cited as examples include at least one support center where similar management activities are performed. In smaller programs it may be most efficient to cluster all program support activities into a single management CC. But in larger programs it is usually desirable to establish one overall program management center, as well as one or more centers that perform subsidiary support functions (such as word-processing, statistics and evaluation, vehicle maintenance).

The production and support centers serve as the foundation upon which all functional budgeting and differential costing procedures are carried out. These procedures pertain to operations that span the entire fiscal period: prospective resource allocation, ongoing implementation and management of resource consumption, and a variety of retrospective cost analyses (the latter two topics are discussed in later chapters).

Differential Resource Allocations

We turn now to the principles involved in differentially allocating resources among the CCs. Allocation of line-item object costs by functions is commonly required by funders as part of the original budget request. But even if it is not required, it must be done *before* the start of the fiscal period. Otherwise the program will begin operations without having planned the integrated use of its resources. We again point out that we have chosen to treat this subject separately from budget development only because its importance is not thoroughly understood and it is typically handled mechanically or perfunctorily. It also deserves separate attention because the thinking and techniques employed go

---

[3]We must also distinguish between the Management/General or Administration function of a single program, and the administrative and other support functions of an entire agency. In addition to their own support functions, programs often depend on essential services that are most efficiently provided through the parent organization for all of its programs. For example, basic accounting services for all programs are typically provided by agencies through a centralized accounting office. The costs of these "outside" support services are in general represented by the Overhead/Indirect line-item in the program budget.

well beyond those necessary for estimating the costs needed by the entire program, as presented in Chapter 3.

Allocate means to set apart or earmark things, or parts of things, each for a specific purpose; to allot, that is, to measure out or to apportion things; to parcel out according to a plan. Therefore, in prospective resource allocation we set aside available resources for each cost center, giving each a differential proportion of every line-item resource, according to the planned purposes of each cost center relative to the others.

There are two main dimensions to the task of differential allocations. We can think of the first dimension as the horizontal, because it has to do with apportioning each line-item element or resource properly *across* a program's several cost centers. The second or vertical dimension has to do with balancing the mixes among resources *within* each center. Each dimension is essential and intertwined with the other, and we discuss each in turn.

PROPORTIONAL ALLOCATIONS: THE HORIZONTAL DIMENSION

When allocating any resource among two or more cost centers the issue is one of *apportioning* it with regard to each center's proper and required share of the total amount of that resource. Here we are dividing a limited and finite line-item resource into proportions across the columns of a functional budget. The line-items are retained, and columns— one for each cost center—are spread horizontally across the budget form. The allocated shares are almost never equal, because the centers' differing functions call for variable amounts of resources to carry out their distinctive activities. We are faced, first, with deciding which center requires *more* and which requires *less* of each resource—and then *how much* more or less.

The proportions to be allocated are best figured in terms of the units of the resource at hand—for example, of staff FTEs, of square footage, or of typewriters or telephone lines. Proportions may also be determined as percentages of each line-item's total units or of the budgeted dollar subtotal of a given resource, but this method carries some risks. Using percentages of line-item dollars obscures variations in the costs of elements *within* the item subtotal. Thus, Personnel dollar subtotals (or percentages of total salary dollars) do not reflect differences in FTEs and salary rates among positions. Two lower-level staff may be employed at the same cost as one higher-level position, and thus apportioning dollar percentages would not indicate the numbers of staff members (and which positions) intended by the allocations across the CCs. With this caution in mind, however, percentages of line-item units or dollars can be used for certain purposes. As *first approximations* in the allocating process, they provide a rough and ready way to begin tackling apportionment decisions. At the end of the process they are commonly employed to summarize the results of allocations among centers, using percentages of both line-item units and dollars.

RELATIONAL ALLOCATIONS: THE VERTICAL DIMENSION

The second or vertical dimension of the allocation process involves making decisions about relations between the amounts of line-item resources *within each center* (between the amounts of particular line-item resources in each column of the functional budget). If, for example, we allocate so many staff FTEs to Cost Center A, how much space, equipment, and supplies should we then allocate to achieve the best possible balance among all the line-items in that center?

Percentages have very limited use in tackling these kinds of decisions; they can be used only to report each line-item's share of a cost center's *total* dollar allocation. However, the percentage of costs allocated to Personnel are often calculated and compared to assess the cost centers' relative needs or uses of this critical resource.

We shall see, however, that ratios, factors, and other measures must be used both for making relational allocations (within centers) and for readjusting the preliminary proportional allocations (across centers). The simple accompanying diagram (Figure 5–2) shows the two allocation dimensions, but to explain allocation more concretely, we next present the main steps in the entire process for a hypothetical program.

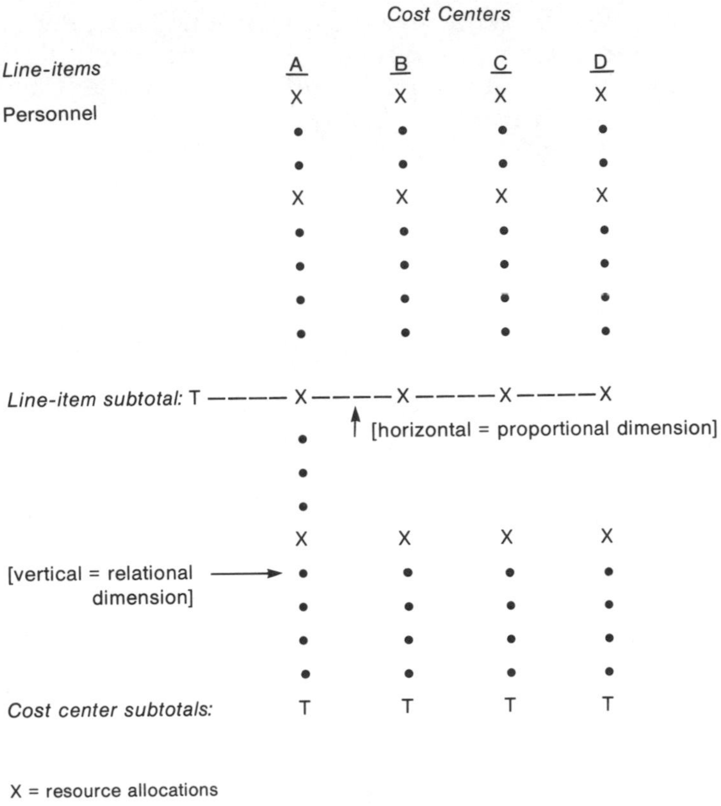

Cost Centers

Line-items	A	B	C	D
	X	X	X	X
Personnel	•	•	•	•
	•	•	•	•
	X	X	X	X
	•	•	•	•
	•	•	•	•
	•	•	•	•
	•	•	•	•

Line-item subtotal: T ————— X ————— X ————— X ————— X

        • ↑ [horizontal = proportional dimension]

	•			
	•			
	X	X	X	X
[vertical = relational →	•	•	•	•
dimension]	•	•	•	•
	•	•	•	•
	•	•	•	•
Cost center subtotals:	T	T	T	T

X = resource allocations

Figure 5–2. Diagram of Proportional and Relational Allocation Dimensions

Defining Program Functions to Establish Cost Centers: An Example

As discussed at the start of this chapter, an agency establishes cost centers that represent distinguishable sets of internal functions or activities, which in turn allows the allocation of resources and then the management of operations. Because we are focusing mainly on programs as responsibility centers within agencies, rather than on organizations as a whole, we shall now consider how functions and centers are determined for a service program within an agency.

We shall address—at some length—the situation at a

hypothetical Job Training Program (JTP) to explain these procedures. Within such a program a number of different kinds of activities would be carried out by personnel having different assignments. These would consume other kinds and amounts of resources, and staff would interact with clients at different points.

It is reasonable to assume that one set of tasks at our JTP has to do with the selection of persons to become trainees, and most programs do establish *admissions* or intake components. Next, every training program must have an *instructional* component in which the training activities actually take place. We have now identified two program functions to serve as cost centers. Let us suppose that JTP also plans to help trainees find jobs after instruction is completed; we shall designate this as a *job placement* function. Finally, we want to recognize the administrative tasks necessary to conduct the program, so we cluster these activities within a JTP *management/general* function.

We have now defined four JTP functions that seem to provide the minimum sets of distinguishable activities for such enterprises. Actual training programs might have additional functions because of the supplementary services they offer, their elaborate relations with schools and firms, their very large size, or for other reasons. For present purposes, however, we shall define only the four listed functions as cost centers to which resources will be allocated.

The core *production* center of JTP is instruction; that is where the primary aims of job training will be pursued. Management/general is the main *support* center, where most of the program's administrative personnel can be assigned and relevant activities will be carried out. In some kinds of programs the admissions component may be regarded as either a production or a support center, depending on one's point of view or prevailing practice in particular sectors of service. We shall regard it as a JTP support center. JTP's job placement activities, on the other hand, will be considered a production center, as this function directly serves program graduates as well as employers.

Having identified the basic functions as cost centers for JTP, we would now like to allocate *all* budgeted resources among them. But it is difficult and risky to do this without specifying the particular activities to be carried out in each center. We faced the same problem in Chapter 3 when developing cost estimates for an entire program. Many experienced persons hold general conceptions of sets of activities appropriate to be basic functions in their own sectors of service; these may be valid for a particular program, such as JTP, but it is unwise to assume so without further deliberation. We have frequently observed that *every* program is unique, and experienced people often disagree about many aspects of program design, operations, and management. For new programs and for persons newly responsible for these matters, it is imperative to go far beyond mere designation of the centers, as we shall see. Indeed, it is best to specify first all the chief program activities, after which the cost centers can be determined by combining sets of related activities into appropriate clusters.

For JTP let us suppose that planning has been well advanced, and the following sets of activities have been specified by centers:

Admissions	Training	Placement	Mgt/Gen
recruitment	curriculum planning	locating jobs	hiring staff
assessment of applicants	basic and advanced instruction	matching jobs to grads	fiscal management
selection of trainees	trainee assessment certification	informing grads and employers	parent agency accountability
assignment to training			community relations

This bare-bones listing is only suggestive of the more rigorous specification and assignment of activities by functions within even a fairly simple program, but it will suffice for our purposes here.

ALLOCATING PERSONNEL TO COST CENTERS

We are now ready to begin allocating personnel resources among the JTP cost centers. We start with the horizontal dimension and assign most of the staff FTEs to the four categories. Let us suppose that prior program/budget planning has determined the total number of FTEs, job titles, salary rates, and so on. To simplify the discussion we shall limit our example to the following full-time staff: a Program Director, one Assistant to the Director, one Curriculum Coordinator, one Admissions and Employment Coordinator, ten Instructors, and six Clerical staff—a total of 20.00 FTEs.

Consider first the question of assuring administrative oversight for all activities in each of JTP's cost centers and for the program as a whole. The Director is, of course, in charge of the total program, and we will assume that the Assistant to the Director and the services of a full-time Secretary are needed to help with the administrative tasks. All these staff positions can be assigned to Management/General. But the Director cannot effectively oversee daily staff activities in all components of the program. Other designated persons must be immediately responsible for each, reporting regularly to the Director.

We can assure proper supervision by designating the Curriculum Coordinator to be in direct charge of Training activities and responsible for supervising teaching, instructors, trainees, and so forth. We shall also decide that the Admissions and Employment Coordinator should be directly responsible for both the Admissions and Placement centers, and that the Instructors are exclusively assigned to teaching duties in the Training center. These initial staff duty assignments now result in the following distribution:

Admissions	Training	Placement	Mgt/Gen
Adms/ Emp Coord.	Curric. Coord.	Adms/ Emp Coord.	Director
	Instructors		Ass't to Dir.
			Secretary

This plan seems to exclude instructional staff from involvement in any other function, which may not be desirable. We want some instructor participation in setting policies and criteria for both the Admissions and the Placement centers, thus to improve the integration of services for trainees. We provide for this by assigning such duties to an instructor and allotting the necessary time.

It should now be obvious that the primary basis we have used for allocating personnel—JTP's most critical resource—has been the different sets of tasks to be performed in each of the cost centers. Distinctive tasks require particular and appropriate competencies. Because the resource being allocated consists of staff with these distinctive competencies, we seek to match them to the tasks. The seeming inevitability of allocating instructors to the Training function may suggest that the tasks automatically determine allocative issues. But there was nothing automatic about the assignments of other personnel, nor did teaching tasks absorb all the instructional staff in our plan.

CLERICAL STAFF

It is time now to consider clerical duties and assignments. If we were to use only a "pool" arrangement at JTP, all clerical staff would be assigned to the Management/General center without any specific cross-category allocations. To exemplify the kinds of problems that typically arise, we prefer to make these decisions more concretely and to designate a minimum level of clerical support for every function. A full FTE has already been allocated to Management/General; each of the other CCs will now be allocated one-half of a clerical position (.50 FTE) to handle basic typing duties, maintain files and related materials, and so on. Thus we have now decided the assignments for two and one-half of the six clerical FTEs.

To report and assess all the staff assignments so far, let us display the FTEs by cost centers:

Admissions	Training	Placement	Mgt/Gen
0.50 Adm/Emp Coord.	1.00 Curric. Coord.	0.50 Adm/Emp Coord.	1.00 Dir.
0.25 Instructor	9.50 Instructors	0.25 Instructor	1.00 Ass't to Dir.
0.50 Sec'y	0.50 Sec'y	0.50 Sec'y	1.00 Sec'y
1.25 FTEs	11.00 FTEs	1.25 FTEs	3.00 FTEs

Keeping in mind that we are considering only full-time employees and positions, it is apparent that this preliminary plan requires the Admissions/Employment Coordinator and one or two of the Instructors to divide their time between two cost centers. Supervisory staff assignments have been made to each center, and each has been given at least minimum clerical help. The allocations result in very different FTE subtotals and mixes of positions across all the cost centers, reflecting the division of labor considered appropriate.

There are 3.50 clerical FTEs yet to be allocated. Assuming that all the centers could benefit by additional support, on what bases can we determine just where the remaining clerical services can best be used?

RESOURCE RELATIONS

Assuming there is no obvious reason to assign the remaining clerical FTEs to a single center, the question before us presents, albeit in microcosm, issues of resource relations and balances. We must now consider not only the demands to be placed upon each of the centers but also the interrelations among the resources we have already allocated to them.

Three bases will be employed in addressing the relational aspect of the allocation decisions presented in the following discussion. To achieve a desirable balance of personnel assignments for each cost center we shall consider in turn (1) the differing tasks to be performed in each ; (2) the support needs of staff already assigned; and (3) the volume of work or effort expected in each center.

First let us examine the clerical support staffing we have already allocated to the centers, in terms of the FTEs and ratios.

		Admissions	Training	Placement	Mgt/Gen
Subtotal nonsec'ys		.75	10.50	.75	2.00
Sec'ys		.50	.50	.50	1.00
Sec'ial ratios	1:	1.50	21.00	1.50	2.00

Although each cost center has been allocated a minimum of half a clerical position, the *relative* levels of clerical to nonclerical staff across the centers are obviously very discrepant, with Admissions and Placement being the most advantaged and Training considerably disadvantaged. One-half of a clerical FTE is in Admissions and another half in Placement to handle the work generated by less than 1.00 FTE nonclerical personnel in these centers, whereas the 10.50 FTEs in Training must rely on the services of only one-half of a support position.

One possibility is to "equalize" clerical assistance *relative to other staff* in each center; that is, each would be allotted the same secretarial/staff ratio (as near as possible using rounded FTE figures). Then *all* clerical FTEs would be allocated as follows:

		Admissions	Training	Placement	Mgt/Gen	Total
Subtotal nonsec'ys		.75	10.50	.75	2.00	14.00
Sec'ys		.32	4.50	.32	.86	6.00
Sec'ial ratios	1:	2.34	2.33	2.34	2.33	2.33

Although this arrangement would provide equal clerical-to-staff ratios in every cost center, it ignores the differing kinds of activities in each and the differing numbers of clients each must serve. It also reduces the *minimum* level of clerical services that we have already decided each center must have.

Another possibility is to divide the remaining 3.50 clerical FTEs equally among the cost centers (resulting in .875 FTE for three centers, and 1.875 for Management/General when added to the initial allocations). But to continue "equalizing" allocations by either method begs questions about differences in the activity and workload requirements *between* the four centers. Thus, for example, perhaps extra clerical staff should be provided for Admissions to handle telephone inquiries and to serve the receptionist role. This would partially recognize the special activity requirements for this program function. Or perhaps we know that extensive new training manuals must be devel-

oped in the Training center, so it might be advisable to provide extra clerical help there. It was, indeed, the special administrative responsibilities of Mgt/Gen that justified its
initial allocation of a full clerical position. But let us assume
these special needs do not exist and we are unable to identify
any other distinctive demands among the cost centers. Each
may deserve more clerical staff, but we must look to different bases for determining their additional needs.

Several features of these JTP centers should now be attended to more thoroughly. We have not yet explicitly examined the support staff needs that are generated by the
core service staff, as is typical in labor-intensive professionalized organizations. This has to do with the clerical
assistance that will be needed by the *nonsecretarial staff*
already allocated to the centers. Presumably secretaries will
not generate work for each other, so we are concerned only
with the proportions of clerical assistance needed and
available for other personnel within each center. The first
ratios reported previously (1:1.50, 1:21.00, and so on) reveal
the disparities in clerical services made available to other
staff across the centers.

Suppose, then, we accept the clerical allocation decisions
initially made, and choose to allocate the last 3.50 clerical
positions *relative to the number of nonsecretarial FTEs* in
each center. This approach allows us to retain the first
secretarial allocations based on the centers' distinctive
tasks, and to apportion the remaining support services in a
way that also seeks to adjust secretarial help to the numbers
of nonsecretarial personnel in each center. The percentages
of total FTEs represented by each center's nonsecretarial
staff provide a basis for this last allocation. We multiply the
3.50 clerical FTEs by each center's percentage of the total
nonsecretarial FTEs, then apply that percentage to the 3.50
FTEs, and add the resulting figure to the FTEs already
assigned.

But we have not yet addressed the extent to which the
numbers of clients (here potential or actual trainees) also
generate activity demands within the centers. All trainees
will necessarily be handled through the Admissions center,
along with other applicants who do not enroll or are not accepted by JTP (not to mention persons who will simply inquire about the program). The Training center will serve a

lesser number: that is, only those who are accepted, actually enroll, and then attend instructional sessions. Some trainees will probably drop out, fail to complete the program, or finish and find their own jobs, so the Placement center will be responsible for serving an even smaller number of graduates. Finally, no trainees are served directly by Mgt/Gen, so the clients-served measure does not apply to this center.

The grand total of those to be served in all centers, then, will comprise the applicants plus the trainees plus the grads, with smaller numbers in each successive group. We shall assume that relatively firm estimates have already been developed for JTP as follows: 299 applicants will be considered for admission; of these, 195 will be admitted, enroll, and begin training; and 156 will eventually finish training, graduate, and receive placement help. This total is 650, which we use to calculate percentages for the "share" that each center will serve: 46, 30 and 24 percent, respectively. These percentages can now serve as an *alternative* basis for allocating the time and service of the remaining clerical FTEs, on the supposition that additional support requirements will be generated in direct relation to the numbers of persons being handled in each cost center.

Now let us compare the percentages we have derived from these two ways of estimating additional clerical activity requirements for the centers:

	Percentages				
Allocation Base	Admissions	Training	Placement	Mgt/Gen	Total
Nonsec'ial staff FTEs	5.4	75.0	5.4	14.3	100.0
No. served	46.0	30.0	24.0	—	100.0

These are clearly very different bases for estimating differential needs for additional clerical assistance and would result in significantly different shares of the 3.50 FTEs remaining to be allocated among the cost centers. To select one basis rather than the other for making the final allocation decision would presume that the needs for supplemental clerical assistance are dependent on either the number of nonsecretarial personnel in a program center *or* on the number of persons to be served in each function—but not on some combination of them. Common sense would argue that both bases probably have some merit. We shall now assume that JTP planners have taken all these considerations into account and have calculated final clerical FTE assignments (see top line on Table 5–1) to achieve a balance among them. Table 5–1 shows the results of their differential allocations.

TABLE 5–1. Result of Assigning Last of Secretarial FTEs

	Admissions	Training	Placement	Mgt/Gen	Total
Final 3.50 FTEs allocated	.75	2.00	.50	.25	3.50
Total clerical allocations	1.25	2.50	1.00	1.25	6.00
Nonsec'ial subtotal	.75	10.50	.75	2.00	14.00
Total FTEs	2.00	13.00	1.75	3.25	20.00
Sec/staff ratios 1:	.60	4.20	.75	1.60	2.33

Even a cursory examination of the figures should reveal a very different pattern of clerical staff allocation across functions from any of those previously considered. The differing results are perhaps most readily apparent when comparing the secretarial/staff ratios, although this measure does not in any way reflect client volume. Despite the modest number of JTP personnel, the alternate allocation methods produce significant variations in the mix or balance of staff resources. And these variations would have important implications for the operations of this program if it actually existed.

The procedures employed in arriving at all the staff allocations deserve review, since they embody those most critical to effective functional budgeting, and we must reapply them in connection with nonpersonnel resources. The first basis for assigning personnel among the JTP cost centers addressed the *different tasks* to be performed in each, allowing fairly straightforward designation of the most appropriate centers for numerous staff. Personnel in positions that denoted distinctive competencies or authority could be readily allocated to those centers whose tasks merited such abilities. Defining cost centers according to their distinctively different tasks, therefore, provides the primary basis for allocating resources to them.

The second allocation basis addressed the *support needs of staff,* in this case for clerical assistance. When we determine where key staff members ought to be assigned, what other available resources must be allocated so they can carry out their activities in each? Paying attention to the requirements of personnel when allocating resources across cost centers should be a familiar matter. This was a significant factor in the "series of demand relations" used to identify needed resources in initial budget development (as discussed in Chapter 3). And we shall apply the same logic when considering the nonpersonnel resources necessary to support staff activities within centers.

The third allocation basis involved the *volume of effort* planned for each center, here represented by the numbers of persons to be handled in each. Different volumes or amounts of work obviously necessitate different levels of resources. The measure of volume should not be limited to persons (or clients), for the tasks defined for certain cost centers involve other kinds of things to be done or worked on, for example, processing files and records, cataloguing books, or maintaining vehicles. Numbers of persons to be served is, however, an important measure of volume in human service organizations and must not be minimized.

Those new to allocation duties often consider volume first, perhaps because it seems to be so tangible or manifest. Regardless of the unit of measure, however, volume in and of itself is not a primary basis for allocation, because the *kinds* of tasks to be performed with, for, or on the persons or things that make up the volume differ greatly between cost centers, programs, and organizations. It is the nature of the distinctive tasks and the resource requirements of personnel who must perform these tasks (our second basis), that mediate the influence of volume. Thus, for example, performing very limited and routine services for a given number of persons usually requires fewer resources than does performing more complex and extended services for the same—or even a smaller—number of persons. We can appreciate this important issue by recalling the Admissions and Training centers in the JTP program: The former will handle more persons and process more applications than the Training center, but training people is far more demanding than processing their applications and therefore requires more staff and other resources. (To grasp the implications of considering volume last rather than first in the allocation process, the reader can go back and reallocate the JTP staff, including the clerical workers, *first* according to the volume figures we used, and *second* according to our descriptions of the tasks for each of these cost centers. The very different results obtained should be carefully considered.)

Differential Allocation of Nonpersonnel Resources

Using the same bases and measures, we shall now examine certain nonpersonnel resources that must be allocated among JTP's four centers. Let us first consider space (occupancy) and then equipment of all kinds.

Space. Presumably space has been budgeted for staff workstations or offices, for classrooms or shops where trainees will be taught, and for some "common use" needs, such as a staff meeting room or lounge, a stockroom, washrooms, and the like. If a facility has already been obtained, then allocation must take into account its actual features (types and sizes of rooms, partitions) since these are usually difficult and costly to modify. If, however, the location has not yet been settled, the allocation process cannot begin until general space requirements are determined and various rental and remodeling options are considered. In any event, the designation of space should be done in terms of the particular uses to which it will be put, and this means a return to the plans for each of JTP's functional categories.

To simplify the problem, we assume that all the common-use space will be assigned to the Management/General cost center and remove that from further consideration (recall that this center serves all components of the program). Now we can consider space requirements appropriate to the distinctive tasks of each center: a waiting room for applicants for the Admissions center; classrooms for the Training center; and ordinary offices for the Placement and Management/General centers. The kind and amount of space needed for the classrooms must depend on the specific instructional activities (special training equipment, cubicles, and so on), as well as on the projected numbers of trainees to be scheduled into the rooms. These matters relate to the distinctive *task* and *volume* bases previously discussed, which are important for determining and allocating actual or planned space. The *costs* for space so allocated can be assigned to the centers in direct proportion to each one's share of the total square footage.

We are now ready to consider how the *support needs* of program personnel affect space planning. Each clerical support person will need a workstation, presumably of about equal size; reexamination of the final staff allocation in Table 5–1 indicates a minimum of one full clerical workstation for each cost center. In addition, the clerical personnel who will work in more than one center (those represented by the fractional FTEs), can also receive one workstation per person. The square footage costs of these workstations can then be allocated in direct proportion to clerical FTE designations.

A similar method can be used to determine space allocations and proportional costs for the offices (probably *not* equal in size) of other JTP personnel: the Director, Assistant to the Director, the Curriculum Coordinator, the Admissions/Employment Coordinator, and the Instructors. These space costs, as before, should be allocated to the centers where the staff and other users are assigned. In this sense space "follows" staff, using the same allocation bases, and sometimes calculated by using factors (such as average square footage per person) to simplify the arithmetic.

It is important to note that the proportional dimension was not directly used for any space allocation decisions. Workstation space was distributed across centers in the same proportions as the clerical FTEs, but this also represents a relational approach; that is, space was allocated in relation to another resource, clerical staff.

In these allocation determinations (and later in assigning costs through accounting) the physical location of the given space is irrelevant, at least within the terms of our hypothetical example. The actual workstation or office for any staff member whose time will be divided between two centers would probably be situated within the operational area of one of these. But the occupancy costs must be allocated to both centers in shares equivalent to that person's activities.

Equipment. Let us assume that JTP's budget includes one-time-only funding for ordinary office furniture, standard office equipment (from typewriters to file cabinets), certain special equipment needed for instructional purposes, and furnishings for the waiting room and meeting room. Given these kinds of equipment, the reader ought to be able independently to determine appropriate bases and perhaps even some trial allocations of such familiar items. In all these instances the reasoning should follow that employed for space and should rely on *relational* rather than proportional calculations.

Assistance to Clients. Some resources should be allocated using narrower criteria, and among these are most forms of Assistance to Clients (see Appendix B: Budget Line-Items), which can be used only as authorized in the budget, that is, only for particular clients and at the times specified. Suppose that JTP had obtained line-item funds to be used on behalf of trainees who merited assistance because of their *particular* circumstances. If such funds were specified as tuition aid for qualified applicants with incomes below a certain level, then all these costs must be allocated to the cost center where the aid will actually be made available (spent), in this case the Training center. The identification and even choice of qualified recipients might be done by staff in the Admissions center, but the funds will be expended in the Training center. Suppose that some funds were also included to supplement wages during the first six weeks of employment for graduates who met the income criterion, who were minority group members, *and* who were to be employed by businesses for which minority recruitment goals had been set. This portion of the budgeted Assistance item should be allocated to the Placement center, because that is the category where qualified recipients would be identified and wage supplements handled. Under these and similar conditions the budget award specifies who can receive such assistance and when, thereby determining the appropriate center for the allocation.

This latter discussion has touched on budgeted resources that should be allocated only to a single cost center. The corollary, of course, is that some centers should be allocated none of certain resources. Common or basic resources, such as personnel, space, and supplies, are usually allocated across most or all centers, but specialized resources, as we have indicated, should be allocated only to centers whose need for them can be fully justified. There is, then, no allocation principle or even rule of thumb that encourages resource apportionment universally among cost centers.

RELATIONAL CALCULATIONS

As was evident from our use of ratios in planning assignments of some JTP clerical staff, allocation desisions may be arrived at by computing resource relations within cost centers (that is, in relational terms) without direct reference to dollars. The dollars are determined only after the decisions are made. Several other measures involving personnel are commonly used in addition to the secretarial ratio, for example, the ratio of managerial FTEs to other personnel within each center or the ratios of various kinds of specialized staff to each other. Furthermore, *rates* may be employed in similar ways to establish the desired relation or balance among several resources within and between centers; for example, allocation of space according to square footage standards or rates and travel or mileage reimbursement rates. Residential programs may plan food costs using accepted dietary or nutritional measures per person per meal or per day. And so on. Eventually, of course, the results of these approaches must be translated into dollars to complete the functional budget, and the final results must conform to the dollar limits of the line-items, as with any budgeted resource.

Funder Requirements

Allocation decisionmaking can be heavily influenced by a variety of requirements and restrictions imposed by funding sources. For example, in addition to Assistance to Clients, numerous other line-items or elements may have particular uses that are concretely specified in authorized budgets, and these should always be allocated (and expended) properly to avoid challenge on year-end audits. Funder stipulations frequently affect the assignment of some personnel to certain functions, and such allocations should faithfully reflect the budget authorizations. Thus, if JTP's budget and program plan provided for the part-time employment of a qualified person to administer skill achievement tests to students to certify that they had completed their training, this person's salary would necessarily be allocated to the Training center.

Purchase-of-service contracts may also include cost ceilings imposed by funders, as we shall consider shortly. In these circumstances all steps in defining cost centers and functional budgeting must be followed with great care so that actual expenditures can be shown to conform to these ceilings in subsequent cost analyses. The parent agency must necessarily actively participate in these budgeting processes, as well as in center definitions, allocations, and accounting procedures, to avoid inadvertent violations of contract requirements or, equally important, insufficient resources available to support "indirect" or program management activities.

MANAGEMENT/GENERAL COST CENTER ALLOCATIONS

Funders may also require that certain kinds of costs be specifically allocated to an "Administration" or "Management/General" cost center. Among costs to be sequestered in this arbitrary way, those of the program's administrative personnel (program manager and support staff) are often concretely specified, along with nonpersonnel costs directly connected with operational control of the program. Funders may impose these mandatory allocations so they can examine such expenses and note their relation to production costs, and also make comparisons with similar programs in other agencies.

The principle here is the same as that involved in the definition of Overhead/Indirect costs discussed in Chapter 3, that is, the full identification of and accountability for resource consumption by activities that are necessary but are *not* direct production functions or efforts. But it is important to distinguish between the management activities appropriate for a program's Management/General CC and those for the more distant administrative and related functions of the parent agency, which are properly reflected in Overhead/Indirect costs, as mentioned earlier. Specific program-level management resources and costs may appropriately be allocated to Management/General, because they pertain to all other program functions and *only* to them—and this is what was done for the JTP Director, the Assistant, and the 1.25 clerical position salaries—this is the "management" aspect. Certain other program support costs may also be allocated to this center, because they will be shared among most centers, and there is no clear way to determine the actual pattern of sharing in advance—this is the "general" aspect. For example, costs within a line-item for reproduction (e.g. a photocopy machine and its supplies) might be entirely allocated to Management/General, because how the other centers will use this resource depends on actual program experience (logging actual use may permit later cost assignments to the proper centers). Similarly, costs for JTP's "common use" space was assigned to Management/General because it would be used by all the centers, or for storage of all supplies, and so on. However, the Management/General center must not be thought of as a catchall center to which any difficult-to-estimate costs can be conveniently allocated, and in later chapters we address ways that all of these costs should be treated for analysis and other purposes.

Approximation Devices

We noted earlier that "factors" or other simplifying devices are employed in making allocations of some resources. Certain of these are used by experienced persons as methods for obtaining first approximations before undertaking more detailed work. For example, one may prefer to bypass initially the question of centers' particular requirements for standard office supplies and to develop a *preliminary* functional budget by completing all other allocations, calculating each center's percentage of the aggregate Total Direct Cost (excluding office supplies), and then use these percentages to allocate the supplies line-item. Centers' percentages thus serve as the factors for first approximation allocations. This method yields an initial set of figures and permits the final allocation of supplies to be applied using the explicit bases we have discussed. In the kinds of programs addressed in this book, operational functions or cost centers typically vary broadly in their consumption of resources such as supplies, and final allocations should reflect these differences. In most programs every cost center may well require some *minimum* level of such resources, but beyond that level there are likely to be significant differences in particular resource needs, for example, special *training* supplies and equipment for JTP.

We can recall from Chapter 3 that Employee Benefits are usually estimated initially as an across-the-board *percentage* of Personnel costs, with the caveat that the precise cost will depend on the actual composition of staff members employed in each program and cost center. The same percentage or factor can be used to allocate Benefits to centers under functional budgeting. However, as soon as more detailed knowledge of the actual characteristics of each center's staff complement becomes available (e.g. salary amounts for payroll taxes, proportions of full-time/part-time employees), it is desirable to refine the Benefit sums accordingly.

We believe it is unwise to rely too much on approximation devices when making allocations. Programs or agencies with very dissimilar resource requirements will often use the same devices or formulas, which can lead to serious estimating errors that may prove difficult to correct.

Unit Cost Estimates

Service unit costs will be dealt with in detail in Chapter 8, but we must here anticipate that discussion a bit. To simplify the matter for present purposes, one can consider the numbers of persons expected to be served in each cost center as representative of the numbers of "service units" for each. Then, the estimated Total Direct Costs can be divided by this number of service units to get the average cost per service unit for each center. These unit costs, in turn, can be compared across centers—or with those from comparable programs in the same or different agencies—to assess whether the allocations in the functional budget are at reasonably acceptable levels. It may be immediately evident that one or another of the projected unit cost figures is too high—or perhaps ridiculously low—thus providing some direction for modifying the approximate allocations. If one wishes to examine the composition of the preliminary unit costs more intensively, the numbers of units can be further divided into each of the *line-item cost elements* that have been tentatively apportioned to each center. The resulting arrays of averages may aid in reaching decisions about *which* items or elements should be modified across which centers, or in relation to which other line-items in the same center. This method may be especially useful when purchase-of-service contracts specify allowable costs for line-items or for elements within them.

The Problem of "Equalizing"

We have consistently cautioned against budgeting methods that result in equal amounts or proportions of resources for what are essentially *different* and therefore *unequal* activities, services, and line-items. Certainly we would regard allocating equal amounts, proportions, or ratios and rates of any line-item cost across centers as faulty on its face. One may decide to allocate space equally among uses or users, but this would be valid only if it were determined by applying the criteria we have set forth. To allocate equally to avoid the painstaking work of functional budgeting, or to avoid intraprogram "political" conflicts over differences in resource allocations, is to beg fundamental questions of apportioning scarce resources rationally. It is both inequitable and unreasonable to equalize that which is not equal. Using some shortcuts or approximations may be necessary when there is too little time for thorough allocation planning, or when proram requirements are uncertain, but it also invites later problems for trimming the budget, for cost analysis, and for accountability.

The Series of Approximations

The process we have described has direct parallels to that recommended for initial program planning and budget development, namely, a series of approximations, reviews, and readjustments until one has achieved the best possible under the circumstances. Further, we have pointed out that funders frequently require that all applications include a functional budget. When this is the case, differential allocations can be regarded as essentially a more demanding and detailed approach to determining resource requirements among all major components of the program. Two things have been added to the budgeting process: One is the careful definition of program functions as cost centers, and the other is the application of additional bases for achieving desirable balances and relations *among* resources in each cost center. These bases or criteria, as well as the use of rates and ratios, can also be employed as aids in initial budget development. They are complementary to the series of demand relations and, in fact, are more determinate and concrete ways of implementing the series. The priority schema proposed for use in assessing preliminary budgets, and in trimming them selectively, is also compatible with differential allocations. The cost centers themselves can be examined within the schema, for the ordering of functions into production and support centers clearly distinguishes between more immediate and more distant sets of object costs. Similarly, as has been implicit in this discussion, a well-prepared functional budget can serve as a powerful tool for use in expenditure control and cost containment; it enables program managers to monitor expenditure experiences in terms that go far beyond watching line-items. When program operations experience yields information about numbers of clients served that can be compared to earlier projections, and average service unit expenditures per item elements are calculated, a basis has been provided for more precise management of both program operations and budgets.

6

EXERCISE PROBLEMS IN RESOURCE ALLOCATION

The Situation at CYS

Where We Left Off.   After returning to Community Youth Services from a leave of absence to attend to family matters, you learn about its progress. The funder indeed approved the Revised Budget, as detailed in Chapter 4, as well as a modified four-month Startup Budget. The formal awards were made to the Johnson Youth Center, and CYS is now into its third month of the initial period. All the parent agency preparations were completed as outlined (see Chapter 4), and most—but not all—activities planned for the initial period have proceeded on schedule, including the hiring of most CYS staff. A few of the planned startup steps may not be accomplished during this period and will have to be carried over into the twelve-month FY.

The Task Ahead.   The JYC Director and the Program Coordinator have decided that a twelve-month *functional budget* should be developed now while there is still time before the FY begins. They want to prepare a full plan for allocating all CYS resources over the first regular program and fiscal year, with as much detail of service activities and operations as feasible. You are still serving in a special administrative assistant role at JYC and have now been assigned to participate in this important work. Other staff will be addressing different features of the general task, and gradually your several contributions will be combined into an overall functional budget for CYS. In addition, the Planning Committee of the JYC Board has indicated its strong interest in the new services, and arrangements have been made for periodic meetings of the committee with staff responsible for program and budget planning.

The tasks to be performed in this exercise section simulate the functional budgeting process in a real organization. Everything you will be asked to do for CYS in the exercise steps directly parallels the approach and methods set forth in Chapter 5. You will have to make many judgments and decisions, because there is no single correct solution for allocating budget resources among program functions.

Allocation at this stage requires thoughtful review of previous plans for program objectives and services, of commitments and constraints imposed by budget award agreements, as well as of the efforts already under way. Concrete decisions must now be made about the kinds of activities that should be performed by all staff members in each of the five cost centers. Once that is done, the amounts of time employees should spend in each center can be determined, and these can be translated into dollar amounts for the functional budget. The kinds and levels of nonpersonnel resources needed for each center can then be settled so this budget can serve as a firm program/fiscal roadmap for the year ahead. Various kinds of information are given below to assist you and the others working on producing budget materials, with exercise steps to help you develop the requisite skills. Where information is lacking, you should make reasonable assumptions based on what you know about CYS, and note these for later reference.

The format for the functional budget has been established, as shown on a later page, and the results of certain allocation decisions have already been inserted on this form. Some results of other preparations and planning are also given: summaries of activities for CYS cost centers, a statement of duties for another staff position, preliminary assignments of some staff to centers, and estimates of the numbers of youth who will be considered for admittance to CYS, accepted through Intake, and routed into program services. Again, all these materials are comparable to those you would work with in any program or agency, and they should be accepted as settled so you can concentrate on the remaining functional budgeting tasks.

Description of CYS Cost Centers

Program policy decisions have not departed from the plans set forth in Chapter 4. The main purpose of CYS is to aid youth who are manifesting behavioral and similar difficulties by helping them use appropriate community resources and services to reduce their likelihood of being formally channeled into the county's juvenile justice system. Emphasis is given to helping these youth gain access to existing community resources and serving them independently only when such resources are lacking. Resources to be mobilized include public schools and other training programs; church, civic, and other voluntary associations; businesses, private employers, and unions; public and private agencies of all kinds; neighborhood organizations; professional bodies; and others.

In Chapter 5 we explained the necessity to clarify cost centers as a first step toward differential allocations, and we turn now to the CYS arrangements, which are based on the functions outlined in the original plans (see Chapter 4).

- All references to CYS personnel have been deleted from the summary descriptions of cost centers presented below, but ordinarily these would be included to clarify staff roles and duties. For purposes of this exercise, we shall address staff activities in the next section, where you will be expected to contribute much of this information. Therefore, as you read the following statements, think about which program personnel should perform these tasks, in association with which others, and at what levels of time and effort. All programs should prepare such descriptions before beginning resource allocations.

Screening and Intake (S/I).   This center will receive prospective in-referrals from community agencies, schools, families, and so on, as well as "walk-in" youth who may be interested in the program. The primary service objective in Screening/Intake is to obtain information from and about these youth and to ascertain whether (1) each is eligible for program service, (2) could benefit from it, and (3) is willing to receive it (with parental consent). Direct interviews will be conducted with all prospective clients and with their parent(s), in their homes when necessary. It is probable that some proportion of youth referred from all sources will, in fact, present trivial—if any—difficulties, and that some will be unwilling to accept program services. These should, therefore, be identified as early as possible to avoid further involvement and costs.

When it has been determined that a youth is eligible, likely to benefit from program service, and willing to receive it, that person will be accepted and a "case" file opened. In selected instances, outside specialists may be engaged to help resolve some problem that would otherwise impede a youth's participation in the program. A decision will then be made about which part of the program is most suitable. This will be explained to the youth (and parents), and, if all agree, the youth will be promptly routed to the proper service center. (See Figure 6–1.) Key personnel in this center will also follow clients as they move between centers. The time needed for such "case management" and activities' coordination should be allocated to other centers where clients are being handled.

Personnel in S/I will actively interpret the program to persons likely to send youth for attention and will contact and visit these sources to gain cooperation and assistance. S/I will also be responsible for handling all inquiries about the program. Assistance from consultants will be obtained as needed, and staff will attend an occasional conference relevant to their jobs.

Referral (Ref). Most youth accepted for CYS service will be routed directly to the Referral center. Using the information obtained at S/I, this service will identify the specific community resources (one or more) most suitable to the particular needs and circumstances of each client. To assure the best match between youth and resource(s), additional information may have to be obtained from or about the youth, and all will be personally interviewed. The youth and parents will then be informed about the resource(s) selected

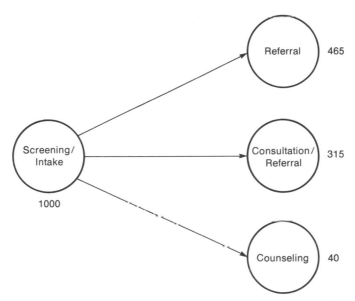

Figure 6-1. Estimated Clients and Case Flow for CYS

so they can make choices and decide whether to proceed. If they agree, efforts will be made to obtain and facilitate access to the chosen resource(s) through direct contact. An "out-referral" will be made to the selected source(s), using appropriate procedures. Basic information about the youth will be forwarded; the youth will receive assistance in locating and reaching the site(s) and may be taken there by Referral staff.

Personnel in this center will be largely responsible for identifying a wide range of community resources and services for the client population, establishing direct associations with their representatives, and actively seeking their cooperation and assistance. In performing these activities staff may draw upon program resources when authorized: consultant and vendor services, client employment or training subsidy funds, local travel, or attendance at an occasional conference.

Consultation/Referral (C/R). This center will pursue essentially the same objectives as Referral but, in selected instances, will supplement the process with more painstaking efforts to connect youth with referral sources. These activities are planned because CYS recognizes that S/I will find some youth who manifest more serious difficulties, and additional services will be needed to effect referrals for them. Further, some community agencies, employers, or other resources may also require continuing support and help from CYS staff, who—in collaboration with the referral source—may be called upon to provide ongoing services to the youth and family *after* the referral has been made. Thus, C/R will maintain a consultative relationship with both the referral source and the client.

C/R will rely on many of the same community resources as Referral, but will seek to develop still other out-referral resources capable of serving these more hard-to-place youth. Given the particular circumstances of those being served, C/R will probably draw more heavily on supplementary program resources, such as Financial Aid and Local Travel.

Counseling (Cslg).   This service will be necessary for a *small* proportion of all accepted youth: those judged eligible but for whom there appears to be no other appropriate community service, and whose difficulties are likely to be resolved through short-term direct personal help. Counseling with these youth (and parents where appropriate) and reliance on other, supplementary program resources will be the main modes of service for this center.

Management/General (Mgt/Gen).   This center will have responsibility for overall management of CYS and its full range of activities, community endeavors, and relations with JYC. It will conduct no activities that can properly be assigned to any other center but, rather, will undertake those necessary to ensure the operation of the entire program. Included here are such responsibilities as overseeing personnel practices, assignments, workloads, and evaluation; defining program policies (in concert with JYC), procedures, and standards; directing development of cooperative relations with community agencies, other resources, and the community at large; handling fiscal management and budgeting tasks; maintaining files and records; and submitting activity and fiscal reports to JYC, the funder, and others. *Supervision of direct services to clients, case management, and other operational oversight tasks will be performed by designated staff within each of the other centers.*

(*Note:* The nature and organization of services, staff activities, and flow of clients and work at JYC are both similar to and significantly different from those of the hypothetical Job Training Program used in Chapter 5 and other program examples throughout the book. This accords with our main theme that the basic procedures can be adapted to meet the differing requirements of various kinds of programs and agencies.)

IDENTIFYING SETS OF ACTIVITIES WITHIN CENTERS

Position descriptions have already been developed for most CYS jobs and used in the process of selecting and hiring staff. A description of the Program Coordinator's position was included in the budget application (see Chapter 4), you drafted one for another position (Step 4, Chapter 4), and more staff information was given in the Self-assessment Guide (Chapter 4). A position statement for the Screening Supervisor is given below. None of these statements is detailed enough by itself to settle allocation decisions: They include only the obvious, or they do not make distinctions critical for assigning positions across centers. Therefore, you will have to make reasonable assumptions when you proceed in the important task of deciding on personnel assignments among the centers.

All the materials presented here, and those referenced from Chapters 3 and 4, should be reviewed, just as you would do given your task in any agency. The materials you developed for phasing in staff in Chapter 4 are also relevant, because they too include notions of who should be doing what within CYS. The next step in functional budgeting, as discussed in Chapter 5, involves identifying the essential *sets of activities* that must be performed within each cost center, then determining *which personnel* should be assigned to each of these activities in *each center.* The results of your work on these two matters will provide the foundation for allocating all remaining personnel. Additional information about CYS service activities and key assignments is given in connection with the exercise steps.

Screening Supervisor (SS). This person will provide direct supervision of Screening/Intake activities, and will make or confirm decisions to accept (or not accept) youths into the program. The SS will supervise the Intake Worker and secretarial staff in their contacts with individuals, families, and in-referral sources, and will personally conduct some interviews with them. Other duties include assistance to staff responsible for interpreting program services to potential in-referral sources; case management across the entire program; consultation with and assistance to the PC in managing program operations, determining policies/procedures, and supervising some staff.

Division of Administrative Responsibilities. CYS is sufficiently large that the PC must rely on a senior associate to share oversight duties, substitute when the PC is away, and advise and counsel other staff. Thus it has been decided that some of the PC's administrative duties should be shared with the SS.[1] The PC will be especially active in community relations, assuming general responsibility for developing, guiding, and nurturing them, and will directly represent CYS in interactions with JYC, the funder, community planning bodies, and the like. Major responsibility for managing crucial aspects of *internal* program activities and operations must be assigned to the SS. This person will be especially active in "case management" duties in the centers: monitoring and guiding staff activities vis-à-vis youth and dealing with outside units on behalf of particular youths; making or confirming most key decisions about the youth (e.g. accept, route, terminate); assuring prompt handling at all points; and authorizing use of special resources for clients. The PC will share in some of these "case management" duties and in a variety of direct service activities, to become familiar with the clients, basic services, staff practices, implications of policies, and to avoid overload on the Screening Supervisor and others.

CYS is too small for exclusive specialization by any staff

---

[1] Note, however, that assignments of administrative duties for the Job Training Program followed a somewhat different pattern.

in a single center, and most personnel will be assigned to work in two or more centers. This pattern will make it easier to integrate services, move clients between centers, and exchange information and expertise. Further, all staff will assist in various support tasks, as needed, to relieve (or fill in for) the secretaries, to simplify office practices such as recordkeeping, and to assure prompt program response to critical situations.

The Functional Budget Form and Allocation

Only your final dollar allocation figures should be entered on the Functional Budget Form; the results of all other work should appear on other pages. When all costs have been allocated, the total for each line across columns 2 through 6 *must* equal the amount showing on that line in column 1; and line entries for each column must add up to the column subtotals you show on lines 9 and 11. Sums are always rounded to the nearest full dollar on budget forms, and no cents should appear on this form. This may cause you some difficulty in getting "perfect" line or column subtotals after rounding, and it is permissible, therefore, to note that subtotals may be off by $1.00.

PARTIAL COST ALLOCATIONS

Some resource allocation decisions have already been reached by the Program Coordinator (and confirmed by the JYC Director), and the results of these are reported on the form. You are expected to accept these determinations even though you may not understand the reasoning behind all of them. Because, either as the reader or as an administrative assistant, you lack full information, you would be unable to make valid determinations about most of these items, and some constraints are likely to be imposed in any organization. The most important of these allocation decisions are discussed below. You should review the descriptions of the program's centers and the partial listings of staff duties, and

JOHNSON YOUTH CENTER

For Internal Use Only

Program ___Community Youth Services___

FUNCTIONAL BUDGET

Line Item		Budget Award Col. 1	Screening/ Intake Col. 2	Referral Col. 3	Con/Ref Col. 4	Coun- seling Col. 5	Mgt/ Gen Col. 6
Personnel	FTEs						
Prog. Coord.	1.00	24,000	4,320			720	4,080
Scr. Super.	1.00	21,000	10,500	3,570			1,050
Intake W.	.80	14,720	13,615			0	0
Liaison Wkrs.	3.30	57,750	12,830		18,619		1,143
Counselors	2.00	32,400	0			5,832	0
Secretaries	2.00	24,000	8,640				960
	10.10						
1. Total Sal/Wages		173,870	49,905				7,233
2. Employee Benefits & Payroll Taxes		34,774	9,981				1,446
3. Professional Fees		4,200	1,037			878	210
4. Supplies, Communications, & Reproduction		6,500	2,998				845
5. Occupancy: Rent		12,000	3,660				1,080
6. Travel: Local		4,925	943				168
Conference		800	379	145	121	0	155
7. Equipment		3,000	0	0	0	0	3,000
8. Assistance to Clients: Vendor Charges		3,600	700				0
Financial Aid		3,800	0				0
9. TOTAL DIRECT COSTS		247,469	69,603			*	14,137
10. Overhead / Indirect		44,544	12,529				2,545
11. GRAND TOTAL		292,013	82,132				16,682

Special Note:

   *$15,000 cap on Counseling TDC

think about how the partial allocations on the form were determined.

The PC has decided that *not more* than $15,000 in Total Direct Costs (TDC) shall be allocated to the Counseling Center (line 9). This restriction on resources is intended to assure that Counseling's activities are kept to the modest level recommended in previous policy decisions and program planning.

Management/General Support Center. Almost all the resources needed for this center have already been allocated and reported on the form. The PC has a good sense of how much time will be needed for the overall responsibilities and also how much time of both the Screening Supervisor and a Secretary will be needed to assist in these activities. None of the Intake Worker's or Counselors' time will be needed here, but one of the Liaison Workers will be expected to participate in generally interpreting the CYS program to the community. Similarly, decisions have been reached about how much of the consultant and conference travel resources will be needed in conjunction with the basic management and community relations duties. (All remaining Professional Fees will be used for "case consultations" by other staff and should be allocated to other centers.) All Equipment funds have been allocated to Management/General, because office equipment will be used by secretaries and others for many purposes, and the portions appropriate to each center cannot be estimated without more actual experience. Assistance to Clients resources will not be needed in this center, because clients are not served directly.

Screening Supervisor. The SS's responsibilities and tasks have been discussed in several earlier sections, which should be referred to when apportioning this person's time among the CYS functions.

Cost Factors. Employee Benefits are set at 20 percent of line 1 salary costs for each center, and the Overhead/Indirect rate is 18 percent of each center's Total Direct Costs (TDC) on line 9. No other factors are imposed for this budget. (*Note:* Your salary costs as a JYC employee are covered by the CYS Overhead funds as you work on various tasks throughout the book.)

Other Allocations. Occupancy costs have been allocated to S/I and Mgt/Gen in relation to their proportions of total FTEs *plus* the costs for the waiting room space assigned to

S/I and the other common use space assigned to Mgt/Gen. Still other allocation decisions have been reached and the results already entered on the form. *Do not change any of these: The PC and Director believe they are valid.* However, you should study the pattern of these allocations carefully, because they have significance for your own work: They both ease and restrict the allocation decisions you still have to make.

Exercise Steps

The Director has offered some cautions as you begin allocating program resources, and these are consistent with information in Chapter 5. Because each center will offer differing services to clients, it is probable that varying portions of each staff position and of nonpersonnel line-items should be allocated across the budget columns. It would be unwise, therefore, to allocate costs across several lines according to some arbitrary percentage or formula—except, of course, Employee Benefits and Overhead costs, for which set percentages must be used. And it is improbable that *equal amounts* of particular resources (such as space or supplies) would be needed for two or more centers, or that *all* of some line-item resource would be needed for only one center. Further, you should consider whether to allocate *none* of a resource to a center; that is, one or another center may not require any of a budgeted resource to conduct its activities. (Note, for example, that *no* Financial Aid was allocated to Screening/Intake.) Think carefully about the *pattern* of services and resource requirements for each center, then strive for a *mixed balance* of allocations to reflect the differences in patterns.

With these cautions in mind, your main learning will come as you attempt to apply the differential allocation methods we have set forth. After making very limited use of the "horizontal" or proportional method of allocation, you will need to formulate what you regard as the correct *bases* needed for use of the "vertical" or relational methods. And inevitably, as you proceed you will want to return to many of your preliminary decisions, reconsider them, and modify some to achieve the desired balances within and across all centers.

PERSONNEL ALLOCATIONS

Step 1. *Position activities by cost centers.* Table 6–1 displays the main types of activities to be conducted in all CYS centers (*except* Management/General, whose main activities have been discussed earlier and for which staffing allocations have already been made). The table is completed only for Screening/Intake, all of whose position activities have already been specified (see p. 158).

Step. 1A. First, you should prepare listings of the main service activities for each of the centers. Table 6–1 details only the general *types* of activities across centers, so you must determine the concrete tasks for each. Think carefully about what has already been explained so you can specify each center's essential tasks as part of the total program.

Step 1B. You are now ready to assign each of the main activities you have listed above to designated staff position(s) and enter these on the chart. Again, refer to the information given for the Screening/Intake center and elsewhere for guidance in your work. It will be helpful to list on a separate sheet, under each position, the activities of that position in each center; you will thus have an alternative view of your allocations. Both activities and personnel must be specified before FTEs can be allocated across the centers.

Step 1C. You should now be able to write a short position description for the Liaison Workers and the Counselors (as exemplified for the PC and SS) or at least a brief but full listing of the main duties to be assigned across the program to the individuals in these positions. This will help clarify how their duties will differ from but complement each other in most centers.

Step 2. You are ready to allocate the remaining Personnel FTEs so that basic CYS duties can be performed. A special *workpage* follows to aid in making and reporting the results of your decisions (Table 6–2, p. 159). Some but not all of the salary allocations already shown on the functional budget are given here as FTE check figures. First you should insert information already on the budget but not yet on the

TABLE 6–1. Staff Activities and Duties, by CYS Service Centers

(fill in missing assignments)

Activities/Duties	S/I	Referral	C/R	Counseling
Center Administration[a]				
Policy/procedure planning	PC with SS	PC with SS	PC with SS	PC with SS
Basic staff assignments and performance evals	SS	PC	PC with SS	PC with SS
Basic resource management	PC	PC		
Records/reports/evals	SS	PC		
Community Relations and Outreach				
Search, contact, interpretation, etc. } Mobilize/recruit, negotiate agreements, etc. }	PC + SS + IW + LW			PC + LW
Client Services				
Case management	SS + IW			SS or PC?
Direct contact/service[b]	SS, IW, LW (and Sec. for inquiries)			C
External services[c]	SS + IW + LW			LW (with C)
Resource usage (consultants, ass't to clients, etc.)	SS + IW	SS		SS or PC?
Office Support				
Receiving/meeting persons; answering inquiries;				
Typing & filing forms, correspondence, records/reports;				
Mailing/reproduction; scheduling staff; misc. & other		always secretaries plus others as needed		

[a] Administrative activities immediately connected with each center and not assigned to Mgt/Gen for entire program.

[b] Must be concretely specified for each center; includes all interactions with youth (and families), and all intramural activities on behalf of individual youth (recording, conferring about, and so on).

[c] Includes all communications and contacts from/with outside sources about individual youth, all interactions concerned with them, including arrangements for intake or referral, cooperative agreements and collaboration, and so on.

TABLE 6–2. Functional Budget Workpage

	Totals	S/I	Ref.	C/R	Cslg.	Mgt./Gen.
Staff FTEs:						
Prog. Coord.	1.00	.180				.170
Screen. Sup.	1.00	.500	.170			.050
Intake W.	.80	.74				-0-
Liaison W.	3.30	.733		1.064		.065
Counselors	2.00	-0-	.520		.36	-0-
Secretaries	2.00	.720				.080
Total FTEs	10.10	2.873				
Percent FTEs	100.0	.284				
Sec. ratio 1:	4.05	2.990				
Space:						
% Occup. $	100.0	.305				.090
Supplies:						
% Supplies $	100.0					
Local Travel:						
Traveling FTEs	7.30					
FTE rate $	674.67		675.04			588.82
Estimated Cases:	1820	1000	465	315	40	XXX
FTE-per-case	XXX	.0029				XXX
Hours-per-case (FTE x 1900)	XXX	5.459				XXX

Note: Check figures rounded to third decimal.

workpage: Calculate FTEs and other measures and enter these where they belong. Before going on, make sure you know exactly the total FTEs for each position and your calculations generate the same check figures already on the workpage. In all calculations involving FTEs be sure to retain as many decimals as your calculator permits, and enter them on your work materials to at least the fourth significant digit.

Step 2A. Begin your allocations with *preliminary* figures for the PC and SS, some of whose assignments to centers have already been made on the budget form and reported on the workpage. Consider these results carefully so you can understand what is involved in light of all the information presented above and already developed by you. Then proceed with all other positions *except* the Secretaries and enter your preliminary nonsecretarial FTE subtotals for each column on the workpage.

Step 2B. You are now ready to allocate the time of the Secretaries, using the methods discussed in the chapter. The workpage shows that somewhat more than 1.00 FTE remains to be assigned across three centers. Are there any special tasks these persons must perform in one rather than another of these areas? Should the remaining Secretaries be allocated only in relation to the staff FTEs you have already determined? Or should you also take into account differences in the tasks to be performed by Secretaries and in the estimated client volume across the centers? After you have made your decisions, insert the Secretarial FTEs and the *secretary/staff ratio* figures on the workpage. (Save any alternative solution in the event you decide to make changes.)

Step 3. Add up the FTEs now allocated to each center (return to your unrounded figures), calculate what percentage of the total FTEs you have allocated to each, and enter these figures on the workpage. Sum these across the columns to make sure you have the correct FTE total. Now divide the FTE subtotals by the number of clients in each center to obtain the *FTE-per-case ratios*. These figures are difficult to assess because they are very small; they should be converted to *hours-per-case:* Multiply each FTE figure by 1,900 (the average total hours for a year's work represented by an FTE) and enter the results on the workpage. *Review all these results and think about the implications for the program.* If you decide to make changes, be sure to redo the other calculations and enter the new figures.

Step 4. As a final check on your personnel allocation decisions, you should consider the adequacy of your provisions for administrative oversight in the centers by calculating the ratio of the PC and the SS to all other staff in each center. (Add the PC and SS FTEs in each center, then divide this figure into the subtotal of all other FTEs.) Each center requires some minimum level of administrative staffing and additional oversight according to the kinds of activities to be conducted in each, as well as the numbers of other personnel whose work must be monitored.

Step 5. When you are satisfied with the allocation of personnel, convert the FTEs to salary dollars and enter these on the budget form. Make certain that your line-item subtotals do not exceed those set in the first column.

Self-assessment Guidelines

We now offer some guidelines for assessing your work on these steps. Because personnel are the key program resource and decisions about nonpersonnel costs are heavily dependent on these allocations, we shall pause and deal with the results you have obtained up to this point—as you would in a real situation. The functional budgeting problems in these exercises have no unique or single acceptable solution, and considerable—but not unlimited—variability will occur. The figures that were already set on the budget form have greatly restricted your freedom of choice but have also offered hints to help you.

After reviewing these guidelines and your preliminary work, you may wish to make changes before proceeding to address the next set of steps. The ranges given below exclude incorrect or faulty results but cannot guarantee solutions that are best rather than less good.

A. *Minimum Staffing for Program Centers.* Except for the zero FTE values already entered, no other position lines should show a zero entry. At least some portion of each position will be needed in every remaining center. Assuming the validity of the partial allocations already set, there would be no rationale for denying any center some of each position. For example, the assignment of only .74 Intake Worker FTE to Screening/Intake, but none to Counseling (or Mgt/Gen), means that this person is also expected to perform some duties in either or both the Referral and C/R centers. Because the Referral and C/R activities are very similar but differ in the degree of assistance provided, this person will be needed in both, at least to relay or interpret information about youth that was learned during Intake. *In general,* therefore, if there is reason to allocate some FTEs for the Intake Worker, Liaisons, and Counselors to Referral or C/R, and perhaps to Counseling, then some of each should also be assigned to the other service centers. Your listing of the duties of the Liaison Workers should have been helpful, since it ought to have included activities across centers and distinguished their duties from those of the Counselors.

The cap on TDC for the Counseling center certainly ought to have affected your decisions. Most of this amount must be spent on salaries, but there is too little to allow a sizable staff complement here. Perhaps you overlooked this constraint or attempted to meet it by cutting out other essential personnel. You can reconsider this as we turn next to the PC and SS positions, and then to the Secretaries.

B. *Program Administration.*   The program and position information given above makes clear that some portion of both the PC and SS positions are needed in every center. Part of the reasoning for this was given in Chapter 4, and part in the discussion of the division of responsibilities between these positions.

Given at least their minimum assignments to all centers, we then need to examine the *ratio* of these administrative personnel to other staff, and to client or case volume—two primary bases for assigning these positions. The overall program administrative ratio is 4.05, that for Mgt/Gen is .66, and the range for all other centers ought to fall between 3.20 and 6.50. If any ratio measure falls outside these limits, it means that some center will have too little senior staff time to assure adequate case management and other oversight.

C. *Support Staff Allocations.*   Some secretarial service is of course required in every center. The overall program secretarial ratio is 4.05, that fixed for Mgt/Gen is 3.57, and Secretarial FTEs have also been fixed for Screening/Intake. The ratios for the other centers ought to fall between 4.00 and 9.50. Every center will have some minimum level of file and correspondence materials to be handled by these persons, forms to fill out for one or both of the Client Assistance resources, as well as work connected with other staff. Beyond these minimum requirements, however, Secretarial allocations ought to reflect the kinds of tasks likely to be associated with the centers' particular services. For example, additional Secretarial assistance will be needed in both Referral and C/R to prepare the materials that must be sent to other places as youth are referred. And greater use of other resources in providing services to these youth will require more work in handling purchase orders, travel reimbursement forms, and so on.

After reviewing your results in light of these guidelines, make any changes you think appropriate, then reassess your new figures. If, on reflection, you are convinced that your results have validity even though they do not meet these criteria, you should try to list your reasons, simulating what you would be expected to do in an agency where similar ranges or considerations are stated, but where you believe another, better set of allocations has merit.

Other Personnel Allocation Steps. We offer no criteria for assessing the staff salary and FTE percentages by centers, except to remind you of the necessity to remain under the cap placed on Counseling TDC (*including* the nonpersonnel costs yet to be allocated there). Methods for verifying salary data are given in the previous chapter. Some programs might use percentage ranges for determining allocations to centers, and percentages certainly ought to be examined. But, as discussed in Chapter 5, this represents a *proportional* (or horizontal) measure and by itself has little validity for CYS. Furthermore, the fixed budget figures in this problem, and the criteria already presented, control your staffing decisions sufficiently to assure adequate results. You will need the FTE percentage measure, however, as you work on other steps that follow.

NONPERSONNEL ALLOCATIONS

Step 6. Begin with *Occupancy* costs in view of the attention given this item in Chapter 5. Assume that there will be equal-size workstations for all personnel (if only because you have no floor plan or other space details). We know from the budget that all common-use space has already been allocated to Mgt/Gen except for the small waiting room assigned to S/I. Determine the remaining dollar balance for this item, and divide it by the subtotal of FTEs in the three other centers to obtain the per-FTE sum still available. Multiply this amount by each of these centers' FTE subtotals, and add these results to the dollars already allocated to see that the total is correct. Then enter the dollar figures on your budget—and the line percentage figures on the workpage. Compare the centers' FTE percentages with their percentages of Occupancy costs to decide whether you are satisfied with these allocations. (The costs of the common-use space assignments are represented by the *differences* between the percentages of FTEs and the percentages of Occupancy costs already allocated to Mgt/Gen and S/I.)

Step 7. Now consider *Professional Fees.* This resource is intended to engage the expertise of consultants to advise staff about special difficulties they may encounter in serving some youth. Two service centers have already received their allocations, as has Mgt/Gen (for program development consultants). Presumably the use of these funds should be dependent on the *kinds* of problems requiring such assistance and on the *numbers* of youth in the several centers that have such problems. This should help you make the remaining allocations on relational (vertical) bases. Enter your figures on the budget form and proceed to the *Vendor Charges* and *Financial Aid* items. Again, consider the nature of these resources, the allocations already set, and the bases you would use for reaching decisions about the remaining amounts. Now turn to *Supplies* and make these quite different allocation decisions. Enter all your results on both the budget form and the workpage.

While planning these several allocations, keep in mind that they involve quite different kinds of resources to be used in conducting CYS service activities, each of which will be needed at different levels across the service centers. There cannot be a single basis for their allocation, and you will need to think carefully about the characteristics of youth served in each center and the service activities of each. (You might want to reread the PC's cautions given at the start of the exercise steps.)

Step 8. Only *Local Travel* funds remain to be allocated. Almost all of this line-item will be used to reimburse staff for necessary travel in the community. It is also likely that some youth will need to be given bus fare to reach the places where they are referred. But this will be a small amount, and you have no information that would allow you to plan for this allocation. All Local Travel should be allocated, therefore, in connection with travel by staff to visit youth and their families in their homes, to contact other agencies and in- and out-referral sources, and to accompany youth to these places or to receive special services.

Step 8A. Assume that personnel in two positions, the Intake Worker and the Secretaries, will do *no* traveling for CYS using these funds. Using the workpage, report the FTE subtotals (*excluding the two positions*) that you have already allocated to the centers. These "traveling FTEs" should then be entered on the workpage.

Step 8B. Consider which staff will be traveling for what purposes at varying levels in each center. Now allocate the remaining Local Travel dollars across the centers and enter these figures on another page. Divide the sum in each center by the FTE figure from the previous step to obtain the *rates per "traveling FTE"* that result from your dollar allocations. Examine these rates and carefully consider whether they represent what you believe should be the per-staff use of this resource across the centers. Make any changes that seem necessary to achieve the desirable rates between centers, then enter the final rate figures on the workpage.

Self-assessment Guidelines for the Nonpersonnel Items

D. *Occupancy Allocations.* Because the costs of common-use space were assigned to two centers, S/I and Mgt/Gen, their percentages of Occupancy line-item funds are greater than their percentages of total FTEs. But this means that the remaining centers cannot receive proportions of these funds as large as the percentages of FTEs you have given them. Therefore, if you made the assumptions cited earlier, the percentage of the line-item dollars now allocated to these centers should each represent about three to four percentage points *less* than its percentage of staff FTEs.

E. *Supplementary Program Resource Allocations.* Three of the resources dealt with in Step 7 are intended to be used in connection with service to *particular clients*, depending on their needs and circumstances. As we shall discuss in Chapter 7, discretionary judgments about clients by program personnel reflect differences among staff as much as they do objective variations among clients. Even if individual staff practices were a valid basis for these allocations, nothing is known about the workers, so your planning cannot take their variations into account and must instead address stated differences in center activities, the kinds and numbers of clients to be served, and so on.

The funds already assigned to two centers for these line-items again restricted your decisionmaking to the remaining amounts. We know that as we move across the centers there are smaller estimated numbers of youth to be served, but they represent successively more serious or less ordinary problems. This can offer a general approach to the allocation problem: We can weight the numbers in each center to reflect what might be their relative needs for each of these resources. Let us assume that each youth to be served in Ref will require twice as much of each of these line-items as those handled in S/I; that each in C/R requires three times as much; and each in Counseling requires four times as much. These weighted estimates can be summarized as follows:

	S/I	*Ref*	*C/R*	*Cslg*	*Totals*
Estimated cases	1000	465	315	40	1820
Weights		x 2	x 3	x 4	
Weighted estimates	1000	930	945	160	3035

The weighted estimates reflect differences in both case volume and relative need for a resource within the program. Here we are simply illustrating a technique for reviewing the results of allocation decisions. To use this method, you must formulate your own weights for each resource and each center, because these line-items represent quite different kinds of resources. And further, you must take account of the amounts of these line-items that have already been allocated.

Such weighted estimates can be used to assess line-item allocation results in two ways. First, the weighted estimates can be calculated as percentages of the new total of weighted cases; the budgeted line-item amount can then be multiplied by these percentages and the results compared to the partial allocations. Second, the new dollar figures can be divided by the numbers of estimated cases in each center to yield per-case dollar rates. Final adjustments can then be made in particular allocations to obtain desired results.

F. *Local Travel Allocations.*   If you followed the methods stated in Step 8, your per-FTE travel *rate* figures are already adjusted so that they apply only to those staff members in each center who are expected to travel in the community. Divide the smallest of these rate figures into the largest. If the result is greater than about 2.25 you have probably allocated proportionately too much to some center, and too little to another. Consider the activities that will require persons to travel to/from the CYS offices: contacting potential and actual in- and out-referral sources, visiting clients and parents in their own homes, transporting clients to referral sites or vendor offices, and so on. The smallest amount of such traveling will be necessary for Counseling, because this is largely an internal service and involves little or no contact with outside sources. The most traveling for these purposes will occur in Referral and C/R because of their kinds of activities, as well as of the numbers of youth each will serve. "Most" and "least" here means in net mileage terms, which translates directly into dollars. But "most" and "least" can be stated more precisely in per-FTE terms. The "traveling FTE" rates you developed offer better bases for both reaching and assessing these allocation decisions than do raw dollars or percentages of the line-item total. You were not asked to develop per-case measures for Local Travel, but may want to assess your results in these terms as well. Divide the sums allocated to each center by its estimated number of cases or by some estimates that use different weights. Each of these techniques offers a way to examine the allocation of this resource according to its *relative* use within the program.

G. *Supplies Allocations.*   As stated in Chapter 5, a variety of bases are employed in making allocations of supplies, any of which might be applicable here. It could reasonably be

assumed that supplies will be consumed primarily in relation to the numbers of clients to be served in each center or,
alternatively, to the number of FTEs in each. You may have
used either of these measures or some composite of both, or
even perhaps assumed that the activities in a particular
center required some special supply items that you first set
aside before making the remaining allocations. If you relied
on some other rationale that produced a very different pattern of results, try to answer such questions as these:

- What are the support implications for a center that received
  far less than the proportionate share of Supplies it would
  have received by either the staff or case volume basis?
- How will you justify your decisions if the PC challenges them
  in terms of each center's relative requirements?

When you completed the work represented by the exercise steps, it was time for a session with the Board's Planning Committee, to which you and other staff are reporting
on work-to-date. Committee members had obviously
prepared themselves by reading all materials in advance;
they showed keen interest in the planning and asked
penetrating questions. After listening to your presentation
of the CYS cost center descriptions, the committee chair
posed this question:

> Could you briefly summarize for us the differences between
> Referral and Consultation/Referral? They seem quite similar,
> but I realize they are intended to deal with somewhat different
> kinds of youth and provide somewhat different kinds of help.
> Please tell us how the youth that will be handled in the two
> areas will be different, and how the services they receive will
> be different.

Perhaps you had thought about the matter in these terms,
perhaps not, but you should now be able to offer fairly clear
explanations of the two sets of differences. List your ideas
and consider whether they conform to the planning
materials you have developed, and whether they would
satisfy an informed listener.

The Planning Committee chair thanked you for your
response, then posed another question:

> I think we now have a better understanding of these service
> plans. Let me go one step further, and apply a rough cost

estimating technique I might use in my own business. Suppose I were to take the TDC dollars on line 9 in the Ref column of your preliminary functional budget and divide it by the estimated number of youth to be served there next year. And then I did the same with the C/R figures. That would produce two average per youth figures of $____ and $____ (you fill in the correct figures from your report materials). Are those fair estimates of the average costs to serve kids in these two parts of CYS?

Think about the question, about what your response would be. Is this a valid and helpful way to estimate costs for these two program components?

The meeting ended with the committee's endorsement of the basic directions taken in functional budgeting and affirmation of certain policy emphases; but the committee also expressed concern about several matters that it hoped would receive close attention during the coming year.

7

EXPENSE/REVENUE MANAGEMENT

EXPENSE AND REVENUE management processes have two broad purposes: to link the use of resources to the achievement of objectives and to adhere to accountability requirements. Commonly referred to as fiscal management, these processes embrace other important issues (dollar or market costs, charges and fees, contractual obligations), which are also discussed in other chapters and are raised at relevant points here.

In this chapter we first explore some of the implicit and explicit elements essential for understanding fiscal management; then we describe in great detail the practical procedures for improving fiscal records and for monitoring and managing the flow of resources. Most of the chapter centers on problems related to expenses, but in the last section we also examine similar problems with revenue management. Controlling expenses is dealt with more specifically in the exercise section.[1]

As we have pointed out, administrators in midsized agencies are all too often overwhelmed or confused by the number and complexity of the management procedures

[1] Broadly following Anthony and Herzlinger (1980), we use expenses as the general term to indicate a monetary measure of the amount of resources consumed or used in operations during a given period. We also follow their definition of cost as referring to the amount of resources used for a particular purpose.

171

prescribed for them. Most accept the importance of maintaining separate fund accounts and the value of sound fiscal practices, but they are stymied in their attempts to implement or profit from them. They may not be able to afford knowledgeable support staffs; or they may set up good fund accounting procedures but not know how to extract useful managerial information from them. Others may shy away from handling all those numbers or may prefer to stick to their "tried and true" ways.

We believe such agencies and programs need to use procedures that embody the accounting principles of accurate record-keeping, careful monitoring, and reliable controls. But these procedures must be simple, appropriate, and comprehensive and especially must be useful for linking resource consumption to program services and objectives. Therefore, in this chapter we focus on practical ways to manage resources that will promote what the profit sector also wants from its cost accountants: to "measure performance against plans and feed back information for future planning" (Skigen and Snyder, 1975, p. 3). For those interested in a thorough knowledge of accounting, many texts are readily available.

We do, however, recommend that program managers become familiar with several key references. These include two publications of the American Institute of Certified Public Accountants (AICPA), *Statement of Position on Accounting Principles and Reporting Practices for Certain Nonprofit Organizations* (1978), and *Audits of Voluntary Health and Welfare Organizations* (1974); the *Standards of Accounting and Financial Reporting for Voluntary Health and Welfare Organizations* (1974) published by the National Health Council et al.; two important United Way publications, *Accounting and Financial Reporting* (1974) and *Budgeting* (1975); and "Federal Cost Principles" issued by the Office of Management and Budget. All these guides are designed to help not-for-profit organizations observe sound accounting practices.

Controllable and Uncontrollable Line-Item Costs

Program managers must, at the outset, understand clearly which costs can be controlled and when control is possible.

The way to control costs is contingent on this understanding.

In accounting parlance "controllable" has the same meaning as its everyday definition: able to be regulated, checked, managed, or restrained. A controllable cost in cost accounting is one "reasonably subject to regulation" by a designated head of a responsibility center (Skigen and Snyder, 1975). Thus, if a cost can be changed or affected by the way a program is carried out, that cost is controllable.

As we set out to determine specifically *which* costs in an organization are controllable or uncontrollable, we must recognize that all costs, while uncontrollable at a given level, are also controllable at some level. The efforts to clarify and define what level has what kind of authority have led to the development of responsibility and cost centers. The responsibility center concept requires an overall plan that spells out areas or spheres of accountability—and, by extension, identification of lines of control. Then, within a clearly defined responsibility frame, authority for managing costs can be assigned and shared. In our illustrative agency, CYS is a clearly designated responsibility center (RC) that is authorized to manage its own funds within the limits set by JYC and the funder.

The time factor also has a significant effect on a responsibility center's ability to control costs. At different times during the budget cycle the RC's influence and leverage will vary. For example, during the earliest budget development stage the parent agency will make many important decisions about the extent and use of all resources. As soon as a new responsibility center is established and authority is delegated to its head, the RC can begin exercising responsibility for its own fiscal and operational affairs. During negotiations with funders about modifications, shifts in emphasis, and so on, the new RC will still have considerable leverage, especially over estimations of controllable costs. After the final contract or award, the RC will usually have discretionary control over only certain controllable costs—the uncontrollable ones will have been determined during earlier stages of the budgeting process.

We can see how this works for a program. Its final budget will probably include a specific amount for rent, which will not be controllable during the fiscal year if a year's lease is signed. However, at earlier stages in the budgeting process this cost could have been controllable: A smaller or larger space might have been selected; a shorter or longer lease might have been negotiated; more or less square footage might have been arranged; a different location might have been chosen. The costs for rent were therefore controllable at some time during the budget development process.

Even a cost that is binding by law has some controllable aspects at certain times. For example, Social Security taxes, although fixed by law, are tied to salary costs, which have controllable aspects, so some flexibility exists at some stages in the budgeting process. For example, the salary ranges for some positions might be narrowed, thus affecting some Social Security costs.

We can see, then, that while some controllability may be possible at certain times, uncontrollability is never absent. Thus you might say that controllability represents the variance that is allowed only after uncontrollability is imposed.

RESTRAINTS AND FREEDOM

Controllable and uncontrollable costs both contain variable dimensions of restraints and degrees of freedom of choice. That is, the freedom or lack of freedom to make responsible decisions and to exercise discretion vary not only with timing but, more important, with external and internal conditions, aims, types of costs, and so on.

Uncontrollable costs are commonly subject to two principal types of restraints: what the organization *must* do and what it *cannot* do. In general, both types result from state and federal laws, from funders' or benefactors' requirements, from union contracts, and from professional ethics. Either type may be indicated in general or in specific terms, and both types should have been thoroughly taken into account during budget development.

Restraints on controllable costs are more diffuse and often call for subjective judgments. The following list illustrates some of the varied restraining factors associated with controllable costs:

• Agency goals and policies
• Program objectives

- Client characteristics
- Accountability and evaluation requirements
- Sound fiscal procedures
- Local situations: similar agencies, competition
- Administrative practicality
- Professional practices

At the same time the freedom of choice also associated with controllable costs offers opportunities to enhance these same restrictive factors. Again, subjective judgments based on a total view of the program are called for. Remember that *decisions* about expending controllable costs can be made at any time; *fiscal transactions* can occur only during the fiscal period. The following list indicates some positive aims toward which discretionary decisions may be directed.

- Enhancing program objectives
- Achieving efficiencies
- Improving working conditions, incentives, and staff morale
- Improving administrative operations
- Enriching relations with community
- Upgrading staff

Thus, for example, the program may choose to spend some of its controllable personnel funds on salary increases rather than on planned temporary staff (strengthening work incentives and improving morale). Or it may choose to hire fewer but more qualified persons (upgrading staff). Or it may decide to enhance program objectives by committing a larger proportion of controllable funds to one particular service function. Or it may decide to improve administrative operations by assigning more of the controllable supplies and equipment budget to setting up a computerized payroll system.

Table 7-1 illustrates the range of controllability and uncontrollability for various object costs in a typical not-for-profit agency (including our illustrative CYS program). For this chart we assume three critical facts: *that a final budget has been agreed upon and awarded; that only minimal shifts are allowed between line-items; and that the fiscal year has already begun.* Although only three points are specified on the range, a five-point continuum is implied: fully controllable, mostly controllable, partially controllable, rarely

TABLE 7-1. Range of Controllability and Uncontrollability for Line-Item Object Costs

Line-Item	Fully Controllable	Partially Controllable	Fully Uncontrollable
Professional salaries & clerical		x	
Temporary staff	x		
Employee health & retirement benefits		x	x
Payroll taxes			x
Professional fees	x[a]		
Supplies			
General office	x		
Telephone		x	
Postal	x		
Duplicating	x		
Special	x		
Occupancy			
Rent/mortgage		x	
Mortgage interest			x
Utilities		x	
Taxes			x
Licenses/permits			x
Maintenance supplies		x	
Misc.	x		
Equipment			
Purchases	x		
Maintenance/repair		x	
Printing & duplications			
Printing		x	
Graphics, records, etc.	x		

Subscriptions x

Publication purchases x—————

Public
information/media x

Travel

Conference x

Per diem x—————

Local for clients x—————

Local for staff x

Leased vehicles x

Emergencies x—————

Conferences, meetings x

Specific assistance
to clients x—————

Memberships, dues

Individuals x

Organizations x—————

Miscellaneous

Insurance x—————

Recruitment x

Bonding x—————

Bank charges x

Fundraising x—————

Note: The *line* indicates the common range for most programs; the *X* indicates the most typical point within the range.
[a] Except for contracts, special purchased services, auditors, accountants, attorneys.

177

controllable, and uncontrollable. For some of these costs the restrictive and discretionary aspects are implicit in their placement on the continuum. *How* the discretion may be exercised is not included.

Financial Records

Today most service agencies and programs recognize the need to keep accurate records of financial transactions. The sophistication of their bookkeeping and accounting systems will depend on resources, size, previous experience, funder requirements, and other factors. Most recognize their fiduciary responsibilities as custodians of resources and as stewards of property belonging to others. They know they must keep multisource funds separate and must usually conform to a functional as well as to a line-item budget. Most also observe standard bookkeeping practices, keep journals and ledgers, and prepare balance sheets. Some may even be tied into computer services that provide detailed monthly revenue and expense summaries. But all agencies set up some method—whether primitive or complex—for keeping track of expenses and revenues.

We applaud these efforts to improve financial record-keeping and to follow accepted procedures. However, some additional important points need emphasis:

1. Financial records should be as complete and accurate as common sense and feasibility indicate. Good records do not necessarily require sophisticated systems.
2. Information output is only as good as information input.
3. The smallest program will need many of the same kinds of basic information from its records as the largest agency. The difference in *amount* of information involved affects the structure and size of the information system—not necessarily its purposes or uses.
4. Financial records should be kept up to date and scrupulously documented for audit.
5. In addition to all the above, the records must be *useful* to the director, executive committee, or board accountable for the program and responsible for future planning.

The last point is discussed thoroughly in this chapter,

because very often program managers do not know *how* to tie fiscal and program records together to get this kind of useful information. No matter how detailed the records, how specialized the system, how well-documented the transactions, if the fiscal information is not integrated with the flow and purpose of program activities, it cannot be useful for reviewing, assessing, and projecting the effects and results of these operations.

GENERATING AND USING INFORMATION

What kind of information is needed to achieve this fifth objective, and how can it most efficiently be obtained? Standard financial records are a necessary but not sufficient component of an integrated record system. They should minimally include payroll journals, a voucher system, receipts journal, check register, accounts payable ledger, deposit slip journal, and so on. All these are thoroughly discussed and explained in the United Way's *Accounting and Financial Reporting* (1974), and its recommendations can be tailored to fit the needs of most programs. A full-scale double entry ledger and journal system is not necessarily essential, but safeguards similar to those incorporated in such a system are indispensable.

To ensure sufficient joint fiscal/program information, however, a number of nonfiscal records can be used to generate important additional fiscal information and to provide supportive data. Although our discussion here centers on information for *internal* fiscal management, the same kinds of backup data are usually also essential for preparing ongoing and final financial and operations reports for external funders. In fact, the wise administrator will aim at integrating the requirements for both to improve efficiency and completeness (see lists of required documentation in Appendix A). In many cases, efficiency can be obtained by modifying existing nonfiscal records so they will yield the necessary fiscal information. In other words, administrators should seek multiple capabilities from all types of records. With a few additions or alterations, the same base information can often be cast in several ways to serve different, but compatible, purposes. By first attempting to build on existing records, paperwork can be reduced and efficiency increased.

We shall first look at some examples of ways fiscal records can be modified to furnish additional important information. Then we shall explore some ways to elicit fiscal data from nonfiscal basic records.

Let us start with a very simple example: the Petty Cash Receipt, a printed form, which looks like the sample in Figure 7–1.

This form, available in every office supply store, is a perfect example of a necessary but not sufficient standard record of a cash disbursement. It is an equally perfect example of a record readily amenable to modification for furnishing additional information. Typically, the line "For" might say, "trip for client" or "postage," or "manila envelopes," and so on. The "Charge to" line will show the account number and might say "travel" or "postage" or "supplies." At the end of a reporting period, each cash disbursement will have to be assigned to a line-item and a cost center; and the program manager will then have to go back either to the persons who approved or received the money or will have to guess where to assign it. With a few changes, much useful information could be included in the first place. For example, a fully detailed Petty Cash Receipt—manageable at the time of the transaction when memories are fresh—could contain all the information shown in Figure 7–2.

Purchase orders or other vouchers should also include similar details (account number, line-item, cost center), plus other relevant information, like check number, interest

---

No. _____   Amount _____

RECEIVED OF PETTY CASH

For _____

Charge to _____

_____

Approved by   Received by

Figure 7–1.   Petty Cash Receipt

```
No.    116                 Account No.   420-PR           Amount $    1.50

                                                       No. of    Total
         Purpose            Date          Base Rate     Units     Cost
       Trip for job         1/7/xx       .75 per fare     2       $1.50
       interview

              Line-Item/Code             Function/Code      Re Case No.
Charge To:      Aid to Clients 077         Placement 420      67421

Receipt(s) Attached            Yes  X        No _____

    If no, why not _____

Payment Date    1/31/xx

Approved by                Paid out by                 Received by
   S.S.S. Coordinator           P.D.                      Jack Jones
```

Figure 7–2. Modified Petty Cash Receipt

charges, discounts, delivery charges, date of receipt of goods, and vendor invoice number. In short, whenever possible a transaction record should serve internal, funder, and audit needs. A review of all these needs would be a sensible starting point for determining the kinds and amount of details that must be collected. It is also important to gain staff cooperation in supplying these details. Therefore, staff should be given simple how-to instructions and told why the details are essential.

Now let us look at some ways to extract fiscal data from nonfiscal records. Staff activity logs are generally required in most organizations. These logs trace the actual use of staff time carrying out specific program activities for specific clients; they are also usually needed for final reports and audits to demonstrate how and where staff dollars were expended. The logs thus chronicle nonfiscal information that has vital fiscal relevance, and they can be readily modified to combine both kinds of information. We look first at a typical example of a staff activity log for Jane Doe, who works in several cost centers (Table 7–2).

From such an activity log, a cumulative monthly fiscal summary can be made for each person (Table 7–3, p. 183). From these individual cumulative summaries, fiscal data for total staff can be compiled month by month, which will be especially useful when summarized by cost centers (see Table 7–4, p. 184). A yearly summary can then easily be prepared (see Table 7–5, p. 185).

TABLE 7-2. Staff Activity Log

Name: Jane Doe
S.S.: 000-00-0000
Responsibility Center Code: 3

For Period: Jan. 1-30, 198x
Title: Contact Worker II

First Day of Activity This Month	Case No.	Client Name	Cost Center	Activity Name or Code	No. in Group	Time Unit	No. of Times This Month
Jan. 4	67421	John J	Intake	Assessment 111	1	2	4
Jan. 4	72146	Albert P	Crisis	Intervention 113	1	4	4
Jan. 6	64731 64733 68297	Sylvia S Mary G Alice C	Outreach	Job Preparation 114	3	8	6
. .	. .	. .	. .	. .	. .	. .	. .

TABLE 7–3.   Staff Activity Fiscal Summary

Name: Jane Doe   S.S.: 000-00-0000
Yearly Salary: $16,000   Per Hour Rate: $7.69

Month	Cost Center	Total Hours	Total Dollars	No. of Clients
Jan	Intake	48·	$369.12	12
	Crisis	16	123.04	3
	Outreach	48	369.12	8
	·	·	·	·
	·	·	·	·
Month Totals		—	—	—
		xxx	xxx.xx	xxx
Feb		·	·	·
·	·	·	·	·
·	·	·	·	·
·	·	·	·	·

Operations measures, which are discussed in Chapter 8, provide information more related to results than the activity logs we have been discussing. They, too, can easily be modified to provide additional fiscal information. Whatever record system is used, the same objectives apply: efficiency, sufficiency, verification, accuracy, and explanation.

Monitoring Budget Expenses

Monitoring is inseparable from the processes that go into the development of the budget, and it merges into the processes of maintaining and ensuring control of expenses. The important relation between budget development and monitoring cannot be overemphasized. Monitoring can be firmly based on the budget only if that document was thoughtfully related to the program and if costs were realistically projected. The more reliable and precise the budget estimates, the more the spending patterns will conform to them and the simpler the monitoring tasks. This holds true for both major and minor line-item object costs. For example, a travel item in the budget would be relatively simple to monitor if time and costs for each person going on the trip and reliable estimates for subsistence and other costs of the trip had been well documented. But a budgeted

TABLE 7-4. Monthly Fiscal Summary of Staff Activities by Cost Centers

Month	Cost Center	No. of Staff Reporting	Total Staff Hours	Total Dollars	No. of Clients
Jan	Intake	8	942	$7,649	65
	Crisis	6	620	4,650	21
	Outreach	4	422	3,427	11
	·	·	·	·	·
	·	·	·	·	·
	·	·	·	·	·
Totals		xxx	xxx	x,xxx	xxx

TABLE 7-5. Year's Fiscal Summary of Staff Activity by Cost Centers

Cost Center	Total No of Clients	Total Staff Hours	Total FTEs	Total Dollars	Average Hours per Client	Average Cost per Client
Intake Crisis	850	10,509	5.59	$83,021	12.4	$97.67
.	.	.	.	.	.	.
.	.	.	.	.	.	.
.	.	.	.	.	.	.
.	.	.	.	.	.	.
Year's Total	xxx	xxxxx	xx.xx	xxxxx		

amount for travel based on figures poorly estimated for an indeterminate trip by an unspecified number of people will be very hard to monitor. Even in the best circumstances, however, monitoring calls for managerial skills, ingenuity, foresight, and tact. Very large organizations will require techniques rather different from those of small or medium-size ones. Working through department heads, program coordinators, or section managers calls for skills different from those needed when the organization is small enough for face-to-face talk with every staff person. We shall confine the discussion here to techniques useful in the smaller organizations.

The monitoring function includes three dimensions that the administrator should recognize and understand. The first might be called the temporal dimension: a particular effort at monitoring may occur before, during, or after a cost is incurred, or at selected or haphazard times during the fiscal year. Thus the administrator must decide *when* is the best time for which items. This *when* factor also impinges strongly on expense control.

Another might be called the structural dimension. Included here would be the degree of the organization's independence; the power and role of the board of directors or outside funder; the level of autonomy given to the fiscal administrator; and the amount of fiscal discretion given individual staff members.

The third might be called the discrimination or judgment dimension. This includes recognizing which budget items are the most critical; which monitoring tasks can be delegated; what resources are still available in the category; and the interrelations between the cost centers.

All these and others—like experience, understanding of program operations, knowledge of market fluctuations—intermingle during the monitoring processes. As in many other aspects of management, the administrator must be aware of each and at the same time able to synthesize, sort, and rank them for each monitoring action.

A few examples of some typical situations will best illustrate how administrators blend the various dimensions to solve everyday problems.

The East Side Senior Citizens Center has been in operation for over four years and serves about 115 persons daily. For the past two years it has received partial funding from the city but still relies on contributions, dues, and some fees for most of its revenue. The staff consists of a Director, a Program Coordinator, and some volunteers. The Board of Directors is very pleased with the Center's development from a bootstrap beginning to its present good reputation in the community. Partly from habit and style, and partly from the lack of professional staff, the Board of Directors maintains a tight grip on all aspects of management and program. They have traditionally operated solely on a cash basis and have solved their perennial financial crises with "quick fix" fundraising. The infusion of city money has made life difficult for the Director, who, along with the Board, had never had to plan, monitor, or control a fixed budget. During the first year of city funding they pursued their old ways, until the city demanded drastic changes in their bookkeeping, accounting, and management practices. They were given another chance this year, and the Director is trying to improve their procedures. He has started monitoring funds by limiting monthly expenditures to a fixed one-twelfth of the total in each line-item. The Board has reluctantly agreed to try this "experiment" but is unhappy about giving him even this amount of independent authority. After all, in their view, he is really there only to carry out their instructions, and this fuss is only due to "bureaucracy" anyway.

The not-for-profit Theater Playhouse of Centerville has organized its budget for this season into seven functional categories, representing the five plays on its schedule and its two support centers. Estimated revenue and costs for the first play turned out to be reasonably on target. The Theater Playhouse is now one-third through the run of the second play and has begun preparing for play number three. The Assistant to the Director, who is the budget manager, as is her practice, calls for a meeting of production staff to review their plans and to see how well they fit the budget guidelines. Before the meeting she puts together a detailed summary of all accrued costs and revenues for play number two (accrued costs will be discussed later in this chapter). The timing of these monitoring activities gives her some leeway for taking final remedial steps for play number two and for adjusting the budget for play number three. At the meeting she will be better able to explain *why* certain adjustments may be necessary; *where* production staff can be given a freer hand; and *when* another monitoring session should take place.

The financial manager at the Borough Maternal Health Clinic has given a great deal of thought to the monitoring process. She realizes that it is neither feasible nor economic to monitor every item equally, especially in a good-sized agency. So in addition to a complete knowledge of the budget, she has made it her business to understand thoroughly the program plans and the roles and responsibilities of the more important staff members. Putting all these pieces together, she is able to determine which budget areas she *must* watch and inspect carefully and which can be "managed by exception." That is, where basic fiscal routines can be handled by standard practices and requirements (forms, journals, etc.). She is convinced that, on balance, constant monitoring of less critical or generally predictable items is not worth the cost in her time and effort. Therefore, although she keeps an eye on them and watches the flow of funds, she only intercedes when an anomaly (the exception) occurs in these items. Meanwhile, she actively monitors the important and the troublesome areas. Typically, these include Personnel—especially temporary help—and Consultants, Equipment, and Travel. Personnel must be monitored because it makes up the largest percentage of the budget and is the most complicated; Consultants, Equipment, and Travel because expenditures in these categories easily get out of control and are usually of great concern to funders. She recognizes that program needs vary over the fiscal period and that many kinds of expenditures will not fit a monthly one-twelfth-of-the-budget pattern. Therefore she prefers to project expenditures on the more predictable quarterly curves in program activities and needs. The Clinic does not now have department heads, but either a person or a group is nominally in charge of each of the various functions. The financial manager works closely with all these people and is even able to delegate some monitoring activities to them. For example, since the Outreach Program consumes a good portion of the Travel budget, she and a senior staff person in Outreach developed a plan for each three months of anticipated travel expenses, which the staff person is then able to monitor and control. Similarly, she works with the Clinic's Executive Committee to monitor expenses for Consultants and for full-time staff. All requests for these two areas must first be approved by the Executive Committee, which is kept abreast of the flow of funds from both categories. For part-time and temporary staff the budget plan is used as her base. Every few months she reviews the pattern of expenses for these items for each function and tries to discuss this with the staff in charge—or at least notifies them that trouble may be brewing. Recently, she decided to experiment with a plan to turn over supervision of Supplies to the three senior secretaries. She hopes this will improve the monitoring of a less critical area and perhaps even advance the secretaries' status. She is, of course, ready to step in when and if staff members find it difficult to accept the authority given to the secretaries. The Executive Committee has been very supportive of all her efforts and agrees with her that a good monitoring plan means having a reasonable system in place for handling problems before they get out of hand.

Cost/Expense Management

It has been common practice for many nonprofit organizations to operate on a "cash basis." This means that an expense is recognized and accounted for (recorded) only when funds are actually paid out for a service or product.[2] For example, if an item or service is ordered, it is not recognized as an expense until a bill is received and *paid*. This permits the agency to use simple bookkeeping procedures, but it seriously restricts cost control. However, when a service or product is ordered or received, it has in effect been "bought," even if the transaction is not yet completed and therefore not recorded in cash accounting. In the accrual system, an expense is recognized and recorded at an earlier point, and the money is considered spent at the time it is recorded.[3] Thus the agency has a more complete and accurate picture of its true financial position at any time. Although many not-for-profit organizations may find it more practical to keep their ledgers and so forth on a cash basis, in its *Statement* the AICPA (1978) recommends that at given periods they put together financial statements on an accrual basis. The benefits from accrual accounting far outweigh the effort needed to switch from a cash system. We wholeheartedly endorse the use of accrual accounting and have developed a simple format to assist agencies in preparing accrual summaries on a regular basis, which will be fully discussed in this section.

Assuming that an agency agrees to adopt the accrual method, it must decide *what* to recognize and record as an expense and *when* to record it. The following list illustrates the kinds of expenses for services and products typically encountered in an agency (*what* to recognize). Note the differing levels of obligations and the variety of items involved.

Examples of Types of Expenses and Obligations

Vouchered items:	ordered, used, or received but not yet paid for (from ledger accounts)
Encumbrances:	recorded on vouchers or purchase orders

[2]The steps and documentation of this process within agencies are nicely depicted in United Way (1974, p. 132), "Exhibit 6: Chart Showing the Flow of Financial Transactions."

[3]Some of the terms we use here do not always conform exactly to the *specific* definitions given them in accounting texts. We have chosen to use the common, everyday meanings of various terms to clarify their applications and to simplify the discussion.

Binding obligations:	payroll taxes employee benefits salaries per contracts salaries per verbal agreements lease for space mortgage payments insurance premiums
Assorted agreements (various levels of obligation):	rental items: duplicating machines, auto lease, etc. services: vendor services subcontracts consultants office machine maintenance cleaning services computer services
Expected and budgeted expenses, not yet vouchered:	telephone postage client assistance, etc. other budgeted items
Other nonbudgeted items (if funds permit)	

With minor exceptions, we recommend that all expenses and obligations be recorded as soon as possible. For example, when supplies are ordered (vouchered), they should be recorded as an expense; when a lease is signed, the total cost should be recorded; if a subcontract is arranged, the total should be recorded; individual *total* salaries should be recorded as soon as they are agreed upon or contracted; and so on. If an exact cost is not known, estimates should be used. We even suggest that ongoing expenses, like telephone charges, should be recorded as full-year estimates at the start of the year. (Various notational techniques can be used to keep administrators informed about obligations and ongoing expenses, even though an agency's or program's accounting methods do not yet recognize these as completed transactions; examples of these will be given later in the illustrative CYS materials.)

Monthly Budget Summary

We have devised a Monthly Expense Summary as a key tool for monitoring expenses and expediting control. As the headings in Table 7–6 show, the Summary is set up to discriminate between and separately identify current-month expenses, cumulative past expenses, projected recognized and recorded future costs, and estimated balances. The first column of the summary shows the total budget amount assigned to each line-item and important subitems. The second column shows the dollar and percentage outlay of funds for the current month for each line-item. The third column shows the cumulated dollar and percentage outlays for all line-items for the year to date. The fourth column shows all recognized, recorded, and estimated expenses (including percentages) that have not yet been paid but have been accrued by the program. This column will include some estimated future costs that are not actually certain but are approximate or straight-line projections based on previous activities or experiences. The final column shows the differences when total outlays (Col. 3) plus projected expenses (Col. 4) are subtracted from budgeted line-item amounts (Col. 1).

At first glance readers may wonder what all the fuss is about: "Our form is almost the same as this one." If an agency or program collects, summarizes, and projects all the same information on a regular basis, then whatever form it uses is certainly as comprehensive as this one. However, in our experience too many organizations rely on a scheme that reports only current-month expenditures, year-to-date expenditures, and the remaining balances. The majority of organizations do not systematically put together sufficient information to record, monitor, and control the flow of resources and thus are unable to make sound projections about future spending.

Sometimes percentages or plus or minus one-twelfth fractions are included for each line-item, which gives limited but not necessarily useful information. The one-twelfth expense summary—with or without percentages—lacks information essential for sound fiscal management and projections. Outstanding and ongoing expenses are totally disregarded so that the "balance" shown is misleading and

TABLE 7-6. Sample Monthly Expense Summary

Account No. B-121
Account Name Fairview Retirement Home

Fiscal Period 1 Oct. 198x - 30 Sept. 198x
Report for Month Ending 30 March

MONTH EXPENSE SUMMARY
(For first 6 months)

Line-Item Object Costs	Budgeted Total (12 months) Col. 1	Current Month Expenses Col. 2		Year to Date Expenses Col. 3		Projected (6) Months Col. 4		Estimated Balances Col. 5
		$	%	$	%	$	%	
1. Personnel 1c. Night Super FTEs 1.00	14,000	1,145	.082	6,870	.49	6,870	.49	+260
4. Equipment 4d. Food Service	500	0		720	1.44	0		−220
7. Occupancy 7a. Utilities	2,400	336	.14	2,468	1.03	570	.24	−638

invalid. Thus, for example, if at the end of five months the budget report indicates that 35 percent, 45 percent, or whatever percent of the budgeted total for a line-item has been spent, that information is not useful *unless* the expected, projected expenses for the next seven months are also known and a way exists to show and incorporate them. Furthermore, the one-twelfth expenditure pattern does not reflect actual program operations—with the exception of salaries for permanent staff and rent or mortgage payments. Even payments for payroll taxes, for example, will not be shown regularly as a one-twelfth cost, since they are deposited quarterly.

Occasionally a column is added to an expense summary form to allow for adjustments from a cash system to an accrual report. However, this still will not provide information about expected *future* expenditures.

Why are we emphasizing so strongly the need to synthesize expenditures in a way that reflects program activities *and* expectations? Primarily because it relates so materially to the main thesis of this book: To achieve its program objectives, an organization must be able to *plan* for the most productive use of its resources, and thus must have up-to-date, comprehensive knowledge about where, when, and how they are being consumed. The addition of our one column (Projected Expenses) to the typical form serves a number of vital purposes: It fosters a nontechnical method of accrual accounting; it generates the regular collection of comprehensive fiscal information; it helps tie together program and fiscal operations; it enhances forward planning; it chronicles outstanding, future, and unusual resource consumption; and it helps clarify the *total* financial picture, past, present, and future.

If we now look at the Monthly Expense Summary given for Fairview Retirement Home (Table 7–6), we can see how this works. To simplify the discussion, we have included only a few selected items. On a real summary the same kinds of details would appear for every line-item and subitem (as they will in the exercise section).

In this example we can see *at a glance* that the Home hired a night supervisor at a salary rate a little lower than originally budgeted (Cols. 2 and 3); that someone has served in that capacity since the start of the fiscal year (Col. 3); that the position is filled full time and will continue to be filled at that salary rate for the rest of the year (Col. 4); and that this subitem should show a surplus of $260 at the end of the fiscal year (Col. 5).

When we look at line-item 4d under Equipment, we can see at once that somewhere during the past six months the Home paid out 44 percent more than its budgeted total for food service equipment (Col. 3); that it expects no more costs to accrue for this subitem (Col. 4); and that it has already incurred a $220 deficit in 4d (Col. 5). Deviations from a budgeted amount should be explained by footnote or attachment to the Monthly Expense Summary (as will be described later in the exercises). In this case, a large freezer unexpectedly had to be replaced in January (the fourth month of the FY) as was reported on that month's Summary.

The Utilities subitem (7a) for the Home demonstrates the special value of the Summary form for keeping track of uncertain or volatile items. We assume that the original budgeted amount was based on best estimates obtained directly from the various utilities sources. But we can see from the Summary that either the rates or usage went up over the winter months. Again, the deviations would have been reported each month. The estimated projections would also be explained; for example, that during the next six months (April through September) the chief utility costs —for heat—would be negligible.

With all the information in view, with the reasons for past deviations understood, and with every projected expenditure explained, the estimated balances now have some validity. The administrator will know which items must be closely monitored and controlled, which ones need no special attention, and how and where to set about balancing the budget.

Let us look at a few more examples of the ways the Summary can be used in real life. The "Examples of Types of Expenses and Obligations" listed earlier in this section can serve as a model for most not-for-profit organizations. Both the types and the examples should be recast, as necessary, to depict accurately the basic and idiosyncratic obligations of the organization. Next, using this modified list as a guide, it must be clearly understood that *every* type of obligation on the list must be accounted for somewhere on the Monthly

Expense Summary. If, for example, a vouchered item has been paid for during the month, it will appear in Columns 2 and 3. If, however, it is still unpaid, it *must* appear in Column 4. Also, each staff member's salary for the month will appear in Columns 2 and 3; but the rest of the total amount still due that person for the remainder of the fiscal year must appear in Column 4. The same is true for travel expenditures: Those already completed must appear in Column 2 or 4; those anticipated go into Column 4.

In some instances an obligation may be reported either in Column 2 or in Column 4. For example, if payroll taxes have not yet been paid for the current quarter, they may be reported as part of current expenses or as part of committed future expenses. The same holds for many vouchered items, especially if they have not yet been received. Each organization should decide which ways are most practicable for its needs. However, a consistent routine should be followed—or at least applied to the same items each month. For example, if it makes better sense to report payroll taxes in Current Expenses, then they should be reported that same way throughout the fiscal year.

As was noted earlier, estimations of essential ongoing operational costs—like the telephone—properly belong in Column 4. Some items may well be "iffy," but do not hesitate to include them and report the uncertainties in special notes or attachments. Disregarding probable real future costs can jeopardize control of any item and perhaps the whole program. In fact, including them in Column 4 may expedite management decisions. For example, plans for employing temporary or part-time staff will often depend on the changing commitments detailed in Column 4. A significant plus or minus change in the Personnel portion of that column could increase or decrease the likelihood of hiring such staff. It is far better to include too much rather than too little information in the Monthly Expense Summary, and especially in Column 4. As will be illustrated in the CYS example later, notes, memos, and attachments should be used to detail and explain the bases and reasons for the inclusions.

For a moment, let us look at a common type of monthly expense summary—one from an organization that maintains a centralized accounting department for all its projects and programs (Table 7–7). Although it includes something

TABLE 7-7. Typical Monthly Expense Summary

Budget Report for Account No. 01111

Report Date: 31 July 198x
Budget Period: 1 Jan. 198x - 31 Dec. 198x

	Budget	Cumulative thru Previous Month	Current Month	Total	Budget Available Balance	Encumbrances	Unencumbered Balance
Salaries/Wages	122,000	56,620	11,700	68,320	53,680	--	53,680
Fringe Benefits	23,680	10,992	2,271	13,263	10,417	--	10,417
.	.	.	.	.	.	.	.
.	.	.	.	.	.	.	.
Supplies	7,000	4,060	790	4,850	2,150	150	2,000
.	.	.	.	.	.	.	.
.	.	.	.	.	.	.	.

called Encumbrances (items vouchered and put "on hold"), it contains no equivalent to Column 4.

Despite its impressive columns of numbers, the Table 7–7 printout (from a real organization) is really nothing more than a cash accounting report. Except for Encumbrances (if any), no accrued obligations are recorded. Not even percentages are shown. Unless the head of the project called Account No. 01111 maintains backup internal accrual records and ignores the balances shown in the printout, the project can run into serious financial problems. For example, the balance shown for Salaries/Wages may be sufficient for the next six months; or it may be far more or far less than the project will need. The project head has no way of knowing from this report. At best, it may serve to alert the head to a possible problem area.

Table 7–8 is another typical example of an expense report (from a real agency). This one relates expenditures to a plus or minus variance of the one-twelfth monthly budgeted amount for each line-item. For example, we see that the program has 17 percent more left in Salaries/Wages than had been budgeted for the month (that is, 17 percent less had been spent); and it has 11 percent less left in Fringe Benefits than had been budgeted (11 percent more had been spent). This example is particularly interesting because it seems to give a great deal of information, which, in fact, is useless for planning without major reconstruction. For example, (1) we do not even know the *total budgeted amount* for any line-item unless we multiply the "Budgeted This Month" amount by 12 and assume that is the right total; (2) we do not even know how many months we are into the fiscal year, unless we divide the "Budgeted Amount to Date" by the "Budget This Month"; (3) even when we know that this report is for the fourth month of the fiscal year, we have no idea how it relates to the expected expense flow for the whole year; and (4) the Travel item seems to be in fine shape *except* that without a projection for the next eight months we have no idea what the final variance will be.

We could give many other examples of similar kinds of expense reports, but we have surely now made our point. Readers might wish to examine the reports used in their own organizations and note the advantages and shortcomings.

TABLE 7-8. Sample One-Twelfth Monthly Expense Report

Program: ABC Service Provider

Period: 1 Jan. - 31 Jan. 198x

	Budget This Month	Actual Expend- itures This Month	Percent Variance	Budget Amount to Date	Actual Expend- itures to Date	Percent Variance	Comments
Salaries/Wages	4,875	4,042	17.0	19,500	17,834	8.5	
Fringe Benefits	730	808	(11.0)	2,920	3,566	(22.0)	
.	.	.	.	.	.	.	.
.	.	.	.	.	.	.	.
Supplies	670	700	(4.5)	2,680	2,620	2.2	
Travel	125	140	(12.0)	725	140	81.0	
.	.	.	.	.	.	.	.
.	.	.	.	.	.	.	.

RELATION BETWEEN COLUMN 4
AND ONGOING ACCOUNTING SYSTEMS

Before we move to the problems of revenue management, another issue needs to be considered: How is information collected for Column 4, and how can this be linked to an established accounting system? The assorted information included in Column 4 of the Monthly Expense Summary may well evoke many questions from a program manager. Who is responsible for gathering it? Do our accounting people have this information readily available? If not, how can I work with them to produce it? How can I simplify the collection procedures?

Every sound accounting system will normally gather most of the "raw data" needed for Column 4. In fact, only a few items are not typically at hand somewhere in the organization, and procedures for acquiring these few items can easily be added to the system when what is needed is recognized. The manager's main task will be to work with staff to find ways to turn these raw data into practical management tools.

Some examples of the accessibility of most Column 4 information will be helpful.

First, let us assume that the program is operating on a cash basis. How is it possible to know for any given period what has been committed in Supplies, Equipment, Travel, or Maintenance? Clearly, no obligations can be entered into in any program or agency without some form of authorization. A voucher or purchase order of some kind—whether crude or businesslike—must be filled out, signed or authorized, and filed somewhere. Therefore, arrangements need only be made to see to it that someone is regularly responsible for reviewing all vouchers and totaling the authorized expenditures in each line-item category for the given period. If there is an accounting department, this will be a simple procedure for its staff. If the accounts are computerized, appropriate instructions will produce the information. However, even without these resources, any designated staff person can learn to handle these raw data and generate the necessary information.

It is equally simple to extrapolate accrual information for the Salary and Fringe categories. Individual payroll records must be kept by every program for tax purposes. Usually a payroll summary is also maintained; all the information needed for Column 4 will be available from this summary plus the original budget. Thus, at most such a summary would have to be set up and someone assigned to maintain it.

Occupancy costs will have to be garnered from several sources, all easily accessible: the lease or mortgage contract, actual and estimated utility costs (from bills and budget), and vouchers for upkeep expenditures.

It should be clear that the information used to prepare Column 4 includes both that derived from already existing accounting records (vouchered items, payroll, and so on) *and* that derived by extrapolating known or probable future expenses that have not yet been recorded as financial transactions (e.g. payroll projections, planned or budgeted purchases). The bases for projecting future expenses will usually vary *from item to item,* and the straight-line method (extrapolating an average monthly amount from actual experience) should be used only when a better basis is not available.[4]

The monitoring process merges with the control process in carrying out many of these tasks, and both processes can benefit from gathering, tabulating, and classifying these data. Information for Column 4 that cannot be directly or approximately projected can be estimated in various ways. Discussions with staff persons responsible for specific types of activities can generate estimates of future expenses in travel, client assistance, printing, computer use, publicity, and so on. A session with the finance committee of the board of directors or with the agency's chief fiscal officer can elicit anticipated personnel or fundraising expenses and can sensitize them to consumption patterns, service uses, and needs. It may further alert them to limits, restrictions, or adjustments that may have to be made in future projections.

It is important to keep in mind that this ongoing accrual Monthly Expense Summary is simple to set up with or without a sophisticated accounting system and is equally simple to maintain once a routine is established. It also can

---

[4] With a computerized accounting system, the computer can be instructed to use a variety of projections or variance figures for different line-items or time periods.

be readily aligned with expense records *by cost centers.* The Summary in no way conflicts with accepted accounting procedures; on the contrary, it goes hand in hand with them. All the data required for the scheme should already be part of the basic fiscal information readily available; if it is not, it clearly should be, for sound fiscal management.

Revenue Management

Monitoring and controlling *revenues* pose similar problems and yield to a schematic format similar to the Monthly Expense Summary. Therefore, in this section we shall direct our attention briefly to some ways to deal with revenue resources so as to extract useful information about total program operations while also maintaining strict accountability.

The terms "revenue" and "income" are often used interchangeably. However, current accounting texts reserve "income" to refer to the net balance remaining after all expenses are accounted for. In the not-for-profit sector income has the meaning: "excess of revenue over expenses." The United Way *Accounting and Financial Reporting* (1974) and the *Standards* (National Health Council et al., 1974) consistently use the term "revenue" to mean money received from any source. We also adhere to this definition throughout the book.

Not-for-profit organizations receive and are accountable for many kinds of revenue: grants and awards, allocations, service fees, reimbursements, contributions, dues, interest, bequests, and sales. These may be wholly or partially restricted (designated for specific purposes) or unrestricted. They may be expendable only for current (or future) operations or only for capital improvements. They may be received in lump sums, arrive at specific intervals, or dribble in erratically. Whatever the source, purpose, or timing, revenues must be as scrupulously handled and accounted for as expenses. If necessary, administrators should consult the numerous available books on accountancy procedures. They can then decide which techniques and procedures will be sufficient and efficient for their size and types of revenue sources.

INTERNAL SYSTEMS

Setting up appropriate journals, ledgers, special bank accounts, and so on, is an important first step toward developing an internal management system. Such a system should allow the administrator to

- Ensure the timeliness and accuracy of the records
- Follow the flow of money step by step
- Simplify reconciliation of bank statements with records

A good internal management system should enable staff to know who is responsible for what, and what is expected from each person. It can also help the administrator determine where in the chain something went amiss, and where to begin sorting out problems.

An internal system involves planning transaction records, establishing routes for orderly processing, designating responsibilities and authorizations for each step, separating custody and depositing authority, arranging supervision and review measures, and so on. Such tasks are well worth the modest efforts they entail. Every agency will have some scheme for handling revenue. All we are recommending is that it be orderly, efficient, and inclusive; that it guard against improprieties, and even fraud; that it be able to furnish accurate information for fiscal planning and management; and that it promote accountability. All these recommendations for managing revenues are analogous to those offered for expenses. Since revenues and expenses complement each other, good management of both is necessary for current and future program assessment and planning.

Agencies dealing with cash revenue are especially vulnerable to problems of mishandling, ranging from mislaying receipts to outright chicanery, as evidenced frequently in the newspapers. Prudent internal control should help reduce or eliminate many problems. Again, accounting and bookkeeping texts detail various ways to handle cash. A variety of methods now on the market simplify cash management for service-directed enterprises—both profit and not-for-profit. These can be used for recording receipts as well as expenses and are sold by several different companies. For example, one system uses a pegboard device that allows transactions entered on one form to be simultaneously recorded on several other forms. At the same time a bill is made out, that information is recorded on the client's individual record sheet and on an accounts receivable summary. When the bill is paid, that too is recorded with one entry on the client's record sheet, on a revenue received summary, and on a daily/monthly journal. The same techniques are used for disbursing money, and with the addition of a few column headings one can record receipts and disbursements by appropriate functional or line-item categories.

Revenue/Expense Flow and Balance

Cash flow in the profit sector applies only to the movement of currency (cash) in and out of a business; it does not include credit transactions. However, in common parlance, the term is generally used in the not-for-profit sector to represent the flow of liquid assets into an agency whether by cash or from a funder. Furthermore, the cash flow balance is commonly interpreted in the not-for-profit sector to mean the balance between incoming revenues—whatever their source—and outgoing expenses.[5] Without debating the merits or demerits of this interpretation, we prefer to maintain the classical accountancy definitions and will therefore use the terms "Revenue Flow" and "Revenue/Expense Balance."

Most agencies and programs, especially the smaller ones, frequently have serious problems balancing their inflow and outflow of resources. They have few sources from which to seek advice since most of the information about these topics deals only with the profit sector. We do not pretend to have all the answers to such problems, but we do have some suggestions that recognize the special or different conditions under which many not-for-profit organizations operate.

[5] Additional confusion in terms arises if the agency operates strictly on a cash accounting basis.

REVENUE FROM FUNDERS

Over a fiscal period, payouts of awarded funds into a not-for-profit agency typically match one of the following patterns (or a mix of them for those with more than one source of revenue):

1. A prearranged payment schedule (often quarterly); not based on flow of expenses
2. A monthly installment of one-twelfth of the total budget; also unrelated to expense flow
3. A prearranged payment schedule based on actual expense flow; often biweekly or monthly
4. Postpayment (reimbursement) of actual expenses; at either specified or unspecified intervals

In addition, revenue is received episodically or erratically from contributions, special events, and so on. Programs with several funders frequently must wend their way through the maze of mixed payment patterns. An organization learns—often the hard way—to live with whichever patterns the funder and fee payment plans impose.

Given the diversity of these payment plans and the idiosyncrasies of organizations, we cannot offer specific answers to specific situations. We can, however, share a few ideas for coping with the most common pitfalls.

Every program faces an initial major hurdle: It must survive until the funder delivers the first payment. In this respect, the one-twelfth and the biweekly arrangements offer some advantages; at least staff can be paid more or less on time. Many funders will, however, agree to a payment schedule that provides some money "up front" (that is, money available by the first day of operations). Most federated funding agencies provide a one-twelfth payment in advance. If needed, every program should present its strongest possible case for up-front money whether or not this arrangement is specifically covered in the contract conditions. Similarly, up-front money should be sought from purchase-of-service contracts, fee agreements, and pledged contributions. Even in the best of circumstances the smaller agencies and programs will still have little maneuvering room. Those paid at the one-twelfth rate must plan ahead carefully and husband certain line-item resources to be able to make large purchases, like printing or out-of-town travel. Buying "on time" can be dangerous, as most funders will not reimburse interest charges. Those paid quarterly must be careful to set aside (by at least encumbering on their books) funds they will need farther along in the fiscal year. Those receiving postpayments must try to arrange repayment terms with their suppliers ahead of time to avoid interest charges. Most agencies seek to maintain sufficient operating reserve funds to cushion the effects of these payment arrangements.

But what if the best laid plans go awry and a short-term deficit occurs? What about borrowing money? Borrowing from a commercial source, like a bank, may well be forbidden by a funder, or payment of interest charges from the funder's money may not be permitted. Some of our references suggest that if an agency has several funders, it can borrow from one of its other funds to tide it over. That is possible, but the agency would be well advised to have a superb accounting system in place and to keep absolutely clear records of authorizations and repayment so that all transactions will pass muster during an audit. In recent years the federal government has been tracking down those who used federal funds for interfund borrowing and has declared such transfers illegal, to the consternation of several large organizations. Agencies that collect fees in addition to their revenue from funders are often able to survive short-term deficits by temporarily applying fee revenues to fill the gaps, since the fees are usually not restricted in any way. In fact, some agencies on a one-twelfth schedule regularly use fees as a backstop for large purchases or repayments; again, accurately kept records are essential. A federated funding agency may sometimes be willing to advance a no-interest loan for good and sufficient reasons, but it would be wise not to depend on that too often. A "cash," "working," or "unrestricted" reserve should be attempted to avoid short-run problems; the United Way advises a reserve of three times the average monthly operating costs, especially for agencies that own their own buildings.

Programs that often have to resort to payless paydays or emergency solicitations are in deep trouble. Most likely they did not develop a reliable budget, are not planning ahead, are not monitoring the revenue/expense balance, are not keeping good records, have not adjusted to their revenue payment schedule, or all of the above. We cannot guarantee that doing all these things properly will assure a perfect inflow/outflow balance, but not doing most of them will surely bring about a catastrophe. A simple chronological projection (by chart or graph) of times of expected receipts aligned with times of expected expenses could go a long way toward making the manager aware of the stress points and allow time for figuring out how to cope with them (see Lohmann, 1980, p. 228). The chronological chart might acknowledge the typical "lead time" (often thirty days) for both paying bills and receiving revenue. Problems in balancing revenues and expenses are further compounded these days by sudden large funding cutbacks, which force agencies and programs to shift to other resources—often less reliable ones. In such circumstances even the best-run organization can face a grave crisis.

Monthly Revenue Summary

The typical monthly revenue statement in most organizations parallels its typical expense statement. Each will show how much was received/spent that month, how much has been received/spent for the year to date, and the balance. We have just explained in detail the value of the five-column Monthly Expense Summary, and we believe that similar considerations are relevant to a *revenue* summary. In particular, we assert that a valid, reliable balance must reflect the total fiscal condition whether or not all the transactions have actually occurred. In other words, revenue management should, as far as possible, indicate *anticipated, expected* transactions as well as completed ones. For an organization totally supported by one funder, this is a simple matter, although few revenue summaries show even these expected funds. For those depending in any degree on fees, contributions, and the like, projections of necessity will be approximations. However, the future operation of such programs will depend on the assumptions they make about expected revenue. Concretely expressing and refining these expectations each month will help clarify a program's total financial picture and may even stimulate efforts to collect that revenue.

It is easier to identify many kinds of future expenses (salaries, rent, payroll taxes) than to evaluate anticipated revenues. But, as we have repeatedly emphasized, approximations, even if not completely reliable, are important and very useful. Therefore, we have drawn up an exemplary format for a Monthly Revenue Summary (Table 7–9). Headings for the columns and rows will vary among agencies and programs, but the *kinds* of information included should be generally pertinent.

The Summary form includes two columns we have devised to incorporate an agency's assumptions about expected revenue. Column 4 is called Pledged, Contracted, and Owed for the Year-to-Date. In this column the agency can indicate the amounts it reasonably *expects* to receive in the future from each revenue source, thus stimulating an *accrual* revenue system. For example, in the Service Fees category, Column 4 would show amounts still owing for services already provided, plus other revenue expected on behalf of clients currently being served. Similar projections would be made for the other categories, as appropriate. As for the Monthly Expense Summary, *the bases for the projections* for each revenue source in Column 4 must be carefully detailed each month in special notes or attachments to the report; and adjustments to previous projections in Column 5 must also be explained.

Column 5, Adjusted Expected Total Revenue, shows the estimated cumulative total of expected revenue for the whole year, based on current knowledge and revisions that take into account the defaults or expected delinquent accounts. A memo should accompany the Summary to detail the expectations. Thus, four months into the fiscal year the program might estimate that ongoing experience and activities in progress indicate that the total revenue from Fees, for example, will probably be $12,000 for the year. Then the Balance in the last column can reflect the refined, updated, and adjusted totals shown in Column 5. The plus or minus Balance is arrived at by subtracting the totals for each category in Column 5 from the Budgeted Totals in Column 1. This scheme attempts to produce the same kinds of useful approximations in Columns 4 and 5 that are included in Col-

TABLE 7-9. Illustrative Monthly Revenue Summary

Account No. _____
Account Name _____

Fiscal Period _____
Report for Month Ending _____

Revenue Source	Budgeted Total Col. 1	Amount Received This Month Col. 2	Amount Received Y-T-D Col. 3	Pledged/ Contracted; Owed Y-T-D Col. 4	Adjusted Total Expected[a] Col. 5	Plus/ Minus Balance Col. 6
Federated Funding						
Federal Grants/Awards						
State Grants/Awards						
Service Fees, Memberships						
Third-Party Payments						
Earned Revenue (contracts, charges)						
Contributions						
Other:						
Sales, Special Events						
Interest, Investments						
Bequests						

[a] Includes adjustments for delinquent accounts and defaults.

umn 4 of the Monthly Expense Summary. Both are aimed at deliberately and realistically projecting future estimates in order to remain solvent.

Exercise Problems

It is now early in the seventh month of the full fiscal year, and CYS has received its end-of-sixth-month expense report from the JYC accounting office (part of the services provided from CYS Overhead). The JYC materials include (1) a line-item statement of current and cumulative expenses and balances, with *accrual adjustments* for some items; and (2) an attached brief commentary. JYC, as the parent agency, has furnished similar expense statements to each of its responsibility centers in the preceding months but had never before included any accrual adjustments.

The Program Coordinator at CYS had carefully reviewed each earlier monthly statement and had felt confident that all was going pretty well, because without the accrual adjustments the bottom line had always shown a healthy balance. Besides, the budget had been well planned and JYC was experienced at "keeping the books." However, with the addition of the partial accrual adjustments, some of the healthy balances seemed to have evaporated, and in fact, it looked like CYS might be facing fiscal problems.

The PC therefore decided that it was imperative for CYS to expand on the information from the JYC agency and put together *its own internal, detailed expense summary*, which would include all costs already incurred—whether noted or not on the JYC statements—plus all planned and projected future expenditures and commitments (as discussed earlier in this chapter). This *within-program* expense summary could then serve as a base that would be updated each month. Even though it was now already well into the seventh month and it would take further time to prepare this summary, expenses could be monitored and controlled for Months 8, 9, 10, and 11, a crucial period when the margin for error would rapidly diminish.

After consultations with key staff persons and with the help of one of the secretaries, the PC prepared a new, revised, internal CYS Monthly Expense Summary that incorporated information gathered from (1) the JYC statement and notes; (2) file copies of outstanding purchase orders and vouchers; and (3) consultations with staff. The PC also drafted a detailed memo for the file documenting the fiscal information and explaining the reasons for previous major deviations from the budget and the bases for the estimated

Account No. RA 156–BY

Account Name Community Youth Services

Fiscal Period 1 Sept. 19XX – 31 Aug. 19YY

Report for Month Ending 28 Feb., 19YY

MONTHLY EXPENSE SUMMARY
(for first 6 months)

Line Item		Budgeted Total (12 mo.) Col 1.	This Month Expenses Col. 2		Year to Date Expenses Col. 3		Projected (6) Months Col. 4		Estimated Balances Col. 5
Personnel	FTE's								
Prog. Coord.	1.00	24,000	2,000	.08	12,000	.50	12,000	.50	0
Scr. Super.	1.00	21,000	1,750	.08	10,500	.50	10,500	.50	0
Intake W.	.80	14,720	1,227	.08	7,360	.50	7,360	.50	0
Liaison Wkrs	3.37	57,750	5,395	.09	30,030	.52	32.375	.56	– 4,655
Counselors	1.92	32,400	2,700	.08	14,904	.46	16,200	.50	+ 1,296
Secretaries	2.19	24,000	3,043	.13	14,323	.60	12,000	.50	– 2,323
	10.28								
1. Total Sal/Wages		173,870	16,115	.09	89,117	.51	90,435	.52	– 5,682
2. Employee Benefits & Payroll Taxes 20%		34,774	3,223	.09	17,823	.51	18,087	.52	– 1,136
3. Professional Fees		4,200	504	.12	2,562	.61	2.000	.48	– 362
4. Supplies, Communications, & Reproduction		6,500	815	.13	3,261	.50	3,506	.54	– 267
5. Occupancy: Rent		12,000	2,000	.17	6,000	.50	6,000	.50	0
6. Travel: Local		4,925	542	.11	2,807	.57	2,800	.57	– 682
Conference		800	0	.00	300	.38	500	.62	0
7. Equipment		3,000	195	.07	1,376	.46	1,624	.54	0
8. Assistance to Clients: Vendor Charges		3,600	360	.10	1,512	.42	2,520	.70	– 432
Financial Aid		3,800	532	.14	2,166	.57	2,166	.57	– 532
9. TOTAL DIRECT COSTS		247,469	24,286	.10	126,924	.51	129,638	.52	– 9,093
10. Overhead/Indirect 18%		44,544	4,371	.10	22,846	.51	23,335	.52	– 1,637
11. GRAND TOTAL		292,013	28,657	.10	149,770	.51	152,973	.52	–10,730

Special Note:

The percentages in the columns represent shares of total dollars; they are rounded to the 2d decimal.

projections for the next six months of the FY. The completed revised Summary and the memo, presented here, revealed that a serious budget deficit (cost overrun) would result if all the planned expenses were actually incurred.

MEMORANDUM

To: File
From: Program Coordinator, CYS
Date: 16 March 19YY
Re: Revised, Internal 2nd Quarter Expense Summary and Projection

The attached Monthly Expense Summary and this memo were prepared after I became convinced that CYS as a responsibility center needs to keep its own regularly updated records of current and anticipated expense to avoid dangerous cost overruns.

At the outset it was necessary to establish guidelines for deciding whether an accrued, but as yet unpaid, expense should be included in Cols. 2 and 3 or in Col. 4. To ensure consistency in subsequent months, the criteria for assigning both the accrued and anticipated costs are spelled out in this memo for each line-item category. Any changes in later months should be expressly noted so that dependable comparisons between months can be made. The dollar amounts in Cols. 2, 3, and 4 on the Summary are also translated into percentages of the total budget, because percentages more succinctly describe the expenditure patterns in each category.

Analysis of Line-Items in Columns 2 and 3

Salaries/Wages have been expended at a higher rate than planned for several positions, but the danger of cost overruns was *not* recognized earlier because the JYC expense statements did not include accrued adjustments.

1. The Program Coordinator, Screening Supervisor, and Intake Worker were employed at budgeted FTEs and rates.
2. The Liaison Worker who was budgeted for .30 FTE worked .70 FTE for two months of the quarter because it took more time than expected to make various critical contacts and arrangements with both in- and out-referral sources.
3. One of the Counselors was not hired until the beginning of

the second month of the FY because the first applicants for the job did not fit our requirements. Thus we saved one month's salary on this line.
4. A serious financial problem arose early in the fourth month when the principal, full-time secretary resigned as of the end of the month. This person had come to CYS from JYC and had there accumulated two months of unused vacation time, which had to be paid in full upon termination. This secretary had the major responsibility for running the office, and, therefore, it was decided to hire a replacement for an extra overlapping week to avoid delays and disruption in the office routines. Thus the overrun in this line consists of the two months' vacation pay plus the extra week for the replacement.

Benefits and Taxes reflect the variances in Salaries/Wages. However, it should also be underscored that the second quarter Social Security and Unemployment taxes are *shown as accrued* in Col. 3 even though they had not yet been paid in by the last day of the quarter (payment was due after the start of the next quarter). This practice should be followed in future Summaries.

Professional Fees have been somewhat overspent—especially during the last month. This was due partly to delays in special consultations during the startup period and partly to inadequate guidelines and control procedures.

Supplies and Communications expenditures can be summarized as follows:

1. Office supplies were bought at a very high rate in the past six months (68 percent of the budgeted subcategory); however, a large amount is still on hand.
2. Telephone bills have not been received promptly (we are investigating this matter); and thus only the costs for the first four months of the FY are known and included in Col. 3. Costs for the missing two months have been estimated and appear in Col. 4; but they will be reassigned to Col. 3 in future Summaries when the exact amounts are known.
3. Postage expenditures have also been high (62 percent of budget), mainly because of the extensive public information mailings.

Occupancy costs for the sixth month (Col. 2) are double the proper prorated amount, because JYC mistakenly had charged another of its programs for one month's rent that should have been charged to CYS. This error has now been corrected, as shown in the year-to-date column.

Travel expenditures include a high rate for the Local Travel subcategory and a very low rate for Conferences. Staff found it necessary to make many more local trips than had been envisioned to strengthen working relations with other organizations and to arrange client out-referrals. Also more taxi trips were necessary than had been expected.

Equipment expenditures are right on target. The second quarter charges for the office equipment maintenance contract are not included in Col. 3 because there was a mix-up and the maintenance person did not come in as contracted. He will come early in the next quarter, so these costs are accrued in Col. 4.

Assistance to Clients costs are detailed separately as follows:

1. The Vendor Charges in Col. 3 include (a) only those already paid or (b) billed but not yet paid. Those incurred but not yet billed are estimated in Col. 4. This practice should be followed in subsequent months.
2. Financial Aid has been given at a slightly higher rate than budgeted for the past six months. Included in Col. 3 are *all accrued and authorized* expenditures.

Explanations of Line-Items in Column 4

The projections in Col. 4 are based on a variety of considerations: contractual commitments; encumbered, already ordered, or outstanding items; and estimates based on staff and client records of past activities and services. Some dollar figures are exact and "firm" (e.g. salary rates, rent); others are best estimates or straight-line projections (e.g. Vendor Charges). The bases for each line-item must be understood so that each can be monitored, modified, and controlled during the next six months. We must keep in mind the possible adverse effects of cutbacks and cost control procedures on service delivery.

Salaries/Wages. All staff members are expected to continue at budgeted rates and times except for one Liaison Worker whose time has been increased from .30 to .70 FTE—a continuation of that person's FTE rate during the past two months.

Benefits and Taxes. The rate remains at 20 percent of Salaries/Wages.

Professional Fees. The figure here reflects the recommendations of staff members; this projection has been allowed to stand *temporarily* until the total overrun situation has been further studied.

Supplies and Communication. Few office supplies will be needed in the next six months because of the current high inventory, but telephone costs are projected at a rate approximately the same as that of the first four months of the FY. The estimated cost of the past two months is also included here, since no bills have yet been received for this period. Postage is estimated at a slightly lower per-month cost.

Occupancy. No changes here, as per lease.

Travel. Local Travel costs are projected at the same monthly rate as for the past six months, based on staff recommendations. The money for conferences will be spent as per the budget.

Equipment. The second quarter machine maintenance charge, not yet received or paid, is included here.

Assistance to Clients. Both subcategories are projected at rates about the same as those of the first six months. The additional amount in Vendor Charges represents estimates of costs incurred in the first six months for which bills have not yet been received. Staff members expressed deep concern about maintaining the projected levels of expenditures in these two subcategories, which they believe are critically important for CYS service objectives.

Exercise Steps

The Program Coordinator has called on you, as an administrative staff person, to study the Expense Summary and the memo and to work up a plan for avoiding an overrun while maintaining the integrity of the program. You will be working only with the projections in Column 4 and the balances in Column 5, but will need to check revised balances against Columns 1 and 3.

After a lengthy meeting with the PC, at which the entire situation was discussed, it was agreed that you should:

- Examine staff, case, and fiscal files to review the details of program operations over the past six months
- Then, by moving through a set of steps (corresponding to the following exercise steps), sum up—without prejudgment—the various courses of action that might be taken to eliminate the deficit
- Next, make recommendations for specific reductions, complete with detailed calculations, based on your determination of the best action plan(s)
- Finally, develop proposals for monitoring and controlling future expenses

Step 1. You conclude that six main alternative courses of action are possible to resolve the overrun problem:

- To recover the whole deficit in one line-item category or in one cost center
- To make all the cutbacks on the overrun lines only
- To spread the pain by cutting equally (by dollars or percentages) in each line-item or in each cost center
- To rank line-items (and their elements) from "least damaging" to "most damaging" for clients and objectives—as per the schema in Chapter 3—and then try to make the most cuts in the former ranking and the fewest in the latter
- To follow no hard and fast rule, but to use a judicious mixture of approaches
- To do none of the above before preparing and submitting a well-documented request for additional money from the funder

Step 1A. You feel that you need to have concrete examples of various cost-cutting options before deciding which course(s) to follow. Therefore, on your worksheet *expand on the few examples* given in Table 7–10 by listing for *every* line-item category a selection of possible cost-cutting options—from no cuts to moderate and drastic ones. *Do not prejudge the prudence or wisdom of any option.* Juxtaposing the concrete possibilities will help you focus on their effects on program operations and services.

TABLE 7–10.   CYS Budget-cutting Options

Line-Item	*Options*
Personnel	Reduce some secretarial and/or counselor time Protect staff at all costs . . . .
Supplies/Communication	Purchase no new supplies till stock is depleted . . . . . .
Occupancy	Rent out some of CYS space Try to negotiate lower rent from landlord . . . .

Step 1B. After carefully thinking through the implications of the different options on your list, review the alternative courses of action and select the *two* you believe are most feasible and least damaging. Write a note for the PC giving the four strongest arguments *in favor* of both.

Step 1C. For the record, list the four strongest arguments *against* two of the other alternatives.

Step 2. Now let us assume you decided that one reasonable course would be to make the most cuts in areas least damaging to clients and objectives. But to do this, you need an overall systematic plan into which you can fit suitable options from the list you have just prepared. You conclude that the *priority schema*, which pointed the direction for the original budget plan, could give similar direction and structure for the cutback decisions. This means that all line-item categories (and subcategories) must be ranked, as per the schema partitions, according to their immediate, proximate, or distant effects, and that the immediate costs must receive the most protection. Therefore, before any dollar calculations are made, all items have to be tentatively ordered into the schema. (Readers may wish to review the sample schema in Chapter 3.)

Step 2A. The following represents a view of the schema partitions for CYS consistent with the principles described

in Chapter 3. Vendor Services, Conference Travel, and Occupancy have not yet been entered. Complete the schema by
assigning these three items to the most appropriate partitions.

Distant	Proximate	Immediate
Equipment	Communications	Administrative Staff
Professional Consultations	Support Staff	Contact Staff
Office Supplies	Local Travel	Employee Benefits Financial Aid

Step 2B. Enter on the completed schema the estimated
dollar *deficit* (or surplus) for each line-item shown in Column 5 of the Monthly Expense Summary. Then total the projected dollar deficit for each partition. What *proportion* of
the total deficit is projected for each? As you expected from
the information on the Summary, the largest share appears
in the immediate partition—the one you most want to protect.

Step 2C. On the Monthly Expense Summary label each
line-item (and major subitem) in Column 5 with a D, P, or I to
indicate its location on the schema.

Step 3. At this point you receive an urgent call from the
PC reminding you that the funder allows only 10 percent or
$1,500 dollars—whichever is *smaller*—of any line-item total
to be transferred *from* any line-item to another line-item.
There are no limitations on the amount allowed to be
transferred *into* any line-item from one or more other lines.
Changes may be made as desired within line-items, but no
line-item can be deleted.

Enter on the Summary or on your worksheet the legal
transfer limit for each line-item. For example, the maximum
that could be transferred out of Professional Fees is $420 (10
percent of $4,200); or $1,500 from Benefits/Taxes (smaller
than the 10 percent figure of $3,477).

Step 4. As you study the details on the Monthly Expense
Summary, you realize that you cannot make sensible
judgments about reducing the projected deficit by working
solely with line-items and dollar amounts. You must know

where, by whom, and for what these resources were used during the past six months. Only when you understand something about the patterns of resource consumption and, if possible, the reasons for these patterns, can you begin to make sound decisions about reductions.

Step 4A. Even though you reviewed the files, there is no way at this stage that you can extract and examine every facet of service delivery; so you pick for study three nonpersonnel items (one from each partition) that were over budget during the first six months. Two subcategories, Local Travel and Financial Aid, typify activities where the resources are expended on important interactions between staff and clients; Professional Fees typifies the kind of resource that needs to be watched carefully, as noted in the PC's memo.

After reviewing various file materials, you put together the following cost center information about these three items.

| | Percent of Allocation Spent After 6 Months | | | |
Item	S/I	Ref	C/R	Cslg
Local Travel	.42	.48	.65	.38
Financial Aid	.51	.36	.62	.40
Professional Fees	.66	.44	.40	.64

Step 4B. Because it is impossible to study the spending patterns in every one of these cells, you select out that cell for each line-item that was most over the 50 percent six-month target. You are well aware that the patterns for the next six months will differ from these, but you need to know what factors will help explain them.

- Were the market costs poorly estimated or allocated originally?
- Were the resources used appropriately, but at levels that could not be foreseen?
- Did the overspending occur rather evenly over the course of the six months, or can it be related to particular situations in particular months?

• Were the resources used for appropriate purposes, but in uncontrolled ways?
• Was spending both inappropriate and uncontrolled?

To seek answers, for example, in the case of Consultation/Referral, which spent a large proportion of its total Local Travel funds during the past six months, you would go back to the staff files and travel forms looking for clues to understand what happened. Were most of the trips

• Made by one or two staff members only?
• Made on behalf of certain types of cases?
• Made by private cars even when public transport was available?
• Made for other reasons that deserve consideration?

Let us say you found that most of the trips were made on behalf of a relatively few clients. Then you would want to know from the staff who dealt with these clients: Do they expect the same pattern—with similar or different clients—for the next six months? If so, can they work with you to devise ways to reduce these costs? Do they know if these same clients received a disproportionate share of other resources? If so, where? Was there something unique about these particular clients, or should one always expect such variation for these costs in this CC?

After following a similar process with selected cells from the other line-items, you look the chart over once more to see if you discern any particular *patterns* of *under*spending. This brief observation may reveal some patterns that could sensitize you to variations in case flow or in staff practices. You should now feel more confident that your recommendations for cutbacks will be based on a better grasp of the *process of service delivery* during the past six months.

Step 5. Clearly you cannot resolve all the issues raised in Step 4, nor can you predict every consequence of the decisions you do make. But at this point you are faced with having to decide on specific reductions. CYS is bound by its budget and compelled to avoid an overrun.

Step 5A. With the Monthly Expense Summary and the memo from the PC at hand for reference, you begin to make a concrete plan for reducing the projected deficit. You know that the plan (1) should preserve the perspective of the schema; (2) should be implemented in an *orderly* way with the cutbacks phased in when possible—not ruthlessly imposed all at once; (3) should have some flexibility to withstand the contingencies that will surely occur; and (4) should include suggestions for better control procedures. Therefore you intend to

- Make the most cuts you can in the distant partition
- Offer a *range* of alternatives—from moderate to more stringent—in the proximate partition
- Present modest initial reductions for the immediate partition, perhaps including suggestions for a range of more severe cuts (At the same time, you will recommend ways to improve resource usage based on your study of the CCs consumption patterns.)

This plan allows you to lay out a *progression* of remedial actions while imposing better monitoring and control procedures over the next few months. CYS should be ready to take more drastic steps, but only if and when necessary.

Step 5B. You now go through each line-item (and major subitem) on the Expense Summary, following the plan you laid out in Step 5A, and calculate new Column 4 and 5 figures *with* your reductions. There are many things to remember, so you keep rechecking the PC's memo and recalling all you know about staff practices, types of clients, and so on.

What did you recommend for the Equipment line? Don't forget that a twelve-month contract may have been signed for the copying machine and that CYS has to pay to move it out.

Did you decide you could recoup most of the projected costs for Professional Fees? Don't forget the 10 percent transferral regulation.

Office supplies are a nuisance to control. If you cut down in Column 4, did you propose a plan for monitoring all supplies or only some kinds?

Step 5C. For the items in the *proximate* partition you have to provide some alternatives.

How about the costs of Occupancy? Should CYS consider subletting part of its space if the budget gets *really* tight? Should it start planning for such a contingency? If so, how soon? Outside of moving—which entails all sorts of other expenses—can any reductions be made at this time?

The breakout of Local Travel by cost centers (Step 4) should have helped you decide on some alternatives for this item. For example, given what you learned about resource use, you might have recommended that the total projected amount (Column 4) be reduced by a certain number of dollars or by a certain percentage, *but* the cut should be borne entirely by two or three of the CCs while not cutting back the other(s) at all.

Communications is a difficult item to cut. You may have already been able to reduce Supplies enough to enable you to afford a postponement of stringent cuts in telephone service while trying out for a few months some strong control procedures that you plan to develop immediately with input from staff.

The Support Staff item at CYS consists solely of secretaries, and you are probably not ready to recommend any cuts on this position line. You may, however, want to suggest to the PC that should any secretary leave CYS or request fewer hours, it would certainly help save some money if fewer FTEs were needed.

It is difficult to estimate future costs for Vendor Charges. This is a category that really needs strict guidelines and controls. Perhaps a staff committee could develop tight guidelines for restrained and only essential uses of vendors. You have proposed a modest reduction at this time that would eliminate the negative balance in Column 5 but urge the Program Coordinator to decide very soon about monitoring procedures.

Step 5D. The items in the *immediate* partition, although accounting for most of the deficit, are the ones you least want to cut—and often cannot cut.

You probably proposed a small reduction in Financial Aid for the next two months to give staff time to search for more outside support for this category. However, it may well have to be seriously reduced not later than Month 9 of the FY.

You were not prepared to tackle reductions in the staff complement, with one exception. You recommended that the *additional* time for the Liaison Worker for the next six months, noted in the memo, be deleted and that that person remain at the originally budgeted FTEs. This may be a sticky problem for the PC: Was the additional time already promised, and has that Liaison Worker already started working extra time? But even if this must be implemented a month later, the deletion of the extra time will lower the deficit in Salaries/Wages by a large percentage.

Step 6. Prepare a clean copy of the Monthly Expense Summary that includes new figures in Columns 4 and 5 based on your first-stage recommendations in Step 5.

What is the total deficit still remaining in Col. 5?

List for the PC some of the possibilities that you temporarily set aside as too drastic but that could be partially or fully invoked if necessary.

Step 7. Your final task requires that you briefly describe some ways for the PC—both with and without staff involvement—to monitor and control the projected expenses in Column 4. For this task you might, for example, discuss the pros and cons of:

- Establishing monthly maximum limits for certain things (e.g. travel amounts per person), with a secretary in charge of recording each expenditure, and perhaps cutting off funds when the limit is reached for the month
- Holding monthly staff meetings where fiscal problems are discussed and staff cooperation and input is solicited. For example, what can staff members do on their own versus what must be handled centrally? Where and how do the guidelines need clarification or strengthening?
- Advising staff of specific ways to hold costs down; e.g. recommending that in many cases telephone calls supplemented with confirming memos can replace letters and postage; but also asking for ideas and feedback from them
- Forbidding certain kinds of expenditures; e.g. trips by taxi or long distance calls
- Directing staff members to think through their activities and to present at a meeting the ways they think costs could be reduced by better cooperative efforts, by more feedback, or by stronger directives

In working through the tasks and procedures in these exercises, your fundamental purpose was to manage CYS's resources in ways that would optimize the achievement of its objectives. You began by deciding on a course of action that would best protect these objectives, and only then did you define specific options for maintaining a balanced budget. You next based your concrete recommendations on a progression of remedial actions that were tied to the program plans by means of the priority schema. You related past and future expenditures to patterns of service delivery and sought reductions that were least damaging to those services. Thus you applied the principles of sound fiscal management to all your monitoring and controlling tasks.

8

COST ANALYSIS

Introduction to Cost Analysis

IN THIS CHAPTER we continue our journey through the budget cycle and examine the important processes and procedures associated with the end of the fiscal year. For the original line-item and functional budgets we had to rely on forecasts of probable costs. During the year we had to keep adjusting and revising these estimates as dictated by events and experience. At the end of the year we have the opportunity to find out not only the total *actual* costs but also to break down these costs and look at different facets of resource use, service delivery, and program results.

Many agencies and programs rely on end-of-year (EOY) summaries that show amounts received and spent, and the variances from the award or budget. Such reports show *dollar accountability*, which, although always required and useful for some purposes, are of little help in program planning, because they do not show which kinds of clients consumed which service resources or what results, if any, were achieved. For example, a line-item summary of dollars spent in each cost center tells us about the relative use of the total resources by kinds of activities. But these resources were consumed on behalf of clients and in pursuit of certain results. It is the connections between resource consumption and those efforts and accomplishments that must be traced, integrated, and understood.

Both program and fiscal planners must be able to answer questions of this sort:

- What kinds of services were provided to which and how many clients?
- Which staff spent how much time serving which clients?
- Which clients consumed which resources, and how much of each?
- How much did it cost to provide each kind of service for the average case?
- Were each and all these costs necessary and proper?
- Could equivalent services be given for less cost?

Administrators are concerned throughout the year with parallel questions about program operations. They watch, think about, and assess what goes on all the time. Is the waiting room empty or full? Is the staff fully occupied? Are the phones ringing? Are we getting responses—or criticism—from the public? Cost analysis addresses the same kinds of concerns in *quantitative* terms. It is a mechanism for producing in comparable dollar terms (1) a justification of the uses of resources for demonstrable activities and results and (2) an account of the various interactions and relations among resources, staff, clients, and services. Cost analysis refers to those processes and procedures that allow us to separate total program and fiscal experiences into their component parts, so we can examine and interrelate them, and then reaggregate and integrate them as needed. Thus, cost analysis is aimed at:

- Revealing the flow and patterns of resource consumption through the services of the program
- Hence disclosing activities, performance, and accomplishments
- Which can guide and control future program and fiscal planning

In general, EOY cost analysis offers a two-way perspective: The look backward at historical data helps inform and improve future planning. In particular, this retrospective view can produce powerful and concrete details about the relations between various program operations. A full-scale EOY cost analysis should always be carried out, but programs typically must begin planning the next year's budget and activities around the end of the third quarter of the fiscal year. Even though final actual figures are not available, we strongly recommend that all the procedures described in this chapter be applied at that time, with the full understanding that the figures are *approximate*. Through the final quarter and at the end of the year the projections can be corrected and updated.

Cost provides the link we need to relate the resources to the activities and to the results, because, as Elkin (1980) says, "the dollar provides a single measure which uniformly quantifies a level of effort and resources expended." Thus with cost as a base we can separate out the "moving parts" that make up the program, put a uniform value (the dollar) on each, and then relate the parts to each other in systematic ways.

We need the information garnered from the cost analysis procedures not only to plan ahead but also to make sound judgments about (1) where the least damaging changes or reductions in the program should be made, (2) which services need the greatest protection, and (3) how the program could operate more efficiently and perhaps more effectively.

Another important benefit results from disaggregating and analyzing program operations: Fees, rates, and purchase-of-service or performance contracts can be estimated more reliably, while at the same time the program will be better aware of its full costs even if they are only partially collectible or reimbursable. For example, if we know that it actually cost, on the average, $500 a client to give Service A and $300 to give Service B, it would not be fair to the client (or reimburser) to charge $500 for Service B. Nor would it be safe for the program not to budget for the difference between what a service cost and what is reimbursable. We would all immediately recognize the "fair price" principle if we went to the health clinic for a flu shot. We would not expect to be charged the same as for a whole series of allergy shots. But the same principle applies when the differences between the program's services are not so patently obvious. The cost analysis procedures described later in this chapter allow us to determine more equitable service fees and charges and to plan for nonreimbursable costs, regardless of the type of program.

In addition to these applications, cost analysis is useful for making external and internal comparisons, because when we can disaggregate costs in a variety of ways, we can also reassemble them in a variety of ways. For example, by using measures standard in a given field, it is often possible to compare a program's costs for services or results with those of similar programs. We can also compare the costs for Center A this year with those for Center A in an earlier year by, for example, how much and what kinds of nonpersonnel resources were consumed in each of the years for which kinds of clients.

We must emphasize, however, that cost analysis information should not be sought for its own sake; it must be relevant, purposeful, and useful for assessing past performance and management and for future program and budget planning.

An Operations Framework

With the general purposes of cost analysis clearly in mind, our next question might well be: How does a program go about getting together the necessary information about clients, staff, results, and so on? Again, the three basic files—staff, client, and fiscal—when combined with our cost center information, will furnish almost all the data needed. Not only can we find out about particular clients by status, classification, and the like, but we can also follow their movement through the CCs to reveal the *case flow*. The staff files will show us how much time was spent by which staff doing what, which can then be related to case flow, since the staff records were coded to correlate with the cost centers (as shown in the figures and tables in Chapter 7).

Most organizations are well aware of the importance of maintaining good records because they have for years been putting together what are familiarly known as "service statistics," by which they have sought to describe their operations, to plan changes, and to improve management. Some of these statistics may be mandated by funders or licensing bodies; some may have singular and diagnostic definitions; others may be used to meet internal or special needs or predilections; and still others may be collected because "that's what we always did." Some of these service statistics may tally with or parallel the kinds of backup data needed for cost analysis. Others may need definitional changes to accord with standardized cost analysis terms or changes in reporting or accounting procedures to ensure accurate data collection. But since cost analysis moves a critical dimension beyond simple statistical records, they should be reevaluated to clarify their pertinence and utility.

But what do we do with all this valuable, but still disparate, information from records and files so that we can eventually answer the questions raised at the beginning of the chapter? We need a structure or framework that profiles each program's *continuum of operations* (the "moving parts"), so that all its service activities and fiscal experiences can be *properly identified and related to each other*. Only then can we express the connections that exist and generate measures that will enable us to cost out these connections.

The framework currently used simply sets forth what happens *sequentially* in any program. Thus we know that:

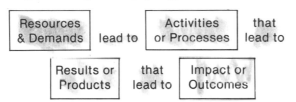

Using "systems" terms, this translates into:

INPUTS--------> THROUGHPUTS----------> OUTPUTS----------> OUTCOMES

The Role of the Cost Centers and Records

Let us recall that (1) all our original program and budget plans were directed toward a course of action that would achieve certain objectives; (2) at the start of the fiscal year we incorporated sets of activities, or functions, into cost centers; (3) these CCs reflected the expected course of operations for the year; and (4) the accounting system was to be made compatible with the cost centers.

Now we should recognize that the continuum of operations, as represented by the framework, mirrors the functional processes we defined at the start of the year by means of the CCs, which themselves had evolved from the original program and budget plans. *Thus we have, in a sense, come full circle.* The framework compresses the CC production functions into their main sequential phases, but it clearly and logically depicts the same processes we tried to encompass in the CCs in the first place. Therefore, the information we have already stored in the CCs can now be matched with the processes expressed by the framework.

We are also able to trace the flow of clients by identifying their movement along the continuum through the CCs (sometimes called "client careers"). This allows us, in addition, to find out which and how many clients received services from more than one CC and which and how many dropped out. The real-life diversity of clients and situations precludes a perfect fit with the CCs. However, the better the CCs were defined, the sharper their boundary points, the more the information that can be aligned, through them, with the framework.

How well the basic files were kept has critical importance, because analysis of costs will be affected by the kinds and consistency of both fiscal and nonfiscal records. For example, determining staff costs for any part of a program's operations will depend on how well staff time was logged or reported. Similarly, determining various costs for an Admissions CC will depend on how accurately records discriminate between those applicants accepted and enrolled and those not admitted; both have used resources that should be counted.

A Priorities List

No matter how ambiguous the definitions of the CCs or how limited and scanty the records, serious efforts must be made to reconcile and align whatever *is* known with the framework, because cost analysis measures and procedures are coordinated with these sequential operations. But even with excellent CC definitions and records, good cost analysis does not require that absolutely everything be counted and costed. Therefore, it is wise to begin by reviewing existing program statistics and noting their possible usefulness and to develop a preliminary list of desired information that fits the framework and reflects the main planning and fiscal requirements and priorities. Included here would be specific kinds of information for the funder, which often must be reported according to predetermined formulas; data especially needed for purchase-of-service contracts; information standard or typical in the program's sector of service; and finally, matters of special internal concern or interest. The last-mentioned might relate to the level of staff time spent in certain CCs or to a sharp increase or decrease in certain types of clients or in service demands. But, more important, planners could be worried about imminent cutbacks and would want to have concrete, detailed information to buttress arguments for support or to make sound decisions about cuts. The list will probably contain a mixture of general and specific items and questions at this stage, which is fine, because it will later be modified, altered, and expanded, depending on the availability of records and accounting data and on the particular cost measures selected for analysis.

Operations Measures

To be able to make use of all the information at hand, it must be expressed in *measures that can be quantified*, that is, can be reliably counted.[1] These measures must be classified or grouped to accord with each phase of the operations framework so that cost analysis procedures can be applied, as desired, within or across the framework. Many measures are available for each phase—as will be illustrated shortly—and all have value for efficiently summarizing important facts about resource use, program activities, and results.

From the numerous possible measures each program will, of course, select for cost analysis those that are most

---

[1] In this context we use the word "measure" solely in the *noun* form; in its verb form, it means to ascertain the quantity of something, for which we use the word "count" to avoid confusion.

telling and informative. However, we have a few general guidelines for all programs. Every measure selected should

- Refer to clearly defined and demonstrable events or objects that are recorded and can be verified
- Be directly germane to the core activities and production processes
- Meet minimum requirements for validity and reliability

Further, we want to emphasize that despite the broad variety of service organizations—with their differing objectives, resources, efforts, and clientele—numerous measures are readily available and applicable to most of them. Even those measures with seemingly distinctive labels can usually be translated across *comparable* programs. However, standardized terms (e.g. FTEs) should be used whenever possible.

When making final choices for the cost analysis procedures, several cautions should be kept in mind:

- Recognize and accept that some desirable data will not be available.
- Conversely, data should not be used solely because they are available. They must have value for the purposes of analysis.
- Totting up numbers is not the point. Illuminating past performance and future directions is the point.

We are now about to go through each phase of the framework and look at examples of typical measures that can be applied to cost analysis procedures, noting especially the web of interconnections among all the measures. As we move through the phases, the bases for developing measures will be explained. We will see how, in the input and throughput phases, we have *sets* or groups of different types of measures, and how *within each set*, when dollar values are added, measures can be costed relative to each other (e.g. measure X versus measure Y in Set A). In addition, we shall be able to see that in some phases *composite measures* are available, which means that the measure itself is a ratio or other relationship between a Set A measure and a Set B measure that yields a new Set C measure. These composite measures are especially useful for making comparisons *across* the framework; for example, the ratio of admitted clients to professional staff FTEs (from two different sets) gives us a composite measure of input that can be related to throughput and output. These and other connections will become clearer as we illustrate the measures.

INPUTS: RESOURCE AND DEMAND MEASURES

Resources can be quantified into measures of dollars, or equivalent values, available directly for operations; *demands* can be quantified into measures that allow us to count the need or desire for the services. We are all familiar with the kinds of resources common to agencies: dollars from all sources; in-kind contributed and donated services or material; physical plant; and equipment. Resources can be quantified into an equally familiar set of measures: (1) staff FTEs, broken down as needed into professional, non-professional, technical, maintenance, support, voluntary, full-time, part-time, and so on; (2) nonstaff personnel, such as consultants, subcontractors, persons on special assignments, auditors, and the like; and (3) physical facilities, supplies and material, or equipment, if these represent inputs crucial to program operations. Examples are square footage or number of beds in a residential facility; number of books in a library; vehicles for a meals-on-wheels program; telephone equipment for a hot line; x-ray machines in a diagnostic clinic; exhibit space in a museum; and special tools for a job retraining program.

In addition, the demands for services from the program represent an important part of input that can and should be quantified. The very existence of the not-for-profit organization implies certain public needs and demands waiting to be met. The existence of a clear demand for its services legitimizes the establishment and support of an agency or program and mandates that the demand be met by means of the funds that are awarded (sometimes by law, as through entitlements). These demands therefore represent concrete inputs in the form of people wanting or needing the services, which results in interactions between them and the organization.

The demands can be quantified by the following set of measures of these interactions: inquiries, requests for service, applications, in-referrals, waiting lists, eligibility interviews or determinations, membership lists, contacts with referral sources, and so on. Each agency must decide which demand measures are sufficiently germane to be recorded and then must define and distinguish each measure. For example, inquiries or requests for service may not be classified as applications until they have been screened or otherwise processed. The processing procedures may also vary among programs. But no matter how they are handled, these demands exact costs that must be calculated.

A set of *composite* measures of input might include the ratio of applicants to nonprofessional staff FTEs; the number of vehicles to requests for services; the nursing home bed capacity to the area population over age sixty-five; or the gallon capacity of the waste treatment plant to the number of households in the community.

Note the sorts of information that can accrue from the web of interconnections described earlier. The staff FTE measure from one set can be used relative to the supplies measure from the same set, or relative to the applications measure from another set; the composite measure of the ratio of applicants to nonprofessional staff FTEs can be used relative to throughput and output measures.

Throughputs: Activity/Process Measures

Throughputs can be quantified into measures of the efforts expended in delivering services and should therefore depict the full range of a program's service activities.

Three main sets of throughput measures are widely used. One set follows on the input resources and denotes the *staff* activities associated with service delivery. These measures include service hours, number of home visits, site inspections, training sessions, number of meals served, continuing education classes taught, miles traveled, sources developed, number of cases out-referred, and others. These measures are often used to set personnel work or production standards and to monitor staff effort. For such purposes they are usually called workload indicators.

Another set of measures follows on the input demands, and we call these *case* measures. They are expressed by (1) types of clients—trainees, patrons, parents, visitors, students, area residents, patients—and/or (2) their statuses as they proceed through the services—enrolled, accepted, certified, new or reopened case, eligible, legally ordered, sick or disabled.

The third set consists of *composite* measures that reflect the interactions between staff and client. For example, contact hours, which identifies the relation between portions of staff effort and persons of certain statuses, or teacher/student ratios, which can be used to trace a variety of relationships, such as, how many staff FTEs were used to deliver which services to what number and what kind of clients.

OUTPUTS: RESULT/PRODUCT MEASURES

Output measures quantify the accomplishments of the program and should denote *what* was produced or achieved as a consequence of the input and throughput processes. Current literature focuses on the importance of output and outcome measures almost to the exclusion of the other operations phases (see the Bibliography). Authors' terminology varies, and some make little or no distinction between outputs and outcomes.

Ideally, the objectives of an organization and its outputs should be couched in parallel terms. For example,

Objective: to inform consumers about the state's weatherization tax rebate

Result measure: number of brochures distributed on weatherization tax rebate

In reality, however, service organizations often have serious difficulty defining and determining valid output measures. Part of the difficulty stems from the newness of the idea of breaking down the flow of operations (via the framework) and quantifying the elements. Historically, the activities themselves have been viewed as the principal "outputs" of not-for-profit organizations. For the most part, however, the difficulty arises from the intrinsic problem of determining what exactly was produced and achieved by the inputs and throughputs. In other words, agencies lack good measures of results because the results they seek often defy specification and measurement. Sometimes the difficulties are compounded by the organization's definitions of its objectives, which tend to be sweeping. But fundamentally the kinds of situations dealt with do not easily yield finite, straightforward conclusions. For example, how does one determine the product or result of home visits from a home health aide—by whether the invalid gets well, dies, sends a thank-you note, or goes to the hospital?

In spite of these inherent and very real problems, some result measures can be designated, even if imperfectly, so that costs can be assigned and analyzed. Very often the program will have to avail itself of an output measure that approximates or stands in for an objective that cannot be reasonably quantified. This is called a *proxy or surrogate* and typically denotes effort rather than a clear-cut result.

The range of currently common product measures is illustrated by the following list:

- Persons who completed training, accepted placements or referrals, graduates, cases cleared from court docket, inoculations, number who completed the course, inspections completed, child-care days, number removed from welfare rolls, new members/subscriptions, licenses issued, permits approved, number able to return to work, persons who completed rehabilitation sessions

All the product measures listed represent attempts to quantify outputs in terms specifically related to program objectives. Thus they specify the particular accomplishments of or on behalf of a *group of clients or cases*, mark their flow through the entire program, and provide a count of successes or failures. By further examination of the client and cost center records, we could also find out how the different CCs contributed to these results.

OUTCOMES: IMPACT MEASURES

The service program is established on the belief that certain needs should be met, and these needs become translated into specific service activities, so the ultimate question is, What demonstrable impact or effects on clients did the program achieve? Although proof of effect is most elusive, programs are now expected to make strenuous efforts to identify it.[2]

The reality, however, is that the actual outcomes sought by a particular program frequently call for changes in personal qualities or behavior, in attitudes or values, or in public policies. An objective of "cleaner air" or "reducing poverty" or "controlling alcoholism" will call for unmeasurable judgments about impact. Such broad aims have validity, but a service organization must learn to convert them into narrower targets or into throughput surrogates that have a chance to be quantified. This, "cleaner air" could become "reducing the amount of pollution or discharge of X substance from ABC plant by Z percent." "Reducing poverty" could become "training and placing 120 AFDC mothers in jobs by X date." "Controlling alcoholism" could become "conducting 12 group counseling sessions for 50 convicted drunk drivers."

Even when limiting the scope of the objectives, we are still left with the problem of *proving* impact. Thus, even if we place the 120 AFDC mothers in jobs, will they still be working three, six, or whatever months later? And how long is long enough to prove success?

This raises an even more difficult problem in determining impact. Most agencies and programs have time, scope, and task limits and boundaries imposed on them in many ways: by law, by funders, by licensors, by jurisdiction, by professional standards, by community understanding, and certainly by restraints on resources and capabilities. Hence it is almost always impossible for them to keep track of what happens to clients after the output stage. And, as important, it is rare indeed that a program's long-term impact can be distinguished from the host of other influences that affect outcomes for an individual, group, or situation. For example, how does one separate out the influences that result in recidivism?

Nevertheless, because the quest for measures of impact seems here to stay, we must do the best we can to accom-

---

[2] Efforts to analyze impact have typically been linked to broad policy questions ("Should Congress appropriate more money for Literacy Program Type A than for Type B?"); to cost/benefit studies using economic models; to idiosyncratic case studies; or to "evaluation research" studies of causality or intervention theory.

modate to it. The following examples—many of which are necessarily surrogates—might be considered as approximations of outcomes measures.

- • Number or percent: of trainees that found or were placed in jobs; of graduates that found jobs in their specialty; of placements still employed/referred/ adopted after X months; of eligible households that were interviewed/counseled/brought into the program; of target population attending workshops; of inoculated persons receiving booster shots; of increase/decrease in library use or books loaned; of former drug users still free of drugs X months after counseling; of improved waste disposal methods

Operations Measures as Service Units

The costs of service organizations are associated with the *acts and results* of giving services to and for clients, thus the *throughput* and *output* measures when applied in costing procedures are commonly known as *service units* (SUs) because in human services, we are concerned with units of the service delivery system (Elkin, 1980, p. 3). Whatever the entities that make up the service units, their costs can be compared because we use the common denominator of their dollar value. Input measures when applied in costing procedures are known as unit costs—*not* service unit costs—and are key measures for relating resource consumption *along* the operations continuum (see Example 1 below).

SELECTING SERVICE UNITS FOR COST ANALYSIS

A program will usually choose only a few SUs for analysis from the many possible cost measures in each of the operations phases.[3] Therefore, it must make its selections very carefully, taking into account what is:

---

[3] We assume in the following sections that programs will select service units analogous to those listed as operations measures, using appropriate descriptive labels.

- Mandated by the funder
- Standard (and thus comparable) for its service sector
- Important for management decisions and future planning
- Critical for fee and rate setting
- Accessible from the records and accounting systems
- Not too complex or costly to obtain
- Valid and pertinent for describing objectives and efforts

The highest priority must, of course, be given to the mandated and standardized SUs. These often are identical—both the funder and the service sector having learned to agree on definitions—and programs almost always know what they are. Sometimes a program may have to use several SUs to meet requirements and standards, which means that very similar data will have to be broken out and reassembled in several different ways. For example, for the throughput effort of, let us say, the Instruction CC in a Job Retraining Program, the funder may want SU costs per trainee by class hours and by number of sessions, while sector standards may call for the total cost per trainee. Or for the same Instruction CC, the standards may call for a unit cost of staff FTEs in Instruction (input), and the funder may want both the SU cost of contact hours (throughput) as well as the cost per job placement (output). In all such situations service unit costing procedures are efficient: Different SU measures can be applied to the same cost base (here, the line-items and total Instruction CC) to gain different applications from different elements of that base.

We must caution that standardized SU costs are often worrisome, because significant differences in such costs may occur between programs that seemingly provide the same services. A program may be convinced that it had higher SU costs because it gave higher quality or broader services, but usually this is exceedingly difficult to defend and prove. Disparity may also be caused by the exclusion or inclusion of items in the total unit cost. For example, one program may include capital and depreciation costs, while another pays only a minimal amount for rent. However, more and more funders are setting standard SU costs for particular types of service functions that programs must abide by.

Additional service units may be considered necessary to

meet the requirements of current or hoped-for purchase-of-service or performance contracts; to defend, explain, or set fees or rates; to find efficiencies; to prepare for limited or drastic cuts; to take stock of weak links in service delivery or results; or to plan changes or shifts in services or clients. One particular SU may well be able to provide cost information that can be used simultaneously for several of these purposes (by further breakouts or by alternative aggregations or by setting aside certain costs); and it may sometimes be wiser to choose a less precise but more adaptable service unit.

The range in the numbers of SUs that programs apply is broad indeed. Some use only one measure to analyze all their operations, which is fine if it is appropriate for all the services and results, and if all the needed cost information can be obtained. Other agencies go overboard and use a different SU for almost everything they do. This is rarely necessary and makes for time-consuming, costly, and cumbersome cost analysis that, in the end, may produce lots of idiosyncratic and noncomparable information. We suggest a middle-of-the-road course:

Select no more SUs than are accessible, useful for comparisons, fully descriptive of operations, and valuable for program and budget planning, and, if possible, include one measure of output.

No matter which or how many SUs are selected, the program must record *its own definition* of every measure. For example, if the SU is "service hours," then the exact meaning must be made clear: professional staff time only; only hours devoted to particular activities; all time spent on behalf of clients (even a client may have to be defined); only face-to-face time with clients; and so on. A definition may also have to include clarification of procedural matters, such as how something was counted or what was excluded. Precise definitions will help the program sort out the information it needs to obtain from the analysis and will also clarify matters for the funder and board.

USE OF AVERAGES WITH SERVICE UNITS

All unit costing is based on obtaining the *average* cost of something. Although we cannot know the exact cost of service for any one person or thing, averages are highly informative expressions of quantity. An average summarizes data into a representative "one" number, which gives us a condensed view of both the total operation and its parts. We can compare the costs of the parts to each other because the average is representative for each of the parts, and we can make comparisons with other programs because an average represents "one" regardless of the size of the organization. For example, an average cost per inoculation in Agency X, with 2,000 clients, can be compared with the cost per the same kind of inoculation in Agency Y, which has served 400 or 4,000 clients.

Remember, *we are not talking about quality of service or productivity or opportunity costs*—all important matters. We are only asserting that in and of itself an average has validity and practicality for determining and comparing costs.

Service Unit Costing

COST ACCOUNTING

Cost accounting is the term used in the profit sector to describe the system used to relate expenditures and costs to a unit of output. Cost accounting has been known and practiced for more than four hundred years, and today it has a vast literature, its own vocabulary, and practitioners skilled in its many techniques. We purposely do not use this term for the not-for-profit sector, because the procedures we apply in cost analysis do not reflect the complexity and sophistication of current cost accounting systems.

Modern cost accounting methods grew out of the need for better measurement of internal production costs in industrial and manufacturing firms. The term is used to denote the kinds of accounting procedures that produce unit cost figures. The unit cost not only expresses the total cost for an item but also can be used to identify costs of its parts: labor, material, machine, and administration. This information is critical in industry and business for the planning and deployment of resources, for making comparisons with standard costs, and for maximizing profits and minimizing losses.

The cost accounting system is superimposed on and supplements the general accounting system; it dictates what and how many facts should be collected (e.g. by cost centers, by sampling, by special tasks). It fosters ongoing reviews of operations and is capable of producing up-to-date, frequent reports for internal use (management accounting) and for external use (financial accounting). Thus it assists managers and policymakers in planning, controlling, and organizing operations.

At present small and midsize not-for-profit organizations rarely, if ever, have the capability to establish and maintain a full-fledged cost accounting system. But we have incorporated many of its objectives, along with some of its terminology and techniques, into the entire discussion of cost analysis in this chapter. For example, we have emphasized the importance of moving beyond dollar accountability (for assessing past performance and for future planning); the necessity of compatibility between files and cost center records and the accounting system for analyzing costs; the purpose and uses of the operations framework; and the usefulness of unit costing.

Cost Analysis Procedures

In the next few sections we focus on obtaining unit and SU cost information by applying several basic cost analysis procedures; that is, relating costs to measures of input, throughput, and output. An excellent step-by-step outline of the decisions that must be made before implementing these procedures is given by Elkin (1980, pp. 19–21). We concentrate here on exemplifying the principles and techniques of the procedures, which are applicable to all the SU measures. Readers will also be able to work on additional applications in the exercise section.

Note: We do not include support center costs in any of the following examples. In real programs, as well as the following illustrative ones, support center costs must eventually be incorporated into the *final total* SU costs. However, the resources of the SCs (e.g. Management/General, Overhead, Fundraising) are expended on behalf of all other centers—not for clients. Therefore, their costs cannot be translated into operations measures and service units, which reflect the use of resources for providing services to clients. Entirely different procedures are necessary to determine a support center's share of the final total SU costs, and these procedures are detailed in Chapter 9.

EXAMPLE 1: THE COUNTY CONSUMER PROTECTION OFFICE

Cost Analysis Question.   What was the average cost per FTE of staff with duties in the Inquiries CC (*unit* cost of input)?

Solution.   Five persons were assigned to duties in this CC; the portions of their time spent on this activity varied, and some persons had additional assignments to other CCs. From the fiscal files and staff logs coded for cost center activities, the Table 8–1 information on actual time and costs was collected, *excluding* payroll taxes and employee benefits. We can readily determine that the average cost per FTE of staff input in the Inquiries CC was $9,854 ($31,830 ÷ 3.23). (All dollar figures in this and the other examples are rounded.)

TABLE 8–1.   Personnel Costs for Inquiries CC

	Salary Rates	FTEs in CC	Total Personnel Dollars in CC
Mrs. A	$11,000	.33	$ 3,630
Mr. B	11,000	.80	8,800
Ms. C	9,500	1.00	9,500
Ms. D	9,000	.50	4,500
Mr. E	9,000	.60	5,400
		3.23	$31,830

Comments. Here we have used a quantified measure of resources—FTEs—to obtain a *unit* cost of input. Such unit costs can be useful (1) for adjustments of budget allocations to CCs during the year and (2) for planning staff assignments and other resource allocations for the next year. However, such input information would be more useful if it were combined with a throughput measure. For example, to find out (1) the personnel cost (input) per inquiry (throughput):

$$\$31{,}830 \text{ total FTE cost} \div 11{,}200 \text{ inquiries} = \$\,2.84$$
$$\text{personnel cost per inquiry,}$$

or (2) the number of inquiries (throughput) handled by the total FTEs (input), which gives us a *workload indicator* rather than an SU cost:

$$11{,}200 \div 3.23 \text{ FTE} = 3{,}467 \text{ inquiries handled per FTE.}$$

In the next example the service unit costs will include all total direct costs—not just those for personnel.

EXAMPLE 2: THE BEECHWOOD HEALTH OUTREACH PROGRAM

Cost Analysis Question. What was the total cost per visit of the home health aides (SU of throughput)?

Solution. The total direct cost for the Home Health Cost Center was $204,000 (excluding overhead and administration), and a total of 7,686 home visits were made. Thus the SU cost per visit was $26.54 ($204,000 ÷ 7,686).

Comments. The individual line-item expenses that made up the $26.54 per visit cost can also be broken out. For example, of the $204,000, travel costs might have totaled $26,520 or 13 percent, which means that the per visit travel cost was $3.45 (13 percent of $26.54). Breaking out the various component costs within a larger SU cost can be useful for examining their relative shares of the SU cost—information important for deploying resources or for cutting costs. The SU cost based on total direct costs is often used for making cost comparisons with similar services given by similar programs, although, as noted earlier, this may cause problems for the program with above-average SU costs.

EXAMPLE 3: THE NORTHERN BRANCH LIBRARY

Cost Analysis Questions.   What was the cost (1) per staff service hour at the Circulation Desk and (2) per library card transaction (both throughput SUs)?

Solution.   The Circulation cost center personnel records showed that 3.80 FTEs were spent in service activities solely involving circulation loans, for total personnel expenses of $42,447 (*including* payroll taxes and employee benefits) as shown in Table 8–2.

Our first task is to determine the FTE cost per service hour for this CC. Each FTE represents 1,900 *actual* work hours per year following the formula used for CYS (see Appendix C, Personnel Measures). Therefore, 3.80 FTEs times 1,900 service hours equals 7,220 total service hours given by these staff members at the Circulation Desk CC. Thus,

$$\$42,447 \div 7,220 = \$5.88 \text{ cost per service hour.}$$

Comments.   This is a good illustration of the value of unit costs for making comparisons. For example, here at the Northern Branch the personnel costs at the Circulation Desk totaled $42,447; let us say that at the Southern Branch the same kinds of costs totaled $64,220, and at the Eastern

TABLE 8–2.   Personnel Costs for Circulation Desk CC

	Salary Rates	CC FTEs	Total Personnel Cost for CC
Supervisor	$18,000	.20	$ 3,600
Desk Clerk A	13,000	1.00	13,000
Desk Clerk B	12,500	.50	6,250
Assistants	10,000	.90	9,000
Custodian	9,800	.20	1.960
Shelver	8,600	.50	4,300
		3.80	$34,510
			+ 7,937 for Taxes/Benefits
			$42,447

Branch they were $99,966. These gross figures tell us only that it cost more dollars to staff the Circulation Desk at the latter two branches. We can assume that these two had a larger staff complement and that they serviced more people, but we cannot discern the costs of service delivery from these figures. After obtaining the unit cost per service hour at all branches, we might find that at the Southern Branch, 6.4 FTEs worked a total of 12,160 hours (6.4 x 1,900), yielding a $5.28 per service hour cost; and that at the Eastern Branch 8.7 FTEs logged 16,530 hours, yielding a $6.05 cost per service hour. Now we have a base for making comparisons and can, for instance, focus on the reasons for the lower costs at the Southern Branch. Were they the result of a different mix of personnel expenses? Or were more efficient procedures used at the Southern Branch? If so, should these be adopted at the other two branches? And how about the other line-item costs at these Circulation Desks? Frequently the answer to one cost analysis question points us toward other inquiries that are important for program planning, because they provide additional quantitative information about the relations among resources, staff, clients, services, and results (in line with questions raised at the beginning of this chapter).

Now let us turn to our other cost analysis question about the personnel cost per card transaction at the Northern Branch. This is a simple matter to determine. The Circulation Desk handled 37,240 transactions over the year (the number obtained by sample or record tally), and this number is divided into the total personnel cost. Thus,

$$\$42,447 \div 37,240 = \$1.14 \text{ per transaction.}$$

Comments.   This type of measure can be useful when a program is concerned about its efficiency or productivity relative to similar programs. For example, if the per transaction cost at another branch was significantly higher or lower, the reasons for the disparity must be sought. It might be necessary to plan changes in staff complement, assignments, or salaries, or in processing methods or equipment. Note how this relates to the questions just raised about varying costs per service hour. This example illustrates a situation where it would be advantageous to use more than one SU measure, since each can shed important light on the other.

EXAMPLE 4: THE CROSSTOWN JOB RETRAINING PROGRAM

Cost Analysis Questions.   What was the total program cost (1) per enrolled trainee (throughput) and (2) per graduate of the retraining course (output); and (3) what was the cost per graduate who was also served by the Placement CC (output). Here we are being asked to cost two different measures of output, both representing legitimate measures of results. Question 2 assesses the results—within the boundaries of the program—of its major throughput efforts: the completion of a retraining course. Question 3 assesses the results—beyond the boundaries of the program—for a *subset* of these graduates for whom special placement assistance was needed. As we shall see, this last question calls for a further breakout of costs and raises issues that underscore the indivisibility between program and fiscal planning.

Solution.   The Job Retraining Program contained four production centers: *Admissions, Retraining Course, Job Skills,* and *Placement.* The direct Personnel and all other costs for these four CCs totaled $250,000; and 115 people were enrolled in the program. Therefore, Question 1 can be easily answered:

$$\$250,000 \div 115 = \$2,174 \text{ (rounded)}$$
throughput cost per enrollee.

For Question 2 the total costs must be divided by the number of trainees that graduated from the course (the output); and in this case, *100* of the enrollees actually graduated. Thus, the output cost per graduate is $2,500 ($250,000 ÷ 100).

These two SU figures give us a broad, general account of throughput and output costs, and such information is always essential. Very often, however, we have to amplify such SU breakouts to obtain the costs for other important subsets of clients. Rational cost cutting and cost control depend on our knowing the costs of all our principal efforts and results; clearly, such information is also vital when developing realistic cost estimates for purchase-of-service agreements or performance contracts.

Those graduates of the Retraining Course who received special services from the Placement CC certainly represent an important subset of clients. To find out these specific SU costs (Question 3), we must know the SU costs of each of the four production centers. Cost center and client records showed the following:

Production Centers	Total Cost	Persons Served	SU Cost
Admissions	$ 66,175	210	$ 315
Retraining Course	80,875	115	703
Job/Interpersonal Skills	41,200	46	896
Placement	61,750	60	1,029
	$250,000		

From this table we see that the per graduate placement cost was $1,029 (Question 3). Note also how much more cost detail we now have about each throughput cost center. But at the same time we realize that we must know more about the flow of trainees through the program to explain the varying numbers served in each CC. Thus in Figure 8–1 we disaggregate further data about the various subsets of clients and their SU costs within each CC.

Comments.   We can readily see that these additional data can and should be exploited as we make program decisions. Why did 40 percent of the course graduates not use the placement services? Was completion of the retraining course sufficient for them to obtain jobs without special assistance? Were they more able to make use of the services of state employment offices than the graduates who also needed the program's special placement help? And were the jobs these graduates obtained different from those obtained by the graduates needing Placement? Of the 60 who used the placement services, why were only 38 successfully placed in

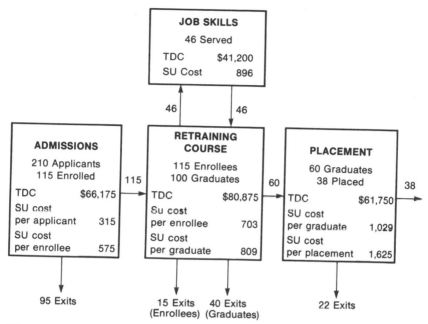

Figure 8–1. Job Retraining Program

jobs? Can this be attributed to the state of the job market, to
the characteristics of these clients themselves, or to both
conditions? These issues would have to be seriously explored when planning the next year's operations and would
be especially critical if, for example, a possibility existed for
obtaining a peformance contract where the funder would
pay only for those trainees who actually got jobs.

   Let us look at still other examples of the management
questions we can glean from Figure 8–1. Given that 13
percent of the enrollees did not complete the course, should
more be enrolled next year if we need to assure a funder a
specific number of graduates? Was a limit set, and could
more enrollees be handled with the same available resources?
If this was not the first year of the program, how do these
figures compare with other years? Further, we accepted only
55 percent of the applicants. Does this represent our typical
pattern? If not, was it because of admissions policies or
criteria, of current local employment conditions, or of the
particular mix of people who happened to apply?

Also, were there time-lag problems (1) between application and enrollment or (2) between acceptance and the start of the course?

What program implications can we draw from the SU breakout for the Job Skills CC? We can determine, for example, that this CC accounted for 16.5 percent of the Total Direct Costs and, if eliminated in a retrenchment effort, would reduce the per enrollee cost from $2,174 to $1,815, and the per graduate cost from $2,500 to $2,088. However, if this CC were cut out, how would the program, and especially the output, be affected? What do we know about this subset of trainees, and would we have to admit more and different types of trainees to ensure a comparable graduate output? How would Admissions policies regarding types and numbers of applicants be affected? Would the retraining course have to be altered? In what ways? Would the Placement efforts have to be intensified or otherwise changed?

We have by no means exhausted the implications and applications for program planning that can be extracted and expanded from the cost analysis information in Figure 8–1 (e.g. class contact hours per trainee, staff/trainee ratios to output). If, for example, we were faced with having to cut the program drastically, the fiscal information in the diagram should alert us to program concerns that must be addressed. But this illustrative Job Retraining Program does illustrate *how* cost analysis allows us to "separate program and fiscal experiences into their component parts, so we can examine and interrelate them" and "make sound planning judgments" (to quote the beginning of this chapter).

Program Applications of Cost Analysis

The foregoing examples demonstrate how the *quantitative* insights elicited by cost analysis illuminate and help define various program issues. But cost analysis does more than merely provoke questions; it also points to directions for finding answers. In this last section we briefly summarize a few of the direct applications of cost analysis to important program planning concerns.

FINDING EFFICIENCIES AND CUTTING COSTS IN PROGRAM OPERATIONS

The program manager is more and more frequently faced with budget ultimatums such as, "costs must be cut by X percent or X dollars" or "find efficiencies so that the program achieves the same results with X percent fewer resources." Instead of blindly slashing the total budget or taking arbitrary across-the-board cuts, the cost analysis procedures permit the manager to cost out the various parts of program operations and make more selective and judicious cuts. For example, after tracing out case flow with its attendant costs, how and where to make the least damaging reductions in operations and services can be more precisely identified. This is not to say that the process will be easy, but it allows managers to focus on program concerns, not merely on dollars. For example, the kinds of questions about program operations and trainees that were raised as a result of the cost analysis at the Job Retraining Program would have to be pondered and resolved if it were decided to reexamine the need for the Job Skills CC.

Cost analysis can indicate efficiencies in operations that not only save money but also improve service delivery. For example, the Admissions CC at the Job Retraining Program, which accepted only 55 percent of the applicants it handled, might well be made more efficient—and thus less costly— by improving procedures for screening or processing applicants, by publishing a clearer statement of entrance qualifications, by speeding up the time between acceptance and the start of the course, or by assigning different personnel to these tasks. Further, if the Job Skills CC were eliminated, the Placement CC might be able to handle some of its functions with some reorganization of tasks and efforts.

COST CUTTING WITHIN UNIT COSTS

Efficiencies can often be pinpointed by breaking out the elements that make up a unit cost. We saw in Example 2, the

Health Outreach Program, that the individual line-item cost within a service unit cost could be separated out, and it is similarly possible to determine the cost of elements that make up a line-item. From such information even more refined cuts and efficiencies can often be determined, not only within one cost center but between cost centers as well. For example, if the total Supplies line-item had to be reduced at the Retraining Program, it might be critical for program objectives that certain kinds of supplies in the Retraining Course CC be maintained as far as possible. By breaking out that element of the SU costs for the other CCs as well as for the Retraining Course, a plan could be made for reducing their share of this element, while protecting the amount in the Retraining Course. Knowing the cost of an individual element can also be useful for controlling or limiting the consumption of such resources by cost centers.

DISENTANGLING SUBSETS OF COSTS

We have stressed the usefulness of cost analysis for finding out which clients used which services with which results. This kind of cost information is becoming ever more critical as programs are forced to supplement or supplant traditional funding sources. Thus, as we have often noted, fees, charges, and purchase-of-service or performance contracts require reliable, accurate estimates of costs of specific services (and results) for specific sets or subsets of clients. With the use of cost analysis procedures the costs for particular sets of clients can be disentangled, and this information can be applied to program plans to ensure that the service needs of a particular group can be met and that fair and appropriate charges are determined.

In sum, the knowledge and insight derived from cost analysis become incorporated in the program and budget plans for the next year and especially in the proportional allocation of resources to the cost centers. Although next year's experiences and clientele cannot be exactly predicted, projections based on cost analysis provide more valid assumptions, and beyond that the techniques can be applied during the year to update and modify plans as dictated by events.

Exercise Problems

For these exercises we assume that all the end-of-year information is in hand. Although continuation budgeting has to be undertaken before final data are available, at some later

Account No. RA 156–BY   Fiscal Period 1 Sept. 19XX – 31 Aug. 19YY

Account Name Community Youth Services

FUNCTIONAL EXPENSE SUMMARY
(for 12 months)

Line Item	FTEs	Total Cost Col. 1	Screening/ Intake Col. 2	Referral Col. 3	Con/Ref Col. 4	Coun- seling Col. 5	Mgt/ Gen Col. 6
Personnel							
Prog. Coord.	1.00	24,000	4,080	7,200	7,920	960	3,840
Scr. Super.	1.00	21,000	10,500	3,570	5,040	1,050	840
Intake W.	.78	14,490	13,331	507	652	0	0
Liaison Wkrs.	3.32	58,905	12,370	24,740	20,499	884	412
Counselors	1.96	31,104	622	6,843	18,662	4,977	0
Secretaries	2.16	26,323	9,081	6,844	9,212	395	791
	10.22						
1. Total Sal/Wages		175,822	49,984	49,704	61,985	8,266	5,883
2. Employee Benefits & Payroll Taxes		35,164	9,997	9,941	12,397	1,653	1,176
3. Professional Fees		3,780	934	754	1,113	790	189
4. Supplies, Communications, & Reproduction		5,950	2,618	1,339	1,131	149	713
5. Occupancy: Rent		12,000	3,840	2,880	3,720	480	1,080
6. Travel: Local		4,853	882	1,471	2,257	97	146
Conference		300	146	51	45	0	58
7. Equipment		2,700	0	0	0	0	2,700
8. Assistance to Clients: Vendor Charges		3,300	627	1,089	1,188	396	0
Financial Aid		3,600	0	1,296	1,584	720	0
9. TOTAL DIRECT COSTS		247,469	69,028	68,525	85,420	12,551	11,945
10. Overhead/Indirect 18%		44,544	12,425	12,334	15,376	2,259	2,150
11. GRAND TOTAL		292,013	81,453	80,859	100,796	14,810	14,095

Special Note:

time the *actual* final data for a fiscal period must be fully recorded and analyzed. These exercises find us at that stage at CYS. We aim in this section to help you (1) to apply the main procedures and techniques discussed in the chapter text and (2) to derive a variety of insights into program operations through cost analysis.

Note: Successive roundings in Steps may cause small number differences between tables. Mgt/Gen and Overhead are excluded here for reasons given earlier.

Your tasks, as an administrative staff person, will involve "separating program and fiscal experiences into their component parts and then reaggregating and integrating them" to "give an account of the various interactions and relations among resources, staff, clients, and services" at CYS (again, quoting from earlier in this chapter). This will enable you to answer for CYS the questions posed for program and fiscal planners at the beginning of the chapter.

Several essential sources of information have been prepared for you (e.g. a Functional Expense Summary, a Case Flow Diagram), but you will be expected to complete some source materials and to develop still others. Most of the solutions to the problems can be derived from familiar basic materials, but in some instances additional file information will be provided (e.g. service hours, contact hours). You will need to develop and maintain your own worksheets, not only for the exercise steps and the calculations but also to record some of the interpretations and explanations given throughout this section.

Step 1. The Program Coordinator, after consultation with the JYC Director, has decided that CYS will apply cost analysis procedures to several measures of throughput and to one measure of output. In the first five steps we concentrate on the throughput measures; in Step 6 we begin dealing with the output measure.

In line with the criteria for selecting service units given in the text, it was agreed at CYS that each client *accepted* into the program and *served* by a CC represented an SU that was applicable to the full range of service activities; was sufficiently standard to be comparable; was accessible from the records and accounting system; and described CYS efforts on behalf of clients. In addition, it would be possible to combine this client measure with a staff measure to arrive at composite measures of throughput (e.g. staff/client ratio, contact hours).

The Case Flow Diagram, Figure 8–2 (p. 256), shows the numbers of clients accepted and routed through CYS. The table below reproduces the information depicted in the Case Flow Diagram. Several important points about these data must be clearly understood and kept in mind as you work on later procedures.

	SUs	Exited/ Placed Cases	Still Active Cases	Routed to Other CCs
S/I	1,052 undup. cases	230	30	792
Referral	448	397	19	32 to C/R
C/R	310 + 32 from Ref	318	24	
Cslg	34	31	3	

1. The 1,052 in S/I is the number of S/I service units *and* the total of *unduplicated* cases. It *includes* those accepted (who consumed resources) but exited before being routed to any other CC (moved away, lost interest, got sick).

Like most admissions centers, S/I also handled various other in-referrals and walk-ins and a host of inquiries about the program. But case files were opened only for the 1,052, and thus only they fit the SU definition of accepted cases.

2. All still active cases *are included* in the totals given for each cost center.

3. The *exits* from Referral, Consultation/Referral, and Counseling received services from these CCs and then (a) were successfully out-referred to other community resources or (b) left CYS for a typical variety of reasons.

4. The 32 cases routed from S/I first to Referral and then rerouted to Consultation/Referral are shown as SUs in both these two centers. In Referral, they are in the 448 SUs; in C/R, they are shown as additions to the 310 directly routed.

Step 1A. Table 8–3 shows the case volume and SU cost data for the four production cost centers at CYS and is based on both the Expense Summary and the Case Flow Diagram

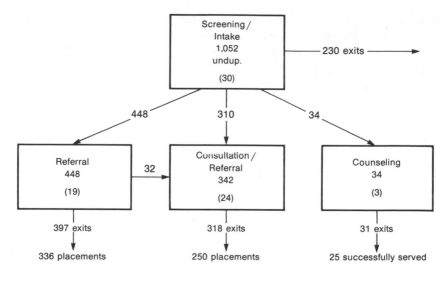

( ) = still active cases

Figure 8–2.   CYS Case Flow Diagram

(Figure 8–2).[4] Fill in the missing data to make certain you understand how they were obtained and their relationship to each other.

The cost analysis priority list for most programs would include a similar analysis, since funders and sector stan-

TABLE 8–3.   Case Volume and SU Costs

	S/I	*Ref*	*C/R*	*Cslg*
1. No. of SUs	1,052	448	342[a]	34
2. Total Direct Costs (TDC)[b]	$69,028	$68,525		$12,551
3. SU cost per TDC	$65.62			$369.15
4. Ratio to cost of SU in S/I	1:1	1:2.33		

[a] Includes 32 cases rerouted from Referral to this center.

[b] Remember that the costs for Mgt/Gen are *not* included in these Total Direct Costs.

[4] In all costing steps the still active cases are given the same weight as the other cases, although most of them would not yet have received the same amount of services. Agencies use various adjustments for costing such cases, depending on their patterns of service and so on.

dards typically require these kinds of basic summary data. Table 8–3 presents an overall view of program operations in which costs of throughput activities are related to the volume and flow of clients, and both are linked by service unit costs. Your completed figures should reveal that the amount of Total Direct Costs for a center obscures the amount of the average cost per case in that center. To grasp this point, compare the TDC with unit cost figures for S/I and then for Counseling. The ratio figures on line 4 express these relationships in a simplified comparable form. Thus, for example, it can be readily seen that it cost 2.33 times as much for a service unit in Referral as it did for one in S/I.

Step 2. You now know the SU cost of providing each kind of throughput service, but you do not yet know the actual patterns of resource consumption by the several groups of clients. Since clients accumulated *differing amounts* of SU costs, you have to determine "which services were provided to which and how many clients"; that is, the "client career" costs. These service pattern costs are pertinent at CYS because all of its clients who proceeded beyond S/I were served by other centers, and thus accrued additional costs. This is true of every program that admits its clients (or members, or the like) through some intake center before routing them to another service center. And it is not unusual for programs to provide two or more types of services to certain clients by design. Because the CYS program plan did not provide for multiple services to clients after their routing from S/I, it is important to account for the thirty-two clients that were first routed to Referral and then had to be rerouted from Referral to Consultation/Referral. They thus consumed more resources than planned and more than were consumed by similar clients who did not require the rerouting. All this has cost analysis implications that we shall consider later.

Step 2A. Therefore, using Table 8–4, you must now calculate the actual cumulative costs for all CYS clients using the Case Flow Diagram together with the SU costs from Step 1. For the "S/I and Referral only" pattern, for example, you *add together* the SU costs for each, which gives the cumulative SU cost; then multiply by the number of SUs to get the aggregate costs for this group. Note that the total of aggregate costs ($235,530) almost equals the sum obtained

TABLE 8–4.   Client Career Costs

Service	No. of Undupl. Units	SU Cum. Costs	Aggregate Costs	Percent of Total Costs	Percent of Undupl. Units
S/I only (230 + 30)	260	$65.62	$17,061	.07	.25
S/I + Ref only					
(448 - 32)	416	218.58	90,929	.39	
S/I + C/R only	310				
S/I + Ref + C/R	32	468.35			
S/I + Cslg only	34			.06	.03
Totals	1,052	n.a.	$235,530	1.00	1.00

Notes: Figures are rounded. The 230 clients in S/I only refers to those served who *did not* go on to any other CC; they consumed costs in S/I but left the program before receiving any other services. The 30 clients in S/I only refers to those accepted cases not yet routed out of S/I (i.e., active cases).

by adding the Total Direct Cost figures for these CCs *from line 9 of the Expense Summary* ($235,524)—but it is slightly off because of successive roundings for all cost figures. These two totals are the same because this method of breaking out costs recapitulates *all* the CYS centers' direct cost information (except Mgt/Gen). Some check figures are given, but you should fill in the missing data.

These service pattern costs reveal the great differentials in resource consumption by groups of clients. For example, the average or unit cost of the resources consumed by the group using S/I plus Referral only was not quite half the average or unit cost of the resources consumed by the group using S/I plus Counseling. After disaggregating and reaggregating these data, we have a perspective on the costs of program operations at CYS different from the perspective gained in Step 1. When we compare these results with the figures given in the previous table, we can see the additional costs accrued as clients were routed from S/I to other service centers. And we can see how each client group's proportion of the unduplicated total compares to its proportion of aggregate TDC costs. The percentage of clients served in S/I and Referral only was almost identical to the percentage of aggregate costs they consumed. The last two career groups listed show small differences between their percentages of unduplicated cases and aggregate dollars, but in both instances these clients consumed twice their proportion of throughput direct costs. We will focus on the thirty-two clients who had to be rerouted from Referral to Consultation/Referral because, as noted before, this was not part of the CYS service plan. Clearly, when seeking more cost efficiency, CYS would want to pursue the analysis of these "crossover" cases even further.

Step 2B. You are therefore asked to calculate *the total dollars and the percent of TDC* that could have been spent differently

1. If all crossovers had gone from S/I to Referral only and had not been rerouted to C/R
2. If all crossovers had gone from S/I to C/R *directly* without going first to Referral
3. If one-half of the crossovers had not been rerouted after going from S/I to Referral, and the other half had gone *directly* from S/I to C/R only

For alternative 1, for example, you would *add* all the crossovers to the S/I and Referral row. Each of the recalculations results in deletion of the S/I + Ref + C/R figures from the table and their reassignment to other centers and career patterns.

Program planners will have to decide how best to avoid crossover problems in the future, but this type of analysis can help them determine the costs of alternative solutions to such problems.

Step 3. Personnel represents the most important input resource in human service organizations, and programs and funders give high priority to knowing where and for whom these resources were spent. You thus continue the CYS cost analysis by calculating the *proportion* of Total Direct Costs in each CC that was expended on Salaries and Wages (excluding Fringe Benefits at this time).

Step 3A. This proportion (or for any line-item) is simple to calculate: You merely have to divide line 1 on the Functional Expense Summary by line 9 (TDC) for each CC. Enter the results on your worksheets.

The results show very much what you might have expected from this labor-intensive program with highly compatible services: that similar percentages of total resources were expended on Salaries/Wages in most CCs. Could you explain to someone why the proportion of Personnel costs for one CC is dissimilar from the others? The general similarities here would not necessarily hold for other programs, but the expected often gives proof of desired results. In this case they prove that CYS adhered in general to proportions originally allocated to the CCs in Chapter 6.

Step 3B. In the next few steps you begin to delve deeper into how and where these Personnel costs were consumed, and you start by determining the *personnel share* (still excluding Fringes) of the SU cost in each cost center.

The total Personnel costs for a CC divided by the total number of SUs for that center will give you the personnel cost per SU. *Select the correct Personnel costs per SU* in each cost center from the following list (which also contains incorrect figures):

S/I	$ 47.51	$ 47.01	$ 46.87
Referral	110.00	111.19	110.95
C/R	181.99	181.24	180.45
Counseling	243.12	242.66	243.88

Step 4. It must always be borne in mind that aggregate personnel costs represent a *mixture* of personnel with diverse tasks and at varying levels. Thus the aggregate and per unit costs of staff within service categories obscure the differential amounts of time (and their costs) among staff positions. Personnel resources are consumed as *staff time*, and the FTE measure is commonly used to denote how much and where staff time (input) was spent in service activities (throughput). In addition, the FTE measure has important program management applications, for example, to judge the deployment of staff resources and, as we shall see in Step 4B, for developing workload indicators.

Step 4A. You therefore continue your analysis of personnel costs by converting the staff dollars on each position line on the Functional Expense Summary into FTEs for each CC, and then totaling them. As you study the Summary, you realize that if a position line contains only 1.00 FTE, its costs across centers can be converted into FTEs with relative ease. For example, in S/I the dollars for the Program Coordinator represent a time equivalent of .17 FTE ($4,080 divided by

$24,000). If, however, a position line contains *more or less than 1.00 FTE*—like the Liaison Workers line—you *first* calculate the *average salary rate* for 1.00 FTE on that line and base your conversions to FTEs on that average salary in each CC. For example, the $58,905 for 3.32 Liaison Workers yields an average salary of $17,742.47 for 1.00 FTE, and this is the figure you must work with for your conversions on that line. Remember to retain all decimals in your calculator in performing these steps and to enter four-place decimals on your worksheets, or the subtotals will not balance.

Complete the following FTE chart on your worksheet; the information already on the chart has been included to help you check your results:

Personnel	Average Sal Rate per FTE	S/I FTEs	Ref FTEs	C/R FTEs	Cslg FTEs
1a. Prog. Coord.		.1700			.0400
1b. Scr. Sup.					
1c. Int. Wkr.	$18,577				-0-
1d. Lia. Wkrs.		.6970			
1e. Counselors				1.1760	
1f. Secys.	$12,187	.7450			
Total FTEs (rounded)		2.88			

When you complete the chart, you decide to look back at the Functional Expense Summary and note how the salary dollar figures obscured the actual staff time expended. Looking at the Counselor and Secretaries position lines in Referral on the Summary, you might have expected that the almost identical dollar figures meant that roughly similar amounts of staff time would have been expended by the staff on these position lines. However, your FTE worksheet shows that the Secretaries spent .131 FTE more than the Counselors—a difference of 30 percent. So if you are concerned primarily with *time* allocations, the FTE information is important; and if you are concerned primarily with *cost* allocations, you must also understand how the FTEs were allocated among positions at differing salary rates.

Step 4B. The FTE measure is often combined with a client measure, as a composite measure, to produce additional information. You are now asked to calculate the staff/client ratio for each CC, so that CYS will have the personnel workload information it needs for future planning (as in Example 1 in the chapter text).

When you fill in the missing data on the first two lines of the following table with (1) the total FTEs for each CC that you derived in Step 4A and (2) the total number of SUs from Step 1, your figures should produce the given staff/client ratios, and you should calculate the correct ratio for Counseling.

	S/I	Ref	C/R	Cslg
Total FTEs (rounded)	2.87	2.88		
Total no. of SUs			342	
Staff/client ratios (rounded)	1:367	1:156	1:93	

Do these workload indicators demonstrate that S/I staff were more efficient than other staff? That they were grossly overworked compared to other staff—especially those in Counseling? Or do they demonstrate in quantitative terms that the nature of the service activities called for differing kinds and levels of staff time across the centers? In the next step we look into this issue.

Step 5. Programs like CYS—and most others in the not-for-profit sector—exist to give services to clients, and those services are transmitted by staff efforts, that is, by staff time. How the time is spent can be separated into *contact and noncontact* time in an attempt to quantify its value for clients. Contact hours are considered to be of especially positive benefit for clients, and thus a breakdown of staff time by contact and noncontact hours is often desired by programs and required by funders.

Step 5A. This matter was included in the priorities list at CYS, and you set about collecting and collating the information. You have also been alerted to the fact that you will be better able to interpret the staff/client ratio (Step 4B) after this analysis is completed.

The exact definition of a contact hour varies among agencies and funders. A variety of equivalent measures are employed among widely differing agencies and programs to define and report uses of the staff time that are considered to be most productive for service results. For example, police departments typically distinguish between officers' time spent on patrol from that spent writing reports, receiving training, or appearing in court. Public schools distinguish teachers' time in classroom teaching from that spent in performing other duties. JYC has elected to define a contact hour as the time that staff spent directly with or on behalf of particular clients, comprising not only face-to-face interactions but also relevant telephone and family interactions (but excluding writing reports or communications, staff meetings, and so forth). CYS staff members recorded their activity time uses on a regular basis, and this information is available for both cost analysis and program replanning purposes. (Note: You should learn the equivalent definition accepted by your own employer and funder, if any.)

Your aim in this exercise step is to find out the *average number of contact and noncontact hours per service unit.* Before you can break out this information, you must determine first the total number of service hours and then the contact and noncontact proportions of these total service hours.

Therefore, (1) using the total *rounded* FTEs for each CC, (from Step 4A) multiplied by 1,900 hours, which is the yearly work/hour figure used by JYC, you first calculate the total work/hours for each CC. Then (2) using the staff activity files, you are able to establish the average proportion of contact to noncontact hours for each CC, which is reported as percentages of staff aggregate work hours in Columns 3 and 5 of the table below. First complete Column 1 using the data from Step 4A, and then calculate the remaining blank cells.

Service	Total FTEs x 1,900 = (Col. 1)	Total Work Hours (Col. 2)	Contact Hours		Noncontact Hours	
			% (Col. 3)	No. (Col. 4)	% (Col. 5)	No. (Col. 6)
S/I	2.87	5,453	.69	3,763	.31	1,690
Ref			.58	3,174	.42	
C/R			.62		.38	
Cslg		931	.72		.28	

With this table completed, you can now determine the *average number* of contact and noncontact hours per SU by dividing the number of hours in Columns 4 and 6 above by the total number of SUs in each CC. You complete the following tabulation.

Service	No. of SUs	Average No. Contact Hours per SU	Average No. Noncontact Hours per SU
S/I	1,052	3.58	
Ref	448	7.08	
C/R			
Cslg			

These data do not account for the varying proportions of contact hours between different positions or the mixtures of positions and personnel among CCs, but they do shed light on the staff/client ratios in Step 4B. Clearly the interactions between staff and clients in S/I and in C/R were of a different character, not just of a different magnitude. Whether contact reflects more complex tasks or less is not an issue you can resolve, but this measure does provide valuable information about the ways staff resources were expended, along with another view of program operations.

Step 5B. You can readily calculate the contact and noncontact *cost per SU* by applying the percentages in Columns 3 and 5 of the first table in Step 5A. For example, the Salaries/Wages cost per SU in S/I was $47.51, and the contact and noncontact shares of this cost—from Step 5A, Columns 3 and 5—were 69 percent and 31 percent, respectively. Thus, the contact hour cost per SU in Screening/Intake was $32.78 ($47.51 x .69); and the noncontact hour cost per SU was $14.73. Calculate the rest of these SU costs for the other CCs and enter them on your worksheets.

Step 6. In the previous steps you focused on different aspects of throughput measures; it is time now to turn to an analysis of the results (output) achieved with all the resources.

The main objective of the CYS program was to deflect boys and girls, confirmed as having difficulties, from the justice system either (1) by matching them with existing community organizations and resources that could give appropriate help in resolving their problems or (2) by direct counseling if it were deemed more appropriate than out-referral. To include the results of both courses of action in their designation of an output, CYS prepared a clear-cut definition of its criteria for the output measure, as follows:

For successfully referred clients (*placements*):

- The youth had to agree to go to the referral agency or resource.
- The youth had actually to arrive at the new agency.
- The resource had to accept the referred youth as its own client.

For the counseled clients (*successfully served*):

- The youth had to complete the series of counseling sessions to the satisfaction of the counseling staff.
- The Screening Supervisor had to "sign off" on the youth and close the file.

Step 6A. The records showed that there were 586 placements (336 from Ref and 250 from C/R) and 25 successfully served by Counseling. Thus, 611 of the unduplicated 1,052 SUs could be classified as output SUs.

The TDC per output can be quickly calculated:

$235,524 (excluding Mgt/Gen) ÷ 611 = $385 per output unit.

Of the unduplicated cases, what was the proportion of outputs?

Step 6B. Attrition is closely related to issues of productivity and efficiency, since resources expended on inputs and throughputs without commensurate outputs may demonstrate low productivity and an inefficient high cost per output. To probe this matter in the CYS analysis, you start by comparing the average cost per accepted case with the average cost per output case:

$235,524 ÷ 1,052 = $224 per unduplicated SU
(versus $385 per output SU).

When you find out the total amount that CYS spent on cases that were *not* successfully served, that is, throughput costs that did not produce outputs, then you will know the cost of attrition. Thus you calculate as follows:

1. Of the 1,052 unduplicated cases, how many were *not* outputs?
2. This number multiplied by the SU cost will tell you the total dollars of consumed resources that did not result in outputs.
3. What proportion of TDC does this amount represent? That proportion is the CYS attrition level; its converse is its success or productivity level.

Step 6C. It should be stressed in any discussion of attrition that its causes are almost as diverse as the clients themselves, and attrition is inevitable in every human service program. Clients will leave town, get sick, become discouraged, lose interest, be overwhelmed by other problems, and so on. And some service programs are deliberately hospitable at intake or admissions, believing it preferable to allow later winnowing by the clients themselves or by staff. Despite these realities, attrition has such serious cost implications for all not-for-profit organizations that they must constantly seek to examine and improve their productivity. You are therefore urged to estimate how much the output cost could be *reduced* if the number of output cases were increased by 10 percent. The 10 percent figure was based on staff judgment of the proportion of the youth who "almost made it" and were unsuccessful because they were not handled as well as they should have been—and can be in the coming year.[5]

You estimate that *if all costs remain the same*, and the 611 outputs are increased 10 percent to _____ (fill in), then the new per output cost would be $_____, for a reduction of $34 per output.

Step 7. To satisfy one JYC Board member's pessimistic view of future funding possibilities, the Director and the Program Coordinator reluctantly agreed to explore the consequences of reducing personnel costs by eliminating the In-

---

[5] All this must not be confused with the idea of increased efficiency through greater volume. We cannot go into this complicated issue, which depends on all sorts of other factors—especially fixed versus variable costs. However, we do assert that in the service sector more volume does not necessarily reduce per unit costs.

take Worker's position. Such a serious issue would also have to be reviewed from important program perspectives, but you are asked to analyze the cost effect of such a step on the Total Direct Costs and on the SU cost in Screening/Intake, since practically all the costs of the Intake Worker were consumed in that CC. In addition, you are to point out any other important consequences for cost or for services. Again, you must assume that all other costs will remain the same.

You immediately recognize that the $14,490 salary cost of the Intake Worker does not represent the total costs for that position. The Fringe Benefit costs of $2,898 must be included as well. The Expense Summary shows that $15,997 of these salary costs were consumed in S/I (13,331 + 2,666). If this subtotal cost were deleted, the Total Direct Cost for S/I would be $53,031, a reduction of _____ percent; and the current SU cost for S/I of $65.62 would be reduced to $_____ or by 23 percent (fill in).

As requested, you ponder the ramifications of deleting an important personnel position.

- Can you assume that *without* the Intake Worker, S/I could handle the same number of clients?
- How will the Intake Worker's responsibilities be handled? If more time must be spent in S/I by the Liaison Workers, what happens to their efforts in the other CCs?
- It is clear from the various analyses that the crossover problem had an expensive effect and must be rectified. Will this be possible if the Intake Worker is eliminated, since S/I was involved in this problem?
- What other problems and ripple effects on the number of clients served in all CCs can you anticipate?

Having completed all these exercise steps, you are satisfied that you have a more thorough understanding of how the parts of the total program and fiscal experiences relate to and affect each other. As you plan and then move through the next fiscal period, you will be far more aware of the links among operations, clients, staff, resources, and results.

9

DISTRIBUTION OF SUPPORT COSTS

THE FIRST ATTEMPTS at requiring fiscal accountability from not-for-profit agencies—especially from those receiving public monies—focused on disentangling and identifying management/administrative kinds of costs, which might or might not include overhead, fundraising, and other support expenses. Despite the lack of efficient methods for distinguishing such costs, it was recognized and accepted that they must be explicitly noted and accounted for as proportions of total expenses. It has thus become standard practice for service agencies to separate and expressly indicate these costs (sometimes following the arbitrary formula of a funding organization).

The need for applying the principles of cost accounting to government-funded service programs has gradually become understood and is more and more a fact of life. Functional budgeting and unit-costing procedures are required more extensively, not only by government agencies and departments but particularly by private insurance companies that reimburse programs for client services. Thus programs have been forced to define and refine their "real" costs. Further, as government and private funding become tighter and costs continue to rise, funders are ever more selective and demanding. For example, a funder might decide to "buy" only a specific "piece" of a program. It is not willing to pay more than its "fair share" of the support costs of the entire program. The funder wants more than the agency's verbal assurance that it will truly be paying only its fair share; it wants fiscal documentation of that fact. In addition, funders want to be able to compare the costs of Program A with those of Program B. To do so, they need some evidence that both programs use approximately the same methods of costing and include the same ranges of costs.

Agencies also have begun to examine the advantages of computing and distributing the support costs equitably. For example, they could judge resource consumption by the various program components more accurately; their budget projections could be based on more comprehensive fiscal information; they could use multiple funding sources more efficiently and to the best advantage of the agency and its clients; they could more clearly define and justify their "true" costs and thus set more realistic, reliable rates and fees; and so on. Since support resources are expended as part of the total actual cost of providing services or doing business, they must somehow be accounted for and incorporated into that homogeneous measure, the service unit cost.

Hospitals were the pioneers in developing procedures for allocating and distributing support costs.[1] Pressures from insurance companies, as costs escalated, forced the hospitals to seek ways to designate and clarify nonrevenue (support) costs and then to distribute them rationally and consistently among the revenue (production) centers. The allocation and distribution methods detailed later in this chapter are derived from hospital procedures. More and more frequently, not-for-profit organizations are required by private and government funders to comply with such procedures (see Copeland, *Managing Federal Money for Children's Services. Manual 4* [New York: CWLA Hecht Institute, 1978]).

In this chapter we focus on the logic and methods for allocating and distributing these real costs, which cannot be

---

[1] See American Hospital Association (1968) and National Institute of Mental Health (1972).

directly assigned to specific activities by routine cost accounting. Only *a full year's* retrospective (that is, historical) expense data are used in these procedures. But the information derived from carrying out the procedures will contribute to a better understanding of total program operations and can importantly influence forward planning.

After a brief review of types of support costs we shall examine in detail the currently used allocation and distribution methods and demonstrate the procedures through illustrative examples. In the exercise section we shall return to the CYS program and concentrate on allocating and distributing its unassignable support costs.

UNFINISHED BUSINESS

In Chapter 8 we learned how to use case, staff, and fiscal records to define and cost out units of service. At the end of a fiscal period we were able, by the techniques detailed there, to determine the amount and the proportions of a program's resources consumed by each cost center. However, administrative and other support expenses *were not included* in determining service unit costs. Clearly, then, we have not yet calculated the *full cost* of a service unit. The Overhead support costs at CYS were determined for each cost center only by an arbitrary formula (18 percent of Total Direct dollars) that cannot precisely reflect *actual use* of these Overhead resources; and Management/General expenditures were identified only by line-item use, not by their actual consumption by the functional categories. We know full well that CYS spent the Management/General and Overhead dollars in support of its services to clients (production). But these costs could not be attributed directly to client services on the basis of standard accounting practices—at CYS or at any other agency. It is essential, however, that these support expenses be included for a program, an agency, a funder, or a potential purchaser of service to know the *full cost* of a service unit. Therefore we must learn to use available current methods for fully incorporating support expenses into service unit costs.

If not done earlier, a final thorough review of case and staff records and line-item expenditures should be undertaken to see if any outstanding support center (SC) costs can be further assigned and distributed to production centers. This *final line-item assignment of expenses* will, of course, be limited since most support costs are by their very nature unassignable directly. However, this final review may reveal some justifiable reassignments to the production centers. For example, another look at staff/fiscal records might show that some equipment costs remaining in a Management/General support center could be further assigned among all the other centers by a more careful assessment of their respective uses of the equipment. Or a record review might indicate that more of a staff member's time should properly have been assigned to specific production activities. Or a review of case/staff records might show a more precise way to assign to the production centers some of the supply costs remaining in a Management support center.

In none of these examples is the actual cost of a person's time or an item at issue—those responsible for accounting procedures will have ensured the accuracy of the costs. We are concerned only with the *assignment* of the cost to the proper cost center, hence we recommend merely a reasonable, limited effort to uncover the more obvious reassignments. When this final line-item review is completed, the remaining support center costs that are unassignable by standard procedures must be allocated and distributed by other techniques.

SUPPORT CENTERS

Let us backtrack for a moment and recall that support centers are distinguished from production centers in that they serve all other centers and are indispensable to the program or the agency as a whole. Their activities are not aimed at directly serving clients or the final products of the organization. Their name, support, most appropriately defines their function: to sustain and uphold all other centers. To illustrate, let us note again the most common sorts of support centers and the most common activities attributable to each.

- *Management/General   (Administration):* Overall program management; preparation of funding proposals;
  negotiations with funders; development of contacts and
  arrangements with outside groups and organizations;
  review of budget and management of revenue and expenses; maintenance of relations with funders and
  parent organization; supervision of staff, including
  meetings; development of internal policies; resolution
  of conflicts inside and outside agency; preparation of
  fiscal and other reports; and so forth

- *Indirect Costs (Overhead)*[2]: Representative of the proportional burden of costs borne by the parent organization (or other accepted controlling agency, like a university) in support of the activities of each of its subsidiary
  programs: includes fiscal supervision and operations
  (payroll, accounting, and so on); insurance; legal and
  audit fees; fundraising; upkeep of buildings and
  grounds; provision of utilities; capital depreciation;
  data processing of records; libraries; and others

- *Fundraising* (if carried out by the responsibility center
  itself rather than by the parent organization; common
  in the private sector, but usually disallowed by government funders): development of promotional campaigns,
  special events, and solicitation drives; distribution of
  public relations information

- *Admissions and Records:* Screening of new clients;
  record-keeping for all clients and other centers; handling of third-party reimbursements from Social Security, Medicaid, and insurance companies; development
  and operation of information systems for maintaining
  records, and so forth

It should be pointed out that the *Standards* (National

---

[2] Funders dislike and sometimes disallow this category, preferring that all costs be
reckoned as direct costs. However, the federal government and many state funders
may permit those programs, projects, and units under the aegis of a larger
organization to assign certain defined costs to such a category. The issue of indirect
costs remains an irritating, familiar problem, and funders' frequent changes in
rules and regulations reflect their search for more satisfactory solutions to the
issue.

Health Council et al., 1974) and the United Way (1974) recognize only Management/General and Fundraising as support centers. However, many not-for-profit organizations will have legitimate, distinctive kinds of support costs and, depending on their size, prefer to substantiate such costs by assigning them to separate support centers. For example, a large organization may have separate SC categories for accounting/financial operations; personnel/payroll; operation/maintenance of plant; membership maintenance; cafeteria; evaluation and assessment; and so on (further examples of SC categories will be given in a later section).

Internal Time/Resources Proportions

This brief review reaffirms our understanding of *what* support costs consist of and *why* they are needed, which brings us to the core question: *How* can we incorporate them reasonably and equitably to determine the full cost of a service unit? A commonsense logic underlies the principal methods that have been developed to accomplish this. Simply put, this logic seeks to connect the consumption of support resources to the distinctive functions of each cost center. That is, cost centers *differentially use* the resources available *from* the support centers. For example, in a day care program the activities of the Education/Child Care production center may consume far more of the resources of the Administrative support center than do the activities of the Food Service production center. In an art museum, the Special Exhibits production center may consume more of the resources of the Fundraising support center than the Permanent Acquisitions production center. Therefore, it is essential that the methods we use to allocate and distribute support center costs to the other cost centers reflect these real differential consumption patterns.

Dollar figures alone cannot reveal the relative consumption of resources among a program's cost centers. For example, if we knew that Management/General had $5,000 of unassignable costs, we would have no idea how much of that $5,000 was used in support of Production Center A (PC-A) versus Production Center B (PC-B). Therefore, we must find a way to apportion to PC-A and to PC-B their fair share of the $5,000, using a base that reflects the function of the support center relative to the functions of each of the two. Since support centers serve all the cost centers and the agency as a whole, the standard techniques for attributing costs to a production center—time logs, purchase orders, travel vouchers, and so on—are of only limited help, and we must seek additional methods.

A Note of Caution.   The procedures detailed in the following sections may at first seem complex, but we make every effort to explain and illustrate them step by step and urge readers to persist patiently. One principal mental hurdle must be overcome at the outset: Readers must accept the idea that the costs remaining in these support centers are not *directly* assignable to the other cost centers on the basis of their actual consumption, *yet they must be assigned and distributed* to these CCs to determine the total cost for a service unit. Since all direct, simple assignments have already been made (e.g. by purchase orders, case records), we must resort to more complicated, arbitrary devices that will serve our purposes rationally and defensibly. Throughout the rest of the chapter we concentrate on these currently approved devices.

Two different, specific terms are used throughout to distinguish two different procedural goals, and readers must keep them in mind.

Allocation is the term we use to describe the methods for *apportioning shares* (percentages) of support center resources equitably among the other cost centers.

Distribution is the term we use to describe the methods by which the shares allocated to each cost center are converted into *dollar amounts* so that total service unit costs can be determined.

Each cost center must first be allocated its proportionate share of support resources. Only then will we have a rational basis on which to distribute the dollar amounts.

Allocation Bases

The most accepted methods for allocation are based on estimations of *the proportion of internal time and resources expended* by each support center vis-à-vis all other cost centers (both support and production centers). So as our first task we must find an appropriate, comprehensive device by which we can estimate the proportions of support time and resources expended *from* one support center *to* all the other cost centers and, conversely, determine the proportions received by each cost center from all the support centers. All present-day methods of allocating SC costs are based on this *from–to* concept.

A device we call the *Internal Time/Resources matrix* serves to organize the estimated allocated shares of from–to exchanges into a cohesive whole from which we can later calculate dollar distributions. But on what foundations can we construct reasonable estimates of these proportions for our matrix? The Internal Time/Resources (IT/R) proportions have to be predicated and developed on *bases* (that is, specific activities or characteristic missions) that are appropriate to both the particular SC to be allocated (from) and the other support and production centers (to). The bases must therefore pertain to actual program activities and processes; must take into account the distinctive cost center functions; and must reflect program operations, types of services, staff roles and activities, and so on.

Common sense and administrative practicality also play a part in determining consistent, defensible bases and estimates. Different SCs will typically call for different allocation bases, and sometimes one SC may properly use a mixture of bases. Concrete examples of the use of various allocation bases will be detailed and amplified as we work through this section. But an illustrative case might be helpful at this point.

Our first task is to decide on the allocation base that will most appropriately denote the character and mission of the support center under consideration. Once this base is determined we can begin to estimate IT/R proportions for that SC. Thus, for an Admissions and Records support center in a hypothetical XYZ program we might well decide that *the number of cases admitted* will serve as a reasonable base. This base legitimately reflects the mission and the activities of this SC relative to all other cost centers, so it is defensible. Also it can be consistently applied, so it is administratively practical.

Once the base is selected, we can begin determining the percentages of the total number of admitted cases that were subsequently served by the other CCs in the program. At this point still another factor must be considered. We have to recognize that some activities of a support center can *never* be reasonably, defensibly, or consistently allocated to any other cost center. Therefore, we must distinguish between (1) the regular, ongoing, basic activities and responsibilities that flow *from* an SC *to* all the other CCs and (2) those "in process" or occasional special activities that must at this point still remain attributed to the SC itself. Remember, these support costs were unassignable in the first place, so it might well be expected that some of them will defy our initial efforts to apportion them to the other CCs.

For our illustrative XYZ case let us say that during the fiscal year the Admissions/Records support center admitted a total of 1,450 clients, most of whom were routed to the various production centers within the program. A review of the number of units routed to and served by each cost center plus, if necessary, an examination of the case records tell us that PC-A received and served 500 of the admitted cases, PC-B received and served 300 cases, and PC-C received and served 400 cases. But this program has one other support center—Management/General—in addition to the Admissions/Records center (which we will call SC-1). Therefore, we must also—using this same base—estimate what proportion of Admissions/Records (SC-1) activities can be fairly designated as support *to* the Management/General support center (SC-2) and what proportion may still have to remain unassigned in SC-1. A study of agency selective screening operations might show that 100 cases were routed to Management/General for resolution of particular policy problems and that SC-1 itself still had 100 cases "in process" plus 50 other cases that it had handled and then turned away. Thus, 100 cases can be attributed to SC-2, and 150 cases must still, at this point, remain attributed to SC-1.

We now have all the information we need to determine the proportionate use of Time/Resources from SC-1 to all the other cost centers using the number of admissions as the allocation base. These same proportions will later be used to distribute the unassignable dollars in the Admissions/Records SC. But first we must convert the number of cases we have assigned to each of the other CCs into allocated shares (percentages) of the total number of cases. Thus, of 1,450 cases

SC-1 (Adm/Records) itself	served	150 cases or	10 percent
SC-2 (Mgt/Gen)	served	100 cases or	7 percent
PC-A	served	500 cases or	34 percent
PC-B	served	300 cases or	21 percent
PC-C	served	400 cases or	28 percent
		1,450 cases or	100 percent

We now see how we used the record information as a *base* to estimate allocated shares of IT/R percentages *from* SC-1 *to* all the other cost centers. Since Admissions/Records deals primarily with the flow of cases, we clearly chose the best possible base. Different measures will be chosen as allocation bases for different support centers, depending on the nature of the support services each provides. One should always try to find the base that best represents the purpose, character, and activities of each support center in its role of providing assistance to all the other CCs. Table 9–1 illustrates (in alphabetical order) some of the variety of credible, relevant allocation bases for different kinds of SCs. In this list some support services have been partitioned into separate categories to demonstrate the point. But large organizations may well need a number of such sub-categories. Remember these bases apply *after* all directly assignable costs have already been accounted for.

In our experience, agencies will choose one base—more often than not it is the percentage of total direct dollars per CC—and use it as the allocation base for every support center. In large part this base is selected because the whole concept of allocating unassignable support costs is not well understood, and this route seems the simplest. We do not oppose this allocation base *per se* but do believe other bases may better denote the true nature of a program's support services and thus will more accurately reflect these costs. The total direct cost base should be used if no other base is as reasonable or practicable.

Since not-for-profit organizations are primarily labor-intensive, the FTE allocation base often seems a logical choice. We shall give a condensed example of the method used to determine Internal Time/Resources proportions with FTEs as the base. (Readers will find this base also used in the exercises at the end of the chapter.) When we use FTEs as the allocation base, we assert that the resources that

TABLE 9-1.   Suggested Allocation Bases for Support Centers

Support Centers	Reasonable Allocation Bases per Cost Center Use
Accounting department	Total direct costs
	Number of financial transactions
Box office	Numbers of tickets sold
Computer services	Data processing time
Director's office	FTEs
Fundraising/Development office	Total number of clients
	Total direct costs
General administration	FTEs
	Staff hours
	Staff dollars
Housekeeping department	Square footage
	Staff hours
Laundry and linen	Pounds of laundry processed
	Pounds of fresh linen issued
Library reference department	Number of requests for service
Payroll department	Number of jobs or positions
	Staff hours
Overhead	Total direct costs
	Total labor hours
Plant maintenance	Square footage
	Work orders
Publications department	Number of items printed, distributed, or sold
Research/Evaluation section	Data analysis costs

came *from* the support center were consumed relative to the personnel time and effort expended within each of the other cost centers, and that FTEs therefore represent a justifiable analogue of actual resource use.

Let us look again at the hypothetical XYZ program and use FTEs as the base to develop the Internal Time/Resources proportions for its Management/General (SC-2) support center (Admissions/Records was SC-1).

The XYZ end-of-year cost analysis summary showed that the program expended a total of 22.25 FTEs on all its activities and that these 22.25 FTEs were consumed by each cost center as follows:

SC-1	SC-2	PC-A	PC-B	PC-C	Total
2.00	1.70	5.25	5.55	7.75	22.25

This FTE base is translated into IT/R proportions by the procedure shown in Table 9–2.

TABLE 9–2. Conversion of FTE Base to Internal Time/ Resources Percentages

FTEs Consumed By	FTE Base	Percent of Total 22.25 FTEs	Rounded Percent for IT/R
SC-1 (Adm/Rec)	2.00	.0898	.09
SC-2 (Mgt/Gen)	1.70	.0764	.08
PC-A	5.25	.2359	.23
PC-B	5.55	.2494	.25
PC-C	7.75	.3483	.35
Totals	22.25	.9998	1.00

Note: We use four decimal places in calculations and only round in the final step; rounding may necessitate adjustments to obtain exactly 100 percent.

We can now put together the proportions we had developed for SC-1 with those for SC-2 and will have the IT/R matrix for the two support centers in the XYZ program (Table 9–3).

TABLE 9–3.   IT/R Matrix of Proportions for XYZ Program

To	From SC-1	From SC-2
SC-1	.10	.09
SC-2	.07	.08
PC-A	.34	.23
PC-B	.21	.25
PC-C	.28	.35
	1.00	1.00

Two different allocation bases were used to construct this matrix. Each was appropriate to the purposes and activities of the support center to which it was applied. The conversions to the IT/R proportions were straightforward, and in both cases only simple arithmetic was needed.

The IT/R matrix for the XYZ program is all set up now, but before any actual dollars can be distributed, one more problem must be solved.

Since the whole point of the allocation process rests on

the need *to distribute completely* all the unassignable costs of a support center, *nothing* can be left in an SC when the allocation/distribution process is finished. If we look at the IT/R matrix just constructed for the XYZ program, we see that 10 percent of Internal Time/Resources could not be allocated to any other cost center and still remains, unallocable, in SC-1. We seem to have arrived at an impasse. On one hand we were unable to allocate the 10 percent to the other centers, but on the other hand we *must* distribute all the dollars represented by that 10 percent. We have to find a way to eliminate this 10 percent remainder before we can begin distributing the dollars. We accomplish this by making the other cost centers *absorb* the support center's remaining 10 percent share (or whatever share) *in proportion to the shares already allocated to them from that SC*. Only when this absorption is completed can we begin distributing the dollars. The same applies to the 8 percent remaining in SC-2.

A simple arithmetic expedient will assure that each CC gets its proportionate share of the to-be-absorbed IT/R remainder in an SC.

1. *We determine the total allocated after excluding the share of the SC that must be absorbed.* For example, if 16 percent must be absorbed from the SC, the total that was allocated is 84 percent; if 20 percent must be absorbed, the total allocated is 80 percent.

2. *We take each cost center's IT/R allocated percentage of the whole to determine its proportionate share of the allocated total.* For example, if a CC has an IT/R allocation of 12 percent of the whole and the total allocated in the IT/R is 84 percent, its share of that total is 12/84. If it has an IT/R share of 15 percent and the allocated total is 80 percent, its share of the total is 15/80.

3. *We now convert each CC's share of the IT/R allocated total (e.g. 12/84 or 15/80) to a percentage so that we can find out its equivalent share of the 100 percent total.* When all the CC's allocated shares have been converted to equivalent shares of the 100 percent total, we will have absorbed *all* the Time/Resources remaining in the SC. To convert the fraction to a percentage of the whole, we divide, for example, the 12 by the 84 and get .1428 or 14 percent; or the 15 by the 80 = .1875 or 19 percent.

4. *We thus know that the 12/84 share of the IT/R allocated total is equivalent to 14 percent of the new absorbed total.* Or if its share of the allocated total is 15/80, its percentage of the total is 19 percent, and so forth.

5. *Therefore we can now allocate 14 percent of the total SC resources to that CC and know that it has absorbed its proportionate share of the SC's unallocable Time/Resources. We call this 14 percent the absorption rate.* With all the proportions that include absorption in hand (which will add up to 100 percent), the distribution of dollars can begin.

Let us see how this applies to the XYZ Admissions/Records SC-1, in which some unallocable resources still remain (Table 9–4). In this example from the XYZ matrix we followed the steps just listed to *absorb* the 10 percent remainder in SC-1: (1) We determined that 90 percent of SC-1's Internal Time/Resources had been allocated; (2) we determined the fraction of that allocated total that had been received by each CC (7/90, 34/90, and so on); (3) we converted these fractional shares to their equivalent shares of 100 percent of SC-1's IT/R (.0777, .3777); and (4) we got a final rounded percentage for each CC (.08, .38) that includes its proportionately absorbed share of SC-1's unallocable IT/R share.

TABLE 9–4.   From SC-1 XYZ Program

To	*IT/R Percent*	*Absorption Rate*	*Percent of Total to be Distributed*
SC-1	(.10)	-----	-----
SC-2	.07	7/90 or .0777	.08
PC-A	.34	34/90 or .3777	.38
PC-B	.21	21/90 or .2333	.23
PC-C	.28	28/90 or .3111	.31
	1.00		1.00

Note: The percentage to be absorbed is always shown in parentheses to distinguish it from the others; all final numbers are rounded here.

We can now use the percentages in the final column to distribute *all* of SC-1's dollars to the other centers.

To summarize this rather complex section: We learned how to select an appropriate base for establishing the proportion of Internal Time/Resources that flowed *from* each support center *to* all other cost centers; by means of the selected bases we constructed an IT/R matrix that showed the proportions of each SC's unassignable Time/Resources that were allocated to the other cost centers; and finally we learned how an SC's unallocable IT/R share could be proportionately absorbed by these other CCs.

After all these tasks are completed, a program can move on to one of the several methods for distributing the actual dollars involved. But no matter which of the following distribution methods is chosen, the Internal Time/Resources matrix, using appropriate bases, remains the foundation for the process. How much of the information in the IT/R matrix is used will depend on which method is chosen, as detailed in the next section.

Current Distribution Methods

Four main methods for carrying out support cost distributions have evolved in the past few years. They are, listed from the simplest to the most complex:

- Direct Distribution method
- Stepdown method
- Double Distribution method
- Algebraic (Simultaneous Equation) method

Which of these four methods is chosen by a program will depend on its assessment of a variety of factors, such as the requirements of the funder, the complexity of the budget, the number of support centers, the rate-setting information desired, and so on. "Playing games" with these methods to increase reimbursements from a particular funder is occasionally attempted under the guise of "practicality." Clearly this subverts the entire procedure.

As we work through these distribution methods, bear in mind that we are left with *only* those support center costs that could not be specifically and directly assigned to the other cost centers, and that for any of the four distribution methods we must have an Internal Time/Resources matrix built on sound allocation bases. We are now about to achieve our main goal: *to distribute the actual unassignable dollars of support centers and thus to find out the full cost of each service unit.*

DIRECT DISTRIBUTION METHOD

To explain the three most common distribution methods we shall conjure up another hypothetical agency and examine each method in detail. Let us say that this agency has three support centers and four production centers and that the matrix of IT/R proportions shown in Table 9–5 has already been developed on appropriate bases for the three support centers. For our purposes here it is not important to know what these are.

TABLE 9–5.   Illustrative IT/R Matrix

To	Proportions from Support Centers		
	SC-1	*SC-2*	*SC-3*
SC-1	(.05)	.05	.05
SC-2	.05	(.15)	.05
SC-3	.10	.05	(.15)
PC-A	.30	.20	---
PC-B	.20	.15	.35
PC-C	.20	.15	.05
PC-D	.10	.25	.35
	1.00	1.00	1.00

Note: For all Tables in this section, the proportions in parentheses could not be allocated to other CCs and must be absorbed by them; and all figures are rounded.

Direct Distribution is the simplest and least comprehensive of the four methods. In this method distributions are made from SCs *only* to production centers. Therefore, all IT/R percentages between SCs are ignored, and the production centers must *absorb the costs of every SC in each column of the matrix,* not just the SC whose costs are being distributed. Thus in our illustrative example only the bottom part of the IT/R matrix can be used for distributing support center costs by the Direct Distribution method. To simplify the discussion, only the proportions for SC-1 are detailed here:

To	IT/R Proportions from SC-1
PC-A	.30
PC-B	.20
PC-C	.20
PC-D	.10
	.80

Now that we have established how much of the table we shall use for Direct Distribution, we can begin actual distribution of the unassignable *dollars* in our illustrative SC-1.

Let us assume that SC-1 had a total of $10,000 in unassignable funds. This $10,000 is now to be distributed among the production centers. Note, however, that in the Direct Distribution method we must do something about the 5 percent, 5 percent, and 10 percent of IT/R shown for SC-1, SC-2, SC-3, respectively. We know that we must absorb the percentage left in SC-1. But now we realize that in this method the production centers must *absorb all* the percentages allocated to all the SCs—in this case 20 percent. The principle of absorption discussed in the previous section applies in each of the three methods we shall illustrate. In this example we proceed as we did for the XYZ example, and we thus allocate 30/80 or .375 of the $10,000 to PC-A, and so on, with the result shown in Table 9–6.

TABLE 9–6. Direct Distribution from Illustrative SC-1 ($10,000)

To	IT/R Percentage	Absorption Rate		Total Dollars Distributed
PC-A	.30	30/80 = .38	x $10,000	$ 3,800
PC-B	.20	20/80 = .25	x $10,000	2,500
PC-C	.20	20/80 = .25	x $10,000	2,500
PC-D	.10	10/80 = .12	x $10,000	1,200
	.80	1.00		$10,000

The same procedures are used to distribute unassignable costs from each of the other SCs. In this hypothetical example we end up with a complete Direct Distribution table (Table 9–7). Only the absorption rates are shown, since we

TABLE 9–7.   Illustrative Direct Distribution
(for three SCs: total budget $185,420)

To	Final Direct Costs	From SC-1 Abs Rate	$	From SC-2 Abs Rate	$	From SC-3 Abs Rate	$	Total Costs
PC-A	$ 50,000	.38	3,800	.27	2,003	-----	--------	$ 55,803
PC-B	40,000	.25	2,500	.20	1.484	.47	2,350	46,334
PC-C	62,000	.25	2,500	.20	1.484	.06	300	66,284
PC-D	11,000	.12	1,200	.33	2,449	.47	2,350	16,999
	$163,000		10,000		7,420		5,000	$185,420

need these to calculate dollars. Readers can readily refer back to the IT/R matrix (Table 9–5) for the originally allocated proportions. The column headed "Final Direct Costs" refers to the total dollars actually expended by the production centers themselves.

In this table we distributed all SC costs. If you add the amounts distributed from the SCs across each row to the final direct costs for each PC (e.g. $3,800, $2,003), you get the total costs for each PC. Then add these sums, and you get the total budget for this agency ($185,420) now completely distributed just to the production centers by means of the Direct Distribution method. We now know the full and final cost of each production center after its fair shares of support center costs have been allocated and distributed by this method.

Stepdown Method

We have just accomplished our goal of distributing all unassigned SC costs, leaving none of these costs in any SC. However, since the IT/R proportions and costs *between SCs* are ignored in the Direct Distribution method, the final cost figures produced from this method only partially reflect the actual consumption of resources between centers.

The next and more complicated method—Stepdown —uses more of the IT/R information, and distributions are made to other SCs as well as to the PCs. However, it does not "yield a unique solution" (Copeland, 1978, p. 38), that is, it does not provide one and only one solution. In fact, a number of alternative total dollar costs are possible in Stepdown, because the final total costs depend on the *order* in which the unassignable funds from the SCs are distributed.

In Stepdown a decision must be made about the *relative amounts* of Time/Resources *given by each SC to the other centers*. This decision is highly important, because the total final costs in Stepdown are based on the *sequence* of cost distribution from the SCs. The SCs have to be ranked, and the distribution sequence should begin with the SC that gives the *most* of its Time/Resources to the other centers and receives the *least* Time/Resources from them. The "most" and the "least" refer to the proportions allocated in the original IT/R matrix, but we must point out that the scant literature available is not precise about this "most" and "least" issue. We recommend that only proportions *between* SCs be considered in making this decision about the order of distribution. Therefore, the SC that "gave the most" *to the other SCs* and received the "least" from them should be distributed first; that SC that "gave the least" to the other SCs and received the "most" from them should be distributed last. The ones in between have to be ranked in the most reasonable order possible. This issue will be further explored in the exercises when we tackle distribution at CYS. Despite the defects of Stepdown, it is a popular and acceptable method.[3] But when setting up IT/R proportions, the consequences and ramifications of the ordering must be borne in mind if Stepdown is to be used.

The next important fact to understand about Stepdown—and this relates directly to the ordering—is that as soon as the funds from any SC are distributed, that SC must be *closed down*. That is, it can no longer receive any distribution (funds) from any other SC, even if the IT/R matrix shows that it had indeed received support from the other SCs. For example, note that our illustrative IT/R matrix (Table 9–5) shows that SC-1 had received 5 percent from SC-2 and 10 percent from SC-3. Once SC-1 is distributed, it is closed down,

[3] Sometimes when an agency gets funds from several sources, and one or more of them have specific "item eligibility" requirements, the agency may be able to order its SCs to achieve the highest rate of reimbursement. However, care must be exercised not to misrepresent or distort Stepdown for this purpose. We emphasize that SCs must be ranked immaculately and with propriety when using this distribution method.

and nothing more can be distributed to it. Therefore, both the 5 percent from SC-2 and the 10 percent from SC-3 will have to be absorbed by the other unclosed centers. This is a critical aspect of the Stepdown method and relates directly to the ordering of the SCs.

After a support center is closed down, the SC next in the most–least ranking has its costs distributed among the centers remaining open. Hence the name Stepdown.

The relevance of the order of distribution now should be clearer. If, for example, we did not at first carefully discriminate among the SCs and did not start with the most comprehensive one, we might get to the second (or third or fourth) support center in the distribution process and realize that a large proportion of its costs ought properly to have been distributed to an SC that is already closed down. Since that SC cannot be reopened, we might have to start all over again with a different rank order. The closing down mechanism will be further discussed as we move along. But first let us refer again to our illustrative example and look at the IT/R proportions in SC-1, which we shall use to illustrate the Stepdown method. Note that this differs from the earlier Direct Distribution method, where no distributions could be made *between* SCs. Here we distribute from the SC to all other cost centers, including other SCs that have not yet been closed down.

To	IT/R Proportions from SC-1	Absorption Rate
(Itself)	(.05)[a]	---
SC-2	.05	.05
SC-3	.10	.11
PC-A	.30	.32
PC-B	.20	.21
PC-C	.20	.21
PC-D	.10	.10
	1.00	1.00

[a] To be absorbed.

After SC-1 is distributed using the absorption rates and closed down, the proportions of the IT/R matrix for SC-2 will be distributed. However, SC-2 now has an additional 5 percent (owing to the absorption factor) that it received from the distribution of SC-1. The dollar equivalent of this additional percentage becomes part of the funds of SC-2 that must be distributed. Since all costs in SC-2 must also be eliminated, these additional funds will be absorbed and distributed during its phase of the Stepdown process. The same holds for SC-3, as it does for whatever number of SCs are involved.

COMPUTING COST DISTRIBUTION IN STEPDOWN

We are now ready to begin to convert the percentages shown in our illustrative IT/R matrix into actual dollars and must consider the *order* of distribution. Since the whole point of Stepdown is to improve the scope of the distributions, remember that distributions are made *between* some SCs in this procedure.

Given three SCs, we have six possible ways to order them:

1-2-3	2-3-1	3-2-1
1-3-2	2-1-3	3-1-2

With more SCs the ordering possibilities greatly expand. These six ways of ordering the SCs will yield six different sets of final production center costs, which is why this method does not produce a single or unique solution. (You might want to calculate the distributions with a different ordering.)

Looking back at the IT/R matrix in Table 9–5, we can see that the order of Stepdown in this illustration should be: SC-1 first, followed by SC-2, and then by SC-3. SC-1 gave the most—15 percent—to the other SCs and received the least, 10 percent. SC-2 gave the next most to the other SCs—10 percent—and also received 10 percent from them. SC-3 gave the same to the other SCs—10 percent—but received the most, 15 percent.

We therefore start the Stepdown procedure by distributing all of SC-1's costs. Following the absorption principle, the 5 percent ($500) unallocable from SC-1 is proportionately shared by all other centers. After the dollars have been distributed, SC-1 is closed down, and its IT/R shares from the other SCs will have to be absorbed by all remaining cost centers. Also note that when SC-2 has to be

**TABLE 9–8.   Illustrative Stepdown Distribution
(for Three SCs: Total Budget $185,420)**

To	Final Direct Costs	From SC-1 Abs Rate	$	From SC-2 Abs Rate	$	From SC-3 Abs Rate	$	Total Costs
SC-1	$ 10,000	(10,000)		-----	--------	-----	--------	
SC-2	7,420	.05	500	(7,920)		-----	--------	
SC-3	5,000	.11	1,100	.06	475	(6,575)		
PC-A	$ 50,000	.32	3,200	.25	1,980	-----	--------	55,180
PC-B	40,000	.21	2,100	.19	1,505	.47	3,090	46,695
PC-C	62,000	.21	2,100	.19	1,505	.06	395	66,000
PC-D	11,000	.10	1,000	.31	2,455	.47	3,090	17,545
	$185,420		10,000		7,920		6,575	$185,420

distributed, the amount it received from SC-1 during its distribution must be added to SC-2's final direct costs; and SC-3 will have accrued additional dollars from the distributions of both SC-1 and SC-2.

DOUBLE DISTRIBUTION METHOD

There are two important problems with the Stepdown method: (1) a high dependence on the distribution order, which precludes a single, "unique" solution, and (2) only partial distribution can be made between support centers because of the "closedown" feature.

The Double Distribution method attempts to solve the second problem. This is accomplished by first distributing *all* the costs in each SC to *all* other centers, based on the IT/R matrix, *without closing down any SCs.* After this first distribution stage is completed, the additional sums apportioned to the SCs are redistributed by the Stepdown method. During the second (Stepdown) stage, the SCs are closed down one at a time after their new costs are distributed. Thus the ordering of SCs still remains an important factor. Table 9–9, using our same example, will help to clarify the Double Distribution method. Note that in neither stage do the SCs retain their own share of the IT/R proportions; these percentages of Time/Resources are again absorbed by the other centers—in both stages—so that all SC unassignable funds can be eliminated. Table 9–9 looks more complicated

TABLE 9–9.   Illustrative Double Distribution

First Stage: SC Distribution Without Closedown

To	Unas-signed Funds	From SC-1 Abs Rate	$	From SC-2 Abs Rate	$	From SC-3 Abs Rate	$	Newly Dis-tributed Costs
SC-1	$10,000	-----	--------	.06	445	.06	300	745
SC-2	7,420	.05	500	-----	--------	.06	300	800
SC-3	5,000	.11	1,100	.06	445	----	--------	1,545
PC-A		.32	3,200	.23	1,706	----	--------	4,906
PC-B		.21	2,100	.18	1,336	.41	2.050	5,486
PC-C		.21	2,100	.18	1,336	.06	300	3,736
PC-D		.10	1,000	.29	2,152	.41	2,050	5,202
	$22,420		10,000		7,420		5,000	$22,420

Second Stage: Stepdown of Newly Distributed Costs with Closedown

To	Newly Dis-tributed Costs	From SC-1 Abs Rate	$	From SC-2 Abs Rate	$	From SC-3 Abs Rate	$	Final Total Costs
SC-1	$ 745	(745)		-----	------	----	------	--------
SC-2	800	.05	37	(837)		-----	------	--------
SC-3	1,545	.11	82	.06	50	(1,667)		--------
PC-A [50,000]	4,906	.32	238	.25	209	----	------	55,353
PC-B [10,000]	5,186	.21	157	.19	159	.17	788	16,590
PC-C [62,000]	3,736	.21	157	.19	159	.06	101	66,153
PC-D [11,000]	5,202	.10	74	.31	260	.47	788	17,324
	$22,420		745		837		1,677	$185,420

Note: All figures rounded. Dollars in brackets indicate original final direct costs expended by each production center.

than it really is. In the first stage all SC costs are distributed (with absorption) according to the original IT/R matrix. In the second stage the Stepdown method is applied *only to the costs distributed in the first stage.* When all the SCs have been closed down, their total costs will have been completely distributed to the production centers. The final column thus shows the accumulated total now incorporated with the PCs' original costs, and we can determine the *full* cost of a service unit.

Now let us compare the final service unit costs resulting from distributions by the three methods in this illustrative agency (see Table 9–10). For convenience, the budget dollar totals are omitted, but they can be readily found in the text.

No dramatic differences appear, but we must recognize we are dealing with a small number of units. Double Distribution is not used as frequently as the other two methods, perhaps because it requires extra calculations. However, since it accounts better for Time/Resources expended between SCs, it may give a more accurate picture of final unit costs. For example, looking at Table 9–9 we see that Double Distribution indicated that SC-2 used resources of $8,257 (7,420 + 800 + 37). In Table 9–8, however, the Stepdown method showed a total resource use for SC-2 of $7,920 (7,420 + 500). Not highly significant, perhaps, but indicative of probably important differences when large numbers of cases or service units—or large sums—are involved. For example, in PC-D the 73 cents of difference between unit costs in Stepdown and Double Distribution represents only a 1 percent difference. But if a large number of units were involved, this could add up to a sizable sum of money (.73 x 6,000 cases = $4,380). Also, the $1.82 unit cost difference between Direct Distribution and Stepdown for PC-D could result in an appreciably higher total cost: $1.82 x 6,000 cases = $10,920.

Unless a specific method is required by the parent agency or funder, a program can choose to use any of the three distribution methods for the fiscal year. With experience, it

TABLE 9–10.   Illustrative Comparison of Final Service Unit Costs (by Three Distribution Methods)

	No. of Units	By Direct Distribution	By Stepdown	By Double Distribution
PC-A	1,200	$46.50	$45.98	$46.13
PC-B	800	57.92	58.37	58.24
PC-C	750	88.38	88.00	88.20
PC-D	300	56.66	58.48	57.75

will be able to determine which method best accounts for its support costs and is also administratively practical.

ALGEBRAIC METHOD

The Algebraic method, also called the Simultaneous Equation method, is considered the most accurate and produces a "unique"—one and only one—solution. For details of executing this method, we recommend that you read *Managing Federal Money for Children's Services, Manual 4* (Copeland, 1978), pp. 56-67. To summarize here: The method requires solution of a series of algebraic equations by means of which all costs between SCs, as well as each one's share, can be more satisfactorily determined and then totally distributed. The method requires computer techniques and may well become more frequently used as computer availability becomes increasingly widespread. The comparison between unit costs given as the example in *Manual 4* does not show significant dollar differences between the Algebraic and the other methods. But that does not negate its possible superiority.

The Algebraic method also *does not* account for transfers of Time/Resources between production centers. Procedures for handling these important transfers, in fact, have not yet become standardized or practicable. It has been suggested that production centers should be structured so that they give as little as possible of their Time/Resources to each other, but we hesitate to recommend that as a feasible management policy.

Exercise Problems

In these exercises we build on the cost analysis in Chapter 8 and allocate and distribute the support center costs at CYS to find out the full service unit costs.[4] CYS is well aware that

---

[4] The exercises here differ from those in other chapters; they are aimed solely at practicing the procedures detailed in the text. These procedures are not difficult in and of themselves, and by working through them in their essentially prescribed order, you will develop the skill and confidence to apply them.

it must know its full SU costs, but in addition certain events have occurred that underscore the need for this information.

At the end of the third quarter of the FY the JYC Board received notice from the CYS funding body about changed requirements for all programs seeking continuation support for the next year. These requirements are detailed in Chapter 10, together with the Board's actions relating to the CYS program. Among the most important changes are (1) the funder's requirement that cost analysis information become part of all applications for program refunding, and (2) its expectation that other revenue sources be developed to support any significant program enhancement or expansion.

The JYC Board, its Director, and the CYS Program Coordinator have already spent considerable energy and time seeking other funding sources, but there appear to be no sources willing to make a fixed sum award like that given by the present funder. However, CYS can now demonstrate its ability to provide distinctive, effective services to its target age group, and another local agency has shown some interest in "buying" services—not yet precisely determined—for a certain number of its clients, perhaps sometime during the next fiscal year. The results of full service unit costing will help meet the funder's requirement and also provide the information needed to advance discussions with the local agency. So CYS goes to work to generate this information.

To provide a total SU cost figure for the potential purchaser of services, CYS has to conform to that agency's accounting procedures and regulations. However, since CYS has kept good case, staff, and fiscal records, it can reassemble these basic data to satisfy the requirements of both the purchasing agency and the original funder.

In this application of the procedures described in the chapter text, we shall adhere to the stipulations laid down by the potential purchaser, which differ from those of the original funder in one critical aspect only:

- The possible purchaser regards Screening/Intake as a *support* center that serves as a necessary first step toward what it considers the true production activities—Referral, Consultation/Referral, and Counseling. Therefore, in this exercise we shall disregard the SU costs for Screening/Intake established in the Chapter 8 exercises and treat S/I strictly as a support center, along with Management/General and Overhead.

Internal Time/Resources Proportions at CYS

The Final Line-Item Assignment

CYS examined its records one last time to see if further support costs could be *directly assigned to the line-items;* some direct assignments might have been overlooked or not precisely known earlier. The unassigned costs left in each of the SCs—by line-item for Mgt/Gen and S/I and by function for Overhead—are shown in the Functional Expense Summary in the Chapter 8 exercise section.

The reexamination of the records produced the following modifications:

- Some of the expenses for Professional Fees in S/I—now considered an SC—really belonged in Referral and Consultation/Referral, because the money had been spent on staff consultations about special problems with particular agencies, whose cooperative relations were needed to assist clients in these two services.

- More than one-half ($1,600) of the $2,700 copying machine and typewriter maintenance costs (Equipment), which had been entirely charged to Mgt/Gen, were reassigned among the other cost centers based on a review of the logs kept of machine use and repair bills.

The review produced no other reassignments, and with these changes the final *Functional Expense Summary* showed the following Total Direct Costs (line 9 on the budget form plus Overhead):

S/I	Ref	C/R	Cslg	Mgt/Gen	OH
$69,453	$69,013	$85,907	$12,751	$10,345	$44,544
		Total budget:	$292,013		

It is not necessary to present the entire Summary here. To simplify the readers' tasks, any changes in SU costs resulting from this final revision are accounted for in the SU costs given later. Any case flow and Personnel FTE information needed will be restated in the appropriate exercise steps; these data do not differ from those given in Chapter 8 exercises.

ALLOCATION BASES FOR THE SUPPORT CENTERS

CYS must now select an allocation base for each of its three SCs, choosing one that is appropriate, administratively convenient, consistent with the particular responsibilities of the SC, and thus defensible.

Management/General.   After considering several possibilities (TDC, service hours), it was decided by the Program Coordinator that the expenditures of staff time and effort, denoted by staff FTEs, best represented the principal activities of this center in relation to the other CCs. The PC further concluded that the nonpersonnel items in this category were typically consumed in proportion to the expenditure of FTEs. TDC and square footage were rejected as indefensible when a more pertinent base was available. You calculated the FTEs for each cost center in the Chapter 8 exercises. Of the 10.22 total, 2.87 was consumed by S/I, 2.88 by Ref, 3.69 by C/R, and .49 by Cslg. Mgt/Gen consumed .29 FTE; *however*, a portion of this .29 was expended on activities *not directly* related to CYS. For example, the PC (with secretarial help) spent time advising the JYC Board and Director on a funding proposal for another possible JYC program; a fair amount of time was also spent by the PC (with the SS) on an assessment of JYC's overall policies on personnel practices. As a result it was determined that .06 of the .29 FTEs should properly be assigned to Overhead.

S/I.   This cost center's principal function in support of all other CCs consisted of determining which potential clients should be accepted and, if accepted, to which services they should be routed. Every client who received any kind of service at CYS had first to be processed through S/I. It was thus readily decided that the *share* (proportion) of the total number of cases *routed* to each CC represented the most appropriate and comparable allocation base for this center. As described in the Chapter 8 exercises, 1,052 cases were accepted by S/I, of which 792 were *routed* as follows: 448 to Referral; 310 to Consultation/Referral (the 32 crossovers were not routed to C/R from S/I); and 34 to Counseling. These same numbers will now be converted into *proportions* for the IT/R matrix. Further, an examination of the remaining 260 cases showed that 30 were still "in process" in S/I, and could not be assigned to any other CCs, and 230 exited. Of these 230, 20 represented a type of case that required a further interpretation of admissions policies from Mgt/Gen. CYS's arrangements with the juvenile court would have been jeopardized if Mgt/Gen had not clarified S/I policies regarding this kind of case. Thus, the costs for these 20 should properly be assigned from S/I to Mgt/Gen.

Overhead.   The costs for this category were determined differently from those of the other CCs in the original budget: The funder had required that the *total* OH costs be set by an arbitrary formula of 18 percent of all Total Direct Costs. Thus, the Overhead costs for each functional center had to be based on this 18 percent formula, although OH resources were not necessarily consumed at that rate by each center. But given this requirement, each CC's proportionate consumption of TDC is the only allocation base that is defensible. The potential purchaser of service is not particularly pleased about this and would have preferred a more definitive allocation base to obtain more precise total SU costs. However, neither JYC nor CYS has any record information about how Overhead resources were consumed by the CCs, so this base must stand. The JYC Director agreed to consult its accountants to try to find a way to itemize or record OH costs in the future.

CONSTRUCTING THE INTERNAL TIME/RESOURCES (IT/R) MATRIX

CYS has now determined the following three bases and can begin allocating shares from each support center for the IT/R matrix.

- Mgt/Gen: the proportion of FTEs consumed by each CC
- S/I: the proportion of cases routed to or served by each CC
- OH: the proportion of Total Direct Costs consumed by each CC

A Word of Caution: To simplify the presentation of the IT/R charts below, we give rounded figures at each stage. When constructing an IT/R matrix for your own organization, be sure to retain all the decimals until the final rounding.

Step 1. The PC, with the help of an administrative staff person in the JYC Director's office, has already begun developing the allocations from each SC, because you have been busy with other important tasks associated with the end of the fiscal year. You are now asked to finish this task by filling in the missing cells. Those cells that are to remain empty are designated by xxx in every chart.

Step 1A.   IT/R Proportions from Mgt/Gen

To	FTE Base	Percent Total FTEs	IT/R Proportions
Mgt/Gen	.23	.0225	(.02)[a]
S/I	2.87		.28
OH	.06		
Ref	2.88		
C/R	3.69	.3611	
Cslg	.49	.0479	.05
	10.22		1.00

[a] To be asborbed.

Step 1B.   IT/R Proportions from Screening/Intake

To	No. of Cases (Base)	Proportion of Total Cases	IT/R Proportions
Mgt/Gen	20	.0190	.02
S/I	240[a]	.2281	(.23)
OH	xxx	xxx	xxx
Ref	448	.4259	.43
C/R	310		.29
Cslg	34		
	1,052 undup. cases		1.00

[a] Includes 30 total active cases still pending plus 210 that exited *after* Screening but *before* routing to PCs.

Step 1C.   IT/R Proportions from Overhead

To	TDC	Proportion of TDC	IT/R Proportions
Mgt/Gen	$ 10,345	.0418	.04
S/I	69,453	.2807	
OH	xxx	xxx	xxx
Ref	69,013	.2789	.28
C/R			
Cslg			.05
Total	$247,469		1.00

Step 2. *Ordering the Support Centers.* Before the allocated shares in the matrix can be used to distribute support dollars to the production centers, the *order* of distribution must be decided, since the order can become a significant factor in the Stepdown and Double Distribution methods. The rule for ordering the SCs was given in the chapter text:

> Distribute first from the SC that gave the *most* services (that is, shares) to the other SCs and received the *least* from them; rank the others by the same rule down to the last SC, which *gave the least and received the most* from the other SCs.

Step 2A.   You find this rule confusing and are not exactly sure how to apply it to constructing the CYS matrix. After thinking it over, you conclude that the "most" and "least" must refer to the shares given to the other CCs—not just to the other SCs. Acting on this premise, which is the order of distribution you decide upon?

Step 2B.   Because you are still not absolutely sure that you understand the rule, you consult an administrative person at JYC to confirm your ordering. She explains that the currently available literature is ambiguous on this matter, but the rule is interpreted at JYC to refer to the "most" and "least" *between SCs only*, because one important aim of the distribution process is to recognize and account for the resources exchanged between SCs.

With this clarification, you reexamine each SC chart and judge that the proper ordering of distribution should be as follows:

- SC-1 should be Overhead, which gave 32 percent to the other SCs and received 1 percent.
- SC-2 should be Mgt/Gen, which gave 29 percent to the other SCs and received 6 percent.
- SC-3 should be S/I, which gave 2 percent to the other SCs and received 56 percent.

Step 3A. You now begin to construct the matrix on your worksheet by relabeling and reordering the SCs. Next you transfer the IT/R proportions from the individual charts to the matrix.

Step 3B. As you get ready to start distributing the dollars in the SCs, you realize that the matrix on your worksheet—with its correct ordering of the SCs—does not show dollar amounts for any of the CCs. You must now add a column showing the dollar totals from the Final Revised Functional Expense Summary (see beginning of this exercise section).

Step 3C. Check your worksheet matrix with Table 9–11. If any of your figures are different, review your work on the previous steps.

Step 4. In the Direct Distribution method, which you now want to apply using the matrix, support center costs can be distributed only to the production centers, even though the matrix may show allocations from one SC to another SC.

TABLE 9–11. CYS IT/R Matrix

| | | Percentages Of | | |
Cost Centers	Total Dollars	SC-1[a] to	SC-2[b] to	SC-3[c] to
SC-1 (OH)	$ 44,544	xxx	.01	xxx
SC-2 (Mgt/Gen)	10,345	.04	(.02)	.02
SC-3 (S/I)	69,453	.28	.28	(.23)
PC-A (Ref)	69,013	.28	.28	.43
PC-B (C/R)	85,907	.35	.36	.29
PC-C (Cslg)	12,751	.05	.05	.03
Total	$292,013			

Note: Parentheses indicate percentages still remaining unallocated in an SC. All figures rounded.

[a] Allocated by proportion of TDC.
[b] Allocated by proportion of FTEs.
[c] Allocated by cases handled.

Therefore the *absorption* problem must be faced and re-solved. You review this topic in the text and firmly fix in your mind the principle of absorption:

> **The SC proportions on the matrix must be absorbed by the production centers so that all the dollars in the SCs can be distributed. In the Direct Distribution method, absorption occurs at the outset; in the Stepdown method, absorption occurs as you step down and distribute from each SC.**

The percentage in a support center is absorbed by each production center in proportion to the share each was allocated on the matrix so that all the PCs together can be charged with 100 percent of the costs of a support center.

Step 4A. For this step, the exemplary model in Table 9–12 should be useful for *practicing* calculating absorption rates. After you have completed the table by filling in the blank cells, you will be ready to work with the actual CYS data.

TABLE 9–12.   Absorption from an SC

Matrix Allocation to	Percent	Absorption Rate	Rounded
PC-1	.25	25/80 = .3125	.31
PC-2	.20	20/80 =	
PC-3	.35		
	.80		1.00

Step 5.   You are now ready to establish the actual proportions *with absorption from* each support center at CYS *to* each production center and distribute these support dollars by the *Direct Distribution* method. Remember that in this method all IT/R shares *between SCs* must be absorbed by the PCs alone.

Step 5A.   You have set up a Direct Distribution table (Table 9–13) based on the IT/R matrix and need only to fill in the missing cells.

TABLE 9–13.   Direct Distribution to Production Centers

	From SC-1 ($44,544)		From SC-2 ($10,345)		From SC-3 ($69,453)	
	Absorption Rate	$	Absorption Rate	$	Absorption Rate	$
PC-A	.41	18,263	.41	4,242	.57	39,588
PC-B	.52	23,163		5,379	.39	
PC-C	.07		.07			2,778
	1.00	44,544	1.00	10,345	1.00	69,453

Step 5B. The *full* service unit costs obtained by Direct Distribution can be calculated now for each of the three production centers at CYS. You divide the full dollar costs by the number of cases served by that PC. Fill in the missing cells in Table 9–14.

TABLE 9–14.   Full SU Costs by Direct Distribution

	Final Expense Summary Costs	Distributed Dollars	Total Costs	No. of Cases	Total SU Costs
Referral (PC-A)	69,013	62,093		448	292.65
C/R (PC-B)	85,907		141,536		456.57
Cslg (PC-C)	12,751	6,620	19,371	34	
			$292,013		

Step 6. The PC wants to make doubly sure that CYS can quote the fairest and most comprehensive per service case charge to a potential purchaser-of-service. Therefore, you are asked to proceed with your calculations and distribute the SC costs by the Stepdown method.

Step 6A. You have already determined the ordering of "most" and "least" (Step 2B), so you get right to work on the Stepdown chart (Table 9–15). Note that (1) the absorption rate is different for this method because you are including some of the costs transferred *between* SCs (as per the IT/R matrix) and (2) as you move through the stepping down order, the dollars accumulated through these transfers must also be absorbed and distributed. Fill in any missing cells on the chart.

TABLE 9–15. Stepdown Distribution

	To Be Distributed	From SC-1		From SC-2		From SC-3		Total Distributed
		Absorption Rate	$	Absorption Rate	$	Absorption Rate	$	
SC-1	44,544	(44,544)		xxx	xxx	xxx	xxx	xxx
SC-2	10,345	.04	1,782	(12,127)		xxx	xxx	xxx
SC-3	69,453	.28	12,472	.29	3,517	(85,442)		xxx
PC-A	xxx		12,472		3,517	.57	48,702	64,691
PC-B	xxx		15,591	.37	4,487	.39		53,400
PC-C	xxx		2,227	.05			3,418	6,251
	124,342		44,544		12,127			124,342

Note: Parentheses indicate SC dollars that must be absorbed by other CCs during distribution process. Nothing had to be absorbed from SC-1, since everything was allocated to the other CCs. However, observe carefully that because of the closedown feature of Stepdown, those shares from SC-2 and SC-3 to other SCs (see matrix) could *not* be distributed to them.

Step 6B. Using the same format as in Step 5B, determine the total service unit costs resulting from the Stepdown method and record them on your worksheets.

Step 7. Someone at JYC was curious enough to use the Double Distribution method, so you can now compare if and how the different distribution methods affect the total SU costs.

Step 7A. Table 9–16 compares final SU costs. You fill in those for Direct Distribution and Stepdown from your calculations in Steps 5B and 6B. The table shows that at CYS, except for Counseling, the results from the three methods do not show large dollar differences. This may well be due to the disparity between the "most" and "least" allocated between the SCs; that is, in this case, little or nothing was allocated to Overhead or Management/General, so the stepping down and closedown had little effect.

TABLE 9–16.   Final Total Service Unit Costs at CYS

	By Direct Distribution	By Stepdown	By Double Distribution	Greatest per Unit Difference
PC-A (Ref)			298.93	$ 6.28
PC-B (C/R)			450.48	$ 7.19
PC-C (Cslg)			542.35	$27.39

The CYS example, however, should alert us to the value of going beyond Direct Distribution, especially when either or both of two conditions exist:

1. Large numbers of SUs are involved.
2. Exchanges between support centers are pronounced or extensive.

Let us look at examples of the effect of both these conditions.

1. A $5.00 difference between two methods, multiplied by 1,500 clients, could have important cost implications. It could add or subtract $7,500 from the cost of providing a particular service, which could certainly be significant when planning and defending a budget or arranging a purchase-of-service contract.

2. To illustrate the second condition, let us say that certain specialized equipment is maintained and charged to the

Planning SC of a city unit and that the central municipal government also used that equipment on numerous occasions for other centers. The cost of the city's other uses should be borne by Overhead—not by the Planning SC—and shares should be apportioned to those other PCs on the basis of their consumption of Overhead costs. This, at least partially, occurs in Stepdown and Double Distribution. However, in Direct Distribution these resources, really consumed by Overhead, are absorbed by the production centers as a cost of Planning, since exchanges between SCs are excluded in this method. This could have serious effects on budget planning and on determining charges for services, since one type of support may be made to carry an unfair burden not based on the true uses of its resources.

The added calculations needed for Double Distribution may or may not be worth the trouble if neither of the two conditions exists. However, we recommend that since a unique solution is not possible with any of these methods, both Direct Distribution and Stepdown should be applied. After comparing the results of both, the program manager can decide which method better expresses the consumption of support costs—but it will still remain a matter of judgment.

10

CONTINUATION BUDGETING AND BEYOND

IN THIS CHAPTER we bring together all the knowledge, understanding, and procedural skills gained from previous chapters and reinvest them in the tasks of developing and submitting a funding reapplication for the next fiscal year. Up to now we have only been looking toward this occasion, being thoroughly busy with the current year's efforts, but this point marks the real beginning of the next full budget cycle. We refer to this phase as "continuation budgeting." "Renewal" is perhaps a more appropriate term, because, as we shall see, there must be a renewal of the program and its financial support, not just a carryover of old patterns.

This chapter differs from the others in several ways. First, instead of presenting one main procedure with its related techniques, we *reapply* known procedures in various combinations. Second, instead of having an exercise section, the familiar CYS program is used as the main model for explaining the processes and procedures associated with continuation budgeting. Readers are also invited to think through certain problems on their own. And third, we move slightly *backward* in the fiscal year to address issues of *forward* planning.

The last point calls for amplification. Previously we introduced each main procedure at approximately the point in the budget cycle or fiscal year when it might have actually been applied and assumed all the needed data were available. But budget development for a succeeding fiscal year must be done *during* a current year to secure uninterrupted continuing support. Thus replanning and reapplication tasks must be completed while the current year's operations are still under way, *before* year-end expense/revenue experiences are fully known, and well before the information from a full year's cost analysis is available. So we now turn backward in time to the point when forward planning should start and consider first the problems and limitations this schedule imposes on all aspects of our tasks.

Major Steps in Continuation Planning and Budgeting

Agencies and programs typically begin rebudgeting work sometime during the third quarter of the fiscal year, depending mainly on when the next budget application(s) must be submitted to the funder(s).[1] The length of the lead time depends on the complexity of the process and the numbers of persons and decisions involved. Here we briefly list the main steps in the continuation budgeting process but hold off detailed discussion for the moment. This list reasserts a fundamental and now familiar theme of this book: Budgeting and fiscal matters are always linked with program and operations, and both must be treated together.

- *First*, collating and reviewing all available current year's expense/revenue experiences
- *Second*, collating and reviewing all program and operational experiences to date
- *Third*, ascertaining and noting *changes* in agency or funder policies and mandates, statutes or regulations, community conditions, client or target population characteristics, and other external developments

[1] Funders' deadlines for submission of continuation or renewal applications vary greatly, of course. Some require receipt of the application three or even four months before the next fiscal year; others set earlier due dates. Subsidiary units of local governments or state agencies, however, may not need to submit their final budget requests until the beginning of the last month of a current fiscal year, but this has usually been preceded by several preliminary reviews through finance officers and higher administrators.

- *Fourth*, identifying and forecasting problematic, likely, and potential revenues for the coming year
- *Fifth*, determining tentative program and budget "targets" that incorporate desired (or expected) changes in both service activities and fiscal conditions
- *Sixth*, evolving a definite program and budget plan for the next year, using a series of approximations, and seeking necessary approvals as work proceeds
- *Seventh*, submitting the completed program and budget application to the funding source(s)
- *Eighth*, revising program and budget proposals in light of funder decisions or subsequent changes in program/fiscal experiences

As Wildavsky (1974) has observed, the budget is, in turn, a plan, a contract, and a precedent. At this point it should be clear that the current year's budget—and program operations—have involved much planning and have been managed with careful attention to the contractual nature of the funding awards that supported it. All this now serves as *precedent* for the next year's program, budget, and funding. The precedent will be extremely unpromising for continuing support, of course, when a program has not honored the assurances given in the original application and the award notice, or when budgeted funds have not been properly and prudently managed.

The Situation with CYS

The continuation budgeting process can be much better understood if we pose matters in fairly concrete terms, using the Community Youth Services and emphasizing common, nonidiosyncratic elements and implications. We know the situation that was confronted and resolved early in the seventh month of CYS's fiscal year. Let us assume that the JYC Director and the CYS Program Coordinator had long ago established a definite schedule for continuation budgeting steps, using the funder's deadline of the first day of the tenth month as the date for submitting the full reapplication. The midyear budget review described in Chapter

7, then, would have been especially critical, since only about seventy calendar days would remain between that review —in the middle of the seventh month—and the new submission dates. We shall refer to this as the *interim period*. It is also reasonable to assume that preliminary cost analysis efforts were begun during this short interim period both for program/budget control and for renewal preparations.

Recalling the four-month startup period, which preceded the current fiscal year, we shall assume that sufficient time has now passed to return to some of the uncertainties with which the CYS program was launched and, further, that the funder expects to see these squarely addressed in the reapplication (see Chapter 4). By this time the PC will also have some definite information about the program's strengths and limitations, and about the vulnerabilities of its emerging cost patterns. For example, progress reports on all aspects of the CYS program had to have been made periodically to the JYC Director and the Board, as well as to the funder; and the Monthly Expense Summaries would have alerted the PC to a variety of cost problems in time to make adjustments.

Given all this, we now learn that the JYC Board has undertaken a policy review of CYS and has determined that its Counseling component is neither fully compatible with the primary community orientation nor defensible from a cost effectiveness viewpoint. Despite objections from some CYS staff, the Board has decided that this component must therefore be terminated at the end of the current year. It has asked for recommendations about how some of the kinds of youth being served in this CC might be handled through other program services and how its resources could be shifted to the other CYS centers to improve their productivity, effectiveness, and efficiency. An important, necessary program change can thus be ameliorated somewhat by seeking to retain and reinvest the support that might otherwise be lost.

About this same time the funder has notified its recipient agencies of new regulations affecting all budget requests and awards for the next fiscal year. Of these, four are most important: (1) Cost analysis information—including service unit costs or estimates—must be included in all future funding requests, but agencies can phase in adoption of these costing procedures over two years; (2) all applicants for continuation funding must demonstrate that they have begun to examine the productivity and cost effectiveness of their programs and are attempting to make the changes needed to improve both; (3) all funded programs must introduce a "reasonable" client fee schedule, and these revenues must absorb at least half of any TDC *increases* proposed in continuation budgets; and finally (4) no additional support will be provided for any program enhancement or expansion, but applicants are encouraged to seek supplementary revenues through purchase-of-service contracts, provided these are full-funded and consistent with each program's aims and integrity.

These are stringent and demanding regulations. Indeed, they may seem unduly harsh and impossible to fulfill. We have introduced them deliberately, however, as illustrative of the kinds of changes in expectations and requirements actually faced by agencies, whether they are dealing with governmental funding sources, foundations, or general contributions. Let us reduce them to their essential and typical terms: (1) budgeting based on more precise and standardized cost information; (2) emphasis on program productivity and cost effectiveness of services; (3) no reduction in support but no funding for program improvement; and (4) movement toward alternative sources of support, including client fees and reimbursement contracting. However difficult it may be to meet these new terms, they are certainly preferable to large-scale program retrenchment or even termination, which will concern us at the end of this chapter. And at least this funder has not (yet) denied any adjustments to meet rises in market costs.

Clearly it will be necessary to make significant changes in the CYS program and services, and even greater changes in its fiscal patterns and procedures. The JYC Board decision to eliminate the CYS Counseling component parallels and anticipates the funder's requirements regarding cost effectiveness standards in future applications. And the new necessity of applying cost analysis data to continuation budgeting is directly in line with the client fees requirement as well as with the possibility of initiating purchase-of-service contracts, since both ought to be based on the same kinds of data, as mentioned in Chapters 8 and 9.

Continuation Budgeting Procedures

With an eye to circumstances such as those confronting the CYS program, we shall walk through the main steps outlined for preparing a continuation budget. Keep in mind that this is the interim period, which spans late month seven through month nine of the program's FY. Long before this time a detailed budget calendar should have been developed, clearly specifying when tasks must *begin* as well as when they must be *completed*. Otherwise, staff are likely to find themselves recruited at the last minute to "drop everything" to help perform some essential task. Of course, this is likely to be the very time when they are also preoccupied with other duties. The result is frantic scurrying at the last minute to throw things together and meet the deadline—which somehow popped up while everyone was busy providing services. In addition, someone should have been designated to monitor the efforts and keep track of the material handed in.

COLLATING EXPENSE/REVENUE EXPERIENCES

Perhaps the most straightforward aspect of expense experiences pertains to the differences between actual market costs for many objects and earlier line-item price estimates. The original cost estimations for all items and elements are in the approved budget document (or backup files), and expense experiences—the actual prices paid—are available from accounting records. The *differences* between these figures should have been noted by management staff during the previous months. Many costs may be higher, but they probably did not rise uniformly; other costs will be the same as expected, or even lower. The monthly budget reviews should have also alerted the program manager to differences in levels or rates of *consumption* (utilization) of line-item resources over the long and the short terms. This compendium of cost information is an enormous advance over what was available when the preliminary budget was being prepared, unless it has been ignored, lost, or misfiled. Thus, past and current market cost information is available *plus* accumulated experience about this program's actual consumption of all items. The fiscal management practices discussed in Chapter 7 are obviously critical for accumulating the kinds and amounts of information we must now rely on.

Planners can assemble these sets of information and ready them for use during later steps in the process. They can also begin to summarize them making certain assumptions (e.g. those resulting from the latest monthly review; no change in program resource needs or uses; no change in market costs) and start initial projections of the next year's resource requirements.

All costs peculiar to the current year or not expected to recur in the next year should be earmarked and set aside. In the case of CYS, for example, one-time-only expenses associated with equipping and launching the new program and any startup costs that continued beyond the first four months should be set aside. (Single source funders are as aware of these "nonrenewable" kinds of costs as agency personnel, so it would be necessary to clarify whether the CYS funder intended the coming year's Total Direct Costs to be reduced proportionately.)

We asserted in Chapter 5 that cost centers must be established before the start of the fiscal year. Thus, client, staff activity, and cost information *must* have been continuously collected during the preceding months, and appropriate service and other units *should* have been defined some time ago. Therefore, preliminary cost analysis methods can now be applied during this interim period with the understanding that only approximations are possible, given the lag in expense accounting and the absence of a full year's operating experience. Despite these limitations, many of the procedural difficulties with costing should have been resolved earlier, and program planners can begin to put together important parts of their unit costs. Funders usually understand such difficulties and will often accept tentative unit cost figures if they are assured that the program is making a genuine effort and that reliable end-of-year unit costs will be presented promptly.

A similar collation and review, and perhaps summarization, should be set in motion with regard to program *revenues*. We have concentrated throughout on single-source funding and a set annual award, but readers relying on other kinds of funding patterns should be well aware of the information needed and developed about revenues, which often directly parallels that for expenses. Patterns of fee and charge payments, reimbursements, contributions, and other kinds of revenue must be examined in the same terms: actual to date compared with initially estimated, and so on.

With this work of collation and review under way, we can turn our attention to program matters.

COLLATING PROGRAM/OPERATIONS EXPERIENCES

We assume records and files have been maintained about all main aspects of program patterns: numbers and types of clients served and services performed, client and workflow patterns, staff activity and time uses, and patterns different from those projected in the approved contract.

We now have considerable recorded information about the particular kinds of youth coming or being referred to CYS, their circumstances and concerns, the availability (and limitations) of community resources for assisting them —and the accessibility or willingness of these resources to accept the out-referred youth. We also know much about the concrete ways in which staff deal with these youth and with outside units: how long it usually takes to reach intake decisions, actual practices in "matching" individuals to particular resources and in obtaining other organizations' cooperation, as well as perceived shortcomings in these and other aspects of CYS operations. It is hoped that we have found it possible to summarize these kinds of information so one can see beyond the trees to the forest—that is, can identify *patterns* as well as idiosyncratic variations among persons (staff as well as clients), situations and problems, practices, and the like. Even if the year to date has worked out much better than anticipated, it will certainly be *different*, and we must be able to apply this information systematically to planning for the next year.

> • *A note on departures from plans and projections:* We have stressed the importance of comparing *actual*

fiscal and program experiences with the plans, estimates, and projections detailed in the approved budget documents. The contractual and precedental implications of these matters have already been pointed out, but we should be equally concerned with the adequacy and limitations of *our internal* ongoing planning methods and results. Miscalculations in any of these areas are likely to be repeated—with more unfortunate consequences—unless we set up some deliberate ways for checking on and correcting the planning processes themselves. Departures and variances are often attributed to the "unexpected" and, by implication, to the "unpredictable," even to the "inevitable" inability to foresee events many months in the future. But it is probable that only some portion of the divergence should be attributed to these "uncontrollable" factors. More likely, a large portion is due to planning errors, failure to take important matters into account, "fudging" both fiscal and program estimates —all factors cited in Chapter 3, and all of which contribute to forward problems and uncertainties about program funding. The planning and decision processes themselves must be self-consciously attended to, and the capacity for learning to improve performance must be developed.

• Because actual experiences *always* differ from plans and expectations, it is important to identify the nature and source of substantial variances, not merely their occurrence. Thus, for example, rises in market prices of certain objects are due to external forces and often cannot be known (though the overall direction of prices can be estimated). This kind of departure from projections is quite different from that caused by much greater consumption of the same resources by program personnel, which may result from inadequate planning or increases in client numbers. And this, in turn, is not the same as finding that without careful reporting or controls, staff practices—and not changes in prices or numbers of clientele—have resulted in cost overruns. (For example, did one or two CYS staff make excessive use of case consultants or vendor services?) These sorts of departures have distinctively different implications for program management and fiscal planning.

We recognize that there is a large gap spanning three to five months during which only projections and estimates of fiscal and program information can be made. But as more of the "missing" information becomes available with each passing week, it should be rapidly incorporated into the experience reviews. Similarly, with the unfolding of *actual* experience the discrepancies from plans, projections, and estimates will become more apparent. By carefully attending to them now, program planning methods can be corrected and better plans incorporated into next year's proposal.

During this interim period four basic kinds of assessments are critical for forward program planning. *First,* a full factual summary of all principal aspects of program operations in the basic terms indicated above. *Second,* an efficient plan for updating projections of operational patterns (and statistics) for the remainder of the current fiscal year. *Third,* identification of the more prominent dilemmas, shortcomings, and problems in the program for which remedies must be found. And *fourth,* a tentative listing of the program features that appear to warrant "enrichment"—not corrections in the sense of remedies, as above—embellishment, or even expansion, *if* additional resources were to become available. Each of these assessments deals with different program management and planning issues, and it is especially important to distinguish between the third and fourth issues, for otherwise the requirements and questions that confront us for the coming year cannot be resolved.

Applications to CYS. Much information about CYS's operational and program experiences has been given in Chapters 7 and 8, and this can be compared with the earlier plans described in Chapters 4 and 6. Some of this information was only emerging at the time of the six-month review, but enough was known to shed light on the first three assessment issues above—and more data would become available with time. We now address only the third set of issues, and only in limited, illustrative terms. One client-related development especially concerns us: the youth who received both Referral and C/R service (eventually numbering thirty-two). Multiple services for clients are often planned and appropriate, whether clients receive them on a sequential or a concurrent basis (e.g. the job training programs presented earlier). But multiple services were not planned for CYS youth beyond Intake; staff must have had particular concerns about these clients, and the PC did not need to await end-of-year data to appreciate the extra time and other resources they were consuming. Without knowing more about the facts, we can surmise several explanations for these "crossover" cases: (1) They were initially misrouted from Intake to Referral; (2) they were properly routed, but the quality or type of service given them in Referral was inadequate; (3) some combination of these reasons; or (4) they represent an early group of youth that out-referral agencies initially were unwilling or unable to serve without supplementary assistance from C/R. The fourth explanation should have led to a resolution of the problem well before this interim period. Either or both of the first two explanations *might* have resulted in resolution of the problems by this time, but the situation probably requires more investigation. As a first step, of course, the files on these youth should be examined to find out more about their characteristics and program experiences, for they may somehow be quite different from other clients. Further efforts might include modifying Intake policies or procedures, monitoring and retraining staff in Intake or in Referral, changing service practices in Referral, and so on, but the crossover problem should not be allowed to continue into the next year.

The cost implications of crossovers for the coming year have to be considered (as they were in the exercise Step 2B in Chapter 8). If the difficulties were limited to the Referral center and have been remedied, such youths can be routed to that CC in the future, appreciably reducing service unit and total program costs (all else remaining constant). However, if such cases should henceforth be routed directly to C/R, it will be possible to avoid only the *extra* costs incurred by misrouting them to Referral first (reducing the unit cost for Referral but not for C/R). Furthermore, some reallocation of staff and other resources may have to be planned between the Ref and C/R CCs to reflect their altered proportions of cases in the coming year. Any of the likely solutions we have suggested would represent a gain in efficiency, because program resources would be conserved without reducing the quality of service.

We are now ready to address the third step in continuation budgeting.

ASCERTAINING CHANGES IN MANDATES, POLICIES, AND EXTERNAL CONDITIONS

We have seen that the JYC Board and the CYS funder reached a similar decision about terminating the Counseling component, and this decision must be accepted as binding for forward planning. The funder's further requirement that all its recipients institute some form of client fees represents a significant policy change with program implications. But what other kinds of changes in policies, laws, and external conditions might also have occurred with comparable influences on planning?

The composition of the CYS target population might also have changed during the year. Perhaps because of rapid economic or demographic shifts in the area, or perhaps because of changes in the practices of the schools, police, and courts. Similarly, agencies, employers, schools, and community bodies, which CYS had relied upon for out-referral assistance, might have undergone changes affecting the program's ability to gain access for its clients. (The establishment of a satellite unit of the county's community mental health center, for example, could raise questions about the proper division of service efforts between the two programs.) Such changes are always occurring, whether slowly or rapidly, and may be welcomed as helpful or salutary, or regretted as intrusive or limiting. But not-for-profit agencies and programs can disregard these "outside" changes only at their peril, and all must learn how to adapt constructively to new conditions and circumstances. As we said in Chapter 2, the annual continuing funding cycle provides a powerful stimulus for agencies and programs to become more sensitive to changing community conditions, expectations, needs, and legitimization.

Quite different kinds of external developments might also be critical: changes in state or federal enactments pertaining to Social Security coverage for employees of not-for-profit agencies (as has happened at the time of this writing); changes in standards for licensing or certification; or changes in any of a broad set of mandatory requirements affecting many agencies and services, public and private. And, as discussed in Chapter 3, all these external conditions and influences must be taken into account in program planning and replanning.

Closer to home, the parent agency may have completed substantial revisions of its personnel classifications, compensation plans, or performance evaluation policies and practices. These can have considerable importance for planning a program's staff cadre, job assignments, and budget. Or the parent agency may have modified its reporting and accounting practices, installed computer-assisted procedures, and otherwise changed many aspects of its system of operations—again for better or worse from the program planners' viewpoint.

FORECASTING REVENUES

The work to be done at this fourth planning step must build on information already developed, particularly that coming from the collation of revenue experiences. If revenues-to-date have been problematic for any reason, this should be known, and forward planning must address the difficulties. Again, they may have as much to do with unrealistic or faulty original planning as with external revenue sources, and corrections must be made as we look forward. But difficulties with revenue sources also may have emerged that could not have been foreseen. For example, the primary funding source may have been compelled to impose a post-award cutback in support; client fees or charges may have been less than expected because of new difficulties in clients' financial circumstances; reimbursement payments may be running farther behind schedule than expected (which causes cash flow problems, not necessarily more limited support); and so on.

As prospects for the coming year are considered, some or all of those adverse shifts may now seem likely to continue. Because the level of funding support sets critical constraints on the scope and quality of services that can be offered, not-for-profit agencies and their programs appear increasingly "budget-driven" in these times. We continue to assert, nonetheless, that such circumstances provide no justification for program planners and managers to abdicate their responsibilities or forfeit their opportunities—however limited—to improve service quality and to conserve resources for needed internal reallocation. Perhaps the most dismaying development in recent years has been the gradual drying up of support once predictably available from a program's main funding sources. Agencies and their programs are fortunate indeed when they are denied *only* price/cost inflation increments in next year's funding from the same source(s). Assuming an agency has not behaved in ways that encourage funders to reduce or terminate their support, little can be done directly to alter the capabilities of resource pools under changing economic conditions and governmental priorities. Because of the considerable lead time needed to identify and develop alternative revenue sources, agency and program personnel would be well advised to start contingency revenue planning *long before* the need presents itself for a given program.

When one scans across states and communities it becomes apparent that almost every *kind* of program has received different types of funding support, even though the preponderance for each may be of a particular type (e.g. federal, foundation, user fees). These diverse patterns argue for as much openness and flexibility as possible in planning to avoid overlooking new support opportunities. National evidence indicates that large shifts have occurred in recent years from reliance on federal or federally derived support to various forms of local support, including increases in cost sharing and user charges (Salamon & Abramson, 1982; Urban Institute, 1983). The funder for the CYS program, as we now know, is requesting that client fees be instituted at some "reasonable" level—on its face, not an unreasonable request. Later on we address the matter of client fees or charges, and only indicate here that this deserves to be explored by agencies that have not, or have only marginally, drawn on this source of revenue. Agencies are increasingly seeking supplemental revenue from other sources; for example, varieties of contractual funding with businesses and employing firms, third-party payments under insurance systems, and development of actual profit activities by agencies. Finally, the level of individual contributions for certain kinds of programs in many communities are not high and may be stimulated by special efforts—except, of course, in localities already disadvantaged by high unemployment, factory closings, and the like. Colleges and universities, as well as some religious groups, have considerably increased their revenues during this period of tightened purse strings. In addition, the very low level of corporate giving (far below the tax incentives for these contributions) should stimulate concerted approaches by not-for-profit organizations.

The careful scanning of such revenue possibilities may offer realistic alternatives that can be incorporated into continuation planning. Efforts to obtain new funding must be launched very early: They will absorb extra parent organization resources, and they should be matched by readiness to consider program downsizing, cuts in services, and so on. Very clear revenue targets for the coming year should emerge out of such planning.

DETERMINING TENTATIVE PROGRAM AND BUDGET TARGETS

At this point we assume that work on the first four steps is well advanced, so preliminary ideas about program changes can now be linked to these estimates of likely funding support. We concentrate here on decisions about the levels and nature of program operations and the fiscal "targets" needed to sustain these new program plans—but *not* on estimates of likely funding support, which we presume have been more or less settled during the first and fourth steps discussed above.

As noted, these estimations of probable support from all sources set critical constraints on planning program operations. It is pointless to develop forward program plans without first determining revenue targets. Plans can be modified to accommodate to a higher (or lower) level of funding *much* more easily than funding can be raised to meet program aspirations and designs.

To help explain what must be done at this fifth step, we should consider three very different *levels of targeted support*. We call the first the *no-change* level, meaning ±5 percent of the current year's budget *after* the most necessary (or "uncontrollable") market price rises have been figured in. Nowadays the no-change level is likely to represent the most realistic prospect for many, perhaps most, agencies. When continuation support is targeted at the no-change level, a comparably circumscribed target must be set for program plans. This in turn should stimulate maximum efforts to find efficiencies and economies in order to "hold the line" or perhaps even to make minimum progress, in the face of cost increases.

Neither expansion nor enhancement of services is possible *unless* significant economies or efficiencies can also be effected. Further, at the no-change level program improvement and expansion are typically juxtaposed: Cost savings may permit one or the other, but not both.

An estimated increase of support *up to 10 percent* for the coming year (after calculating the uncontrollable market cost rises) should be regarded as an *incremental* level. This does allow for planning limited program expansion or enhancement of services—perhaps a little of both if significant economies can also be introduced.

We designate the third, and more distressing, expectation as the *decremental* level, meaning a *reduction* approaching 10–12 percent below current revenues. Now, clearly, it becomes necessary to serve fewer clients, to give less service to each client, or both. These cutbacks are likely to be only partially offset by economies and efficiencies in program operations.

Agencies and programs that have already experienced one or two years of decremental budgets will have been brought to a position of what we consider retrenchment. The *cumulative* effects of even modest decreases combined with still rising market costs cross an important boundary as successive program cutbacks radically alter the scope and character—and probably the quality—of services. Annual decreases of 8 percent over a three-year period result in a cumulative net loss of more than 22 percent—aggravated by continuous price rises over those years—and all slack will have long since been exhausted. We shall address this kind of situation at the end of the chapter, but we refer to it here to underscore the critical importance of searching for economies/efficiencies during *each* year's continuation budgeting process.[2]

Multiple advantages accrue from the successful search for economies/efficiencies, even when not all those identified are immediately introduced. The funds that can be saved may offer opportunities for program improvements not otherwise possible; prepare program planners and administrators for unexpected but not improbable cuts in assured funding during the fiscal year; and allow absorption of proportionate reductions in the following year's funding. Some efficiencies in operations may themselves represent program improvements, particularly when they simplify procedures, reduce time lags, or bring about other changes that directly benefit clients. During these difficult financial times, program integrity can be maintained *only* by finding ways to contain and reduce costs.

Because the expected level of continuation funding so directly affects forward program planning, it is desirable to establish the fiscal target *first*, and then proceed to determine the program targets.

Applications to CYS.   The no-change level of support must be used as the first target for CYS's coming year, *postponing* the question of developing and implementing a plan for obtaining purchase-of-service funding from another source. We know that the plans now provide for terminating Counseling and for "reinvesting" these monies in the other services. A reasonable reallocation of Counseling funds permits a few more clients to be served by the other CCs. Thus, this should be considered both an economy and an opportunity for an increase in productivity. Remedying the crossover problem should be considered an efficiency, also leading to some savings. Necessary market cost rises can be

---

[2] An increase in fiscal support for the coming year exceeding about 10 percent beyond market cost rises should be considered more than incremental. Some may regard a 10 percent decrease for any single year as retrenchment rather than decremental. The issue is more than terminological, as we shall discuss later.

included, but at least half of any Total Direct Costs increase requested for this reason must be derived from client fees or charges, which the funder insists must be introduced. Finally, we shall also assume that market price increases (including JYC merit or other salary raises) have been estimated to amount to a *net* of 5.5 to 6 percent of CYS's *current* TDC.

The monetary values of these matters can be summarized as follows:

Counseling TDC costs	$ 12,551
Resolution of "crossover" problems	6,475
Funds for reallocation	19,026
Current year's TDC	247,469
Market cost rises (at 6% of current TDC)	+ 14,848
Next year's TDC	262,317
Client fee/charge revenues (51% of cost rises)	− 7,573
Next year's request to funder (TDC only)	254,744
Change in funder award (TDC only)	+ 7,275

This summarization of budget amounts needs some explanation. The Counseling costs represent the TDC expenses for this center over the past year. The third alternative offered in the Chapter 8 exercise was selected in estimating the cost avoidance possible from resolution of the crossover problem for the coming year; namely, one-half of such cases will be routed only to Referral and one-half only to C/R. All these cases will proceed through S/I and continue to accrue its service unit cost (32 x $65.62). The first half will then proceed only to Referral (avoiding additional costs of 16 x $249.77 in C/R), and the second half will proceed only to C/R (avoiding additional costs of 16 x $152.96 in Referral), resulting in $6,475 more available for reallocation. Market cost rises for next year are estimated at an aggregate of 6 percent of the TDC. Fifty-one percent of this cost rise is targeted to be offset by client fees to meet the funder's requirement that "at least half" of such rises be offset this way. These estimations involve no other assumptions and are deliberately conservative to avoid introducing complications at this point in the planning.

This approach yields a first budget target of $262,317

(TDC only), of which $7,573 must be generated from client fees/charges and $254,744 will be requested from the funder. Under this funder's requirements for continuation support, CYS must commit itself to obtaining the estimated amount from clients, and this figure must be reported on CYS's next budget application form. And about $19,026 is available for reallocation within this budget.

Now it should be clear why we have characterized this fiscal target as no change. At least one program *problem* will have been resolved, and termination of Counseling means a contraction in the *range* or *type* of services offered, but not in the *volume* of services, because more youth will be served through the other production centers using funds recaptured by these two changes.

Do you see any other program problems that require remedies? Are there more opportunities to conserve resources by introducing other efficiencies? Are there any economies that can be effected without lowering the quality or quantity of services? For example, do you think CYS needs to continue the same amount of either Professional Fees or Vendor Payments, even at the reduced levels shown on the EOY Expense Summary?

If no further economies or efficiencies can be effected, it seems doubtful that services can be significantly enhanced or embellished *if this were to depend on the combined revenues from clients and this funder.* But there should be room for making various improvements in the *quality* of services that do not require more dollars. The all too common discovery that program enhancement or enrichment is impractical without expanded financial support is the main reason for not focusing on these at the start of the continuation process.

Some readers may believe that the availability of more than $19,000 in reallocation funds should permit some improvement, and this may turn out to be true. For example, this is a period when job opportunities for youth are especially problematic. If the year's experience demonstrated that most Client Assistance funds were spent for on-the-job training and other employer subsidies, which actually increased clients' employability, shouldn't this line-item be increased for the coming year? Perhaps, indeed, this can be done, but not until the reallocation of staff and other resources has assured CYS's ability to handle the additional numbers of youth who must be served during the coming year. Whatever remains after these program/budget plans have been settled should, of course, be invested in improvements.

If in this interim period planners were to begin making estimates for supplementary funding (and expansion of services) through purchase-of-service arrangements, they would be moving toward a *second, incremental* budget target. But CYS already has a number of important program and fiscal issues yet to be worked out in detail. These include terminating one program component and arranging to handle or turn away the kinds of clients this center formerly served; implementing the changes resulting from review of the crossover problem; attention to the program's productivity and cost effectiveness; and at least partially applying cost analysis information as the revised program and new budget are developed for submission—an imposing agenda of work.

It will take staff time and consume other resources to develop—and subsequently implement—all these changes, meanwhile preparing the new, full budget application package. We doubt that JYC/CYS has either the capability or the time to undertake still more ambitious planning during this short interim period. Because purchase-of-service contracting usually necessitates direct application of cost analysis information to budgeting, as we shall discuss, these planners would be well advised to develop and apply the data *first* to a no-change continuation budget. They will then be in a far better position to consider a second, incremental budget target. In any event, the option for developing and obtaining a purchase-of-service contract can be retained *beyond* the interim period and into the next fiscal year: The CYS funder is presumably willing to allow program and funding expansion whenever it can be done (subject to the caveats stated).

The other funder requirement—demonstrated attention to CYS's productivity and cost effectiveness—has direct relevance in setting program and budget targets for the coming year. Productivity may take on somewhat different meanings in the not-for-profit and profit sectors; it typically can assume both volume and result implications among human service organizations. Serving more clients at the same level of resources would be a productivity improvement, as would increasing the number of successfully served clients at the same resource level. Both of these would also represent improvements in a program's cost effectiveness.

The Counseling component is to be terminated for policy and cost reasons, and the funder will expect an application that justifies the retention and reallocation of these resources within the budget. It will be necessary for CYS to increase the number of clients handled and/or the number successfully served, *at least* commensurate with the amount of reallocated resources. And, as we shall see, this will require use of cost analysis information. (To simplify matters, we shall examine only the option of increasing case volume and rely on Chapter 8 cost analysis data, rather than interweaving revised data from Chapter 9.) A minimal estimate of the case volume increase is obtained by dividing the amount of Counseling TDC available for reallocation ($12,551) by the cumulative service unit cost for a client served in Screening/Intake and Referral only ($218.58): 57 more cases must be handled through these two centers to meet this condition. But to achieve the expected increase in Referral *more* than 57 youth must be handled in S/I because of attrition in S/I (and year-end active cases).

We projected a first change in the CYS case flow following discussion of a resolution for the crossover matter, but this involved only changes in routing *from* S/I. It did not involve a change in the numbers handled there. The second change requires several calculations: rerouting former Counseling cases to Referral (then only 23 *new* cases must be routed from S/I); using the ratio of all cases routed from S/I to other centers to calculate the increased number of cases that S/I must handle to route 23 more; and finally, making adjustments to reflect the crossover shift as planned (16 fewer routed to Referral and 16 more to C/R, but no increase in S/I).

These planned changes have dealt only with absorbing the reallocated Counseling funds and resolving the crossover problem. But we must also address the funder's concern about productivity improvement. We will propose, therefore, an increase of 30 more youth to be served through

Referral—the core of the CYS program—which will require handling an additional 39 youth in S/I (to account for normal attrition and the year-end active cases). These numbers represent a further increase of about 4 percent in those routed from S/I and slightly over 6 percent in those to be served in Referral, a modest but reasonable effort at productivity improvement.

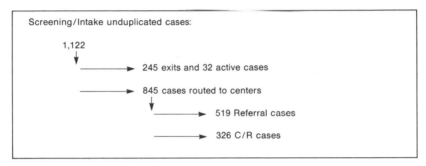

Screening/Intake unduplicated cases:

1,122

245 exits and 32 active cases

845 cases routed to centers

519 Referral cases

326 C/R cases

Figure 10–1.   Projected CYS Case Flow

Figure 10–1 reports the results of these calculations and changes in the projected case flow for CYS next year.[3] This provides a tentative intake and service case volume target for the program that matches the budget target we have already developed.

EVOLUTION OF THE PROGRAM AND BUDGET PLAN FOR NEXT YEAR

This is the point at which continuation budgeting most clearly begins to repeat the final steps in the initial budget development process described in Chapter 3. Many questions and issues remain for resolution, but they are basically

[3] We use several simplifying assumptions in making projections for the next year's operations. These assumptions include: no major change in the kinds of youth coming or being referred to CYS; somewhat more in-referrals from the community; continuation of the basic service patterns and case routings, except as stated; and no major cost changes, except as stated. In actual situations, however, program planners typically introduce still other changes requiring somewhat different assumptions for the coming year; they must also take particular care in projecting service volume and costs to the end of the current fiscal year. All these estimations must then be incorporated into their program/budget plans.

similar to those faced initially. Certain fundamental differences, however, deserve underscoring.

We have already noted that the *precedental* features of the current year's assurances, program and fiscal experiences, and the like, underlie all forward planning and carry great weight in funders' reviews of continuation applications. These application materials should therefore concretely describe and explain the principal kinds of divergences from prior plans and the reasons for them, as well as clearly document how the coming year will be different, and why.

Precedents also encompass a long series of interactions between the funder and the agency (and its program managers). The many exchanges should have engendered (we hope) trust and mutual understanding, which are powerful aids in forward planning. Agency/program planners now simply *know* a great deal more about the funder's expectations, standards, procedures, time schedules, apprehensions, and idiosyncrasies. Where development of the initial budget application had to proceed according to all-purpose guidelines and possibly unreliable interpretations of the funder's intentions and requirements, planners are now on more certain ground and should be able to work with greater confidence and efficiency. Even if relations with the funder have been stressful and less than positive, far more is known than before, and new opportunities exist to improve relations and rebuild mutual trust and respect. At the very least planners should know with fair certainty where problems and risks lie, and what to avoid, and can thus proceed quite differently.

Profound *commitments* were also generated by the current year's endeavors, and these become new sources of constraints on forward planning and activities. Examples are obligations to the community and other agencies and groups—as well as to the clients—and legal and ethical commitments to persons employed within the program. These are subject to continuous change but should not be ignored or denied without justification. Can you identify how the several program changes planned for CYS would affect such commitments, and to whom and how these changes need to be interpreted?

Agency and program staff also have developed certain

commitments: to their now-familiar ways of working, to their own preferences, and to their personal investment in "things as they are." These can readily become sources of bias in assessment and decisionmaking and of resistance to adaptation and change. Only in a symbolic sense does the program "belong" to its operatives, but it is difficult for them to view it dispassionately or from the perspective of others with an equal or greater stake in it: the clients, the larger target population, the community, the policymakers, even the funder. You may want to consider whether changes planned for the CYS program are likely to be resisted by staff, and if so, why.

With these observations and cautions in mind, the sixth, seventh, and eighth steps of continuation planning involve the same series of approximations prescribed for the initial budgeting process. Realize, however, that program and cost estimations should now be firmly based on the extended information generated through cost analysis methods (albeit preliminary) that interrelate operations and cost measures. Out of these efforts should emerge a program and budget plan that meets the funder's requirements, embodies thoughtful decisions based on prior experiences, and balances the realities that confront the planners and their aspirations for a better year.

Let us now return to the task of developing concrete plans for the CYS program and budget that incorporate the changes already discussed. The cost information derived from the EOY Functional Expense Summary and case flow material must be used, simply because that is all we have. But we should remember that during the interim period CYS planners would have to rely on data from six to eight months' operations and fiscal experience, and on estimates to the end of the FY.

Using the service unit costs developed in Chapter 8, we can get a rough-and-ready sense of whether the funds available for next year will be adequate to support the revised case flow plan, as follows:

277	S/I only cases x $65.62	=	$ 18,177
519	S/I and Ref only cases x $218.58	=	113,443
326	S/I and C/R only cases x $315.39	=	102,817
1,122	unduplicated cases		$234,437

This is $1,093 less than the $235,530 TDC costs for these centers (excluding Mgt/Gen and OH) over the past year. The estimation is unreliable, because it ignores the different mixes of resources needed to support the revised program, but it suggests that almost all the funds available for reallocation will be needed, not just the amount gained by terminating Counseling.[4]

The reallocation of funds within an ongoing program employs a procedure known as "cross-walking"—here, shifting the former CYS Counseling resources across the columns of the functional budget. The Chapter 8 Functional Expense Summary shows that Counseling costs represented a TDC value of $12,551. It must immediately be recognized that this includes a number of what are now uncontrollable costs in the sense that they cannot be spent for different kinds of resources. Thus certain personnel positions (certainly the PC and SS) cannot be cut back, and Occupancy or Equipment savings cannot be realized by terminating the Counseling center while expanding other services. However, it *is* possible to think about using some or all of the Professional Fees, Conference Travel, Vendor, and Client Payments funds for other line-items.

The service unit/staff calculations done in Chapter 8 can be adapted and extended to estimate the additional amounts of staff salary (or time) by position that are needed in the S/I, Ref, and C/R centers, where the case volume increases will occur. However, mere inspection of the Functional Expense Summary reveals that sizable amounts become available for only the Screening Supervisor and Counselors—especially the latter—with none for the Intake Worker and very little for the Liaison Workers and Secretaries. We shall look only at the Liaison Workers and Secretaries to assess the limited time that will become available through cross-walking, or reassigning, personnel. Each Referral service unit consumed $55.22 in Liaison Worker time last year; increasing that center's volume by 71 units will require an additional $3,921 in Liaison Worker salary, more than four times the

---

[4] Neither Mgt/Gen nor OH costs have to be considered in this phase of budget development. We have no information about any change in the basis for determining OH costs for the new budget, and we have reason to suppose that the other program changes require no increase in Mgt/Gen costs.

amount available from Counseling. Similarly, each unit in Referral consumed $15.28 in Secretarial time, and the increased volume will require an additional $1,085 for this position, almost three times more than is available. What seemed like sufficient support to handle the revised case flow turns out to be too little of certain critical resources and too much of other, less important ones.

- We recommend that readers use the Chapter 8 Functional Expense Summary to prepare a full chart of service unit costs for each line-item in the main cost centers. These figures should then be multiplied by the *additional units* projected for the remaining centers, and the results compared with the Summary's Counseling column to identify where line-item amounts will be sufficient when cross-walked, and what "deficits" will occur on other lines. This effort will be helpful in understanding the cost implications of program changes and is frequently applied in advance planning. The information developed will also offer further insights into possible solutions for CYS continuation budgeting.

What is to be done in view of these preliminary findings? The rough-and-ready estimates given above indicate that enough *dollars* will be available to support the revised program, but not on the right budget lines. The solution requires several steps. Because the order in which they are taken affects the results, readers may wish to try them in a different order. First, we should realize that even though the FTEs of the Program Coordinator and Screening Supervisor cannot be reduced, it is unnecessary to raise their allocations relative to increases in client volume across centers. The PC's administrative duties do not increase proportionately with modest increments in volume. This probably holds true for some of the SS's duties as well, but if you have prepared the worksheet data as recommended, you already know that almost all the SS's needed salary/time is available from Counseling.

Second, applying the per unit calculations to cross-walk

all Counseling resources will provide a first approximation of the revised budget, and this can help identify precisely where the personnel resources fall short. You will discover that the cross-walked funds "go farthest" in S/I, next farthest in Ref, and the least distance in C/R. You will need, therefore, to try alternative reallocations between the three centers to assess the implications for staff workloads and so forth.

Third, all "extra" nonpersonnel costs in Counseling can be reallocated to increase staff FTEs on critical position lines, once these are identified. But recall the caveat about Occupancy and Equipment costs, which must be moved without change (assuming it is not feasible to contract or expand space to accommodate any change in staffing).

Now it is desirable to reflect on earlier steps that CYS planners presumably took in the continuation budgeting process, particularly those that might have resulted in cost-saving efficiencies and identification of less important resources for the next year. Readers are handicapped by the limited information about CYS program operations and results when considering ways to gain efficiencies in *staff practices*. But it seems likely that up to sixteen months of experience will permit some things to be done better with less effort, and other things to be done without increasing costs. In real situations administrators and staff usually have ideas about ways to simplify procedures, to save time, and to effect other changes that conserve resources.

Rethinking of program procedures and staff practices should also lead to considerations of how personnel assignments can be modified, perhaps to improve service results and certainly to conserve costs. Is some shifting of duties possible between the PC and SS positions in any or all of the centers? How about overlapping duties between the Liaison Workers (who now appear to be too few) and the Counselors (who now appear to be too many)? None of these possibilities involves simple increases in staff workloads, an approach that often seems easiest, especially during periods of program retrenchment. If the client/staff service hours in each center are to be increased, we are proposing that this be done first through simplification of procedures, *not* merely by increasing workloads.

Service Charges and Fees

The matter of charges and fees for services rendered by not-for-profit agencies is part of a larger, highly complex skein of public policies and organizational practices. We can address only limited aspects of this important topic and will preface our discussion with observations about only certain strands in that skein. First, the practice of "user charges" has been evident throughout our nation's history, and there appears widespread support for the notion that beneficiaries of commonweal services should make some contribution—where possible—to their costs. Tolls for bridges, roads, and ferries were once commonplace (and some still are), while charges for parking meters, car and driver licenses, civil court costs, and sidewalk improvements are universal (and universally accepted) in contemporary society. Except for a few classes of citizens, and in some communities, it is routinely necessary to pay some part of the costs of one's health and medical services, attendance at public museums and musical or theatrical events, and so on. And, of course, membership associations of all kinds rely on members' dues for much or all of their support.

We respect the hard efforts to assure the free exercise of every citizen's rights (as in voting) and the access without charge to basic public services (such as free books and study materials in public schools). Nevertheless, public policies provide for only some of these services without charge—particularly at the local level—and in almost every sector user charge practices vary widely.

Despite the variability in practices and viewpoints, two underlying suppositions seem to be widely accepted: first, that services essential to fulfill citizens' basic rights should be available to all, and access should not be impeded by inability to pay; second, that if charges are imposed, they should reflect users' ability to pay. For some, the imposition of a "nominal" fee or charge, as at many state/federal parks, is not regarded as a barrier to anyone, and these revenues may contribute importantly to support those and other facilities. But for large numbers of persons, who are unable to achieve minimum subsistence levels, such charges are scarcely nominal. Besides, sliding-scale fee schedules and other means for adjusting charges according to users' ability to pay involve difficult and contentious procedural problems.

Up to this point we have dealt only with direct payments by users or beneficiaries of services, but we must recognize that other parties also make payments *for* or *on behalf of* persons who use particular services. The best-known examples are the "Blues" or medical insurance plans under private or governmental sponsorship, such as Medicare/Medicaid. In both of these examples a "third party" is charged for portions or all of the costs of certain services received by qualified beneficiaries. The private example is a prepaid insurance system to which the beneficiaries have already made contributions, and in the governmental example an insurance system may include significant proportions of employer tax funds. In the next section we shall deal with other third party reimbursement or purchase-of-service practices. Here we only emphasize that almost all varieties of service payment systems rest on quite common principles and practices. With these observations in mind, we can address these principles and practices for applying user and other charges and fees. Several rationales are given for imposing these charges and come in various combinations. They include:

1. To fulfill the obligation or provide the opportunity for those who directly benefit from a program/service to contribute to its support
2. To shift the burden of program support from the general public to those who actually use it
3. To assure adequate support for a program/service
4. To conform to statutory or other external requirements

The first of these reasons is used to justify clearly nominal charges or fees where these revenues do not substantially cover the costs of providing the service. The second reason may be used when the service is not regarded as a public or governmental obligation, or a necessity for all citizens, even though the program may be conducted by a governmental or semipublic agency. This may be used to justify restriction of the service to those both willing and able to pay, in whole or in part. The more the service is viewed in this light, the greater the relevance of the third reason. Professional associations and religious bodies are prominent examples of organizations that make little or no claim to be rendering services that are public responsibilities. The third rationale is increasingly emphasized as a fiscal necessity, especially given decreases in the proportions of governmental or tax-derived program support. But linking user fees to programs' expense/revenue problems may intrude upon the principles of equal access and ability to pay, which generate some of the most pressing dilemmas in the not-for-profit sector. The fourth reason simply acknowledges that the other reasons may be codified into official policy, and this may sometimes be invoked by organizations to justify their adoption of user charges.

Agencies rely on similar reasons when they consider imposing user/client/beneficiary charges; but determining differing rates and levels of charges usually involves more discrete considerations as well. Agencies often feel compelled to impose or raise fees to maintain services or to offset the loss of other revenues or reduction in program support. Because most agencies conduct multiple programs, however, they face problems in defining the principles pertinent for each and in determining the levels of charges appropriate to each (and to various clients within each), especially when they want to rely on a sliding fee scale related to clients' ability to pay.

PRINCIPLES IN DETERMINING CHARGES AND FEES

The determination of user charges should be guided by several basic principles, which we shall discuss before addressing other issues. Charges and fees assessed for anyone (clients or third parties) may be less than (as is often the case), equal to, or even more than the actual cost of providing a particular service. Therefore, we must clearly distinguish between the *cost of a service* (as discussed in Chapters 8 and 9) and the *charge* (or *price*) set for that service. The relation of charges to cost analysis procedures will become obvious as we proceed.

1. Charges for services should be based on full and true cost analysis information.
2. That information should be developed according to standard cost analysis procedures and should rest on demonstrable and auditable program and financial records.
3. The cost for each service should include only its proper share of support and indirect costs, as determined by standard distribution procedures.
4. Only one cost figure should be determined and declared for each service, regardless of which party pays what share.
5. The proportion of the full and true cost of the service represented by any charge should be clearly stated.

Actual practices of agencies may vary widely from these principles, intentionally or unwittingly. For example, agencies may set differing charges for their services largely in terms of what they think "the traffic will bear"—that is, for different groups of users or for clients with varying ability to pay—with little regard to the true differential costs. Other agencies may establish fee schedules to cover only that part of service costs for which other revenues are (or become) unavailable. An agency may even attempt to declare different service unit costs to different third parties—to some extent based on estimates of probable revenues from external sources rather than from the users.

We believe these approaches are unwise, contrary to generally accepted standards, and sometimes in violation of official regulations. But the reasons for these practices probably have more to do with ignorance of cost analysis procedures than with opportunism. In any event both market conditions (including users' ability or inability to pay) and third party revenue sources are increasingly pressing agencies toward conformity with the principles we have set forth.

PRACTICES IN CHARGING CLIENT FEES

The situation faced in planning the CYS continuation program and budget can help us explore client fee practices. Recall that the funder has insisted on instituting "reasonable" client fees and that the budget target calls for approximately $7,573 to be generated from this new source during the coming year, about 3 percent of the budget TDC. We shall assume that the planners have confirmed projections of the numbers of youth to be served by the cost centers, completed their reallocation of target budget resources and program changes, and can therefore prepare service unit cost estimates for the coming year.

If every youth processed through the Screening/Intake center were charged (and paid) $6.75, that would produce revenues sufficient to meet this part of the target (1,122 x $6.75). But there is an obvious flaw in this arbitrary approach: Few clients will be motivated to pay such a sum on their initial contact with CYS, nor does it seem reasonable to impose a charge on persons who may well have been referred by others or may not actually proceed through the program (e.g. the 260 who did not proceed beyond S/I). Persons familiar with roughly similar service programs would probably warn us that a client's commitment to receiving services is usually far too tenuous and uncertain to impose any fee during the intake process. (This is not the situation for programs offering highly valued services sought out by potential beneficiaries. But even for them an initial charge may bar entry.)

Let us consider, then, imposing a fee at the later point when the youth has been accepted for CYS service, completed Intake, been routed to Referral or C/R, and been informed of the particular service(s) ready to be offered. Our estimate is that only 845 cases would reach this point and wish to continue. The average charge would then be $8.96. Should this be imposed on all these youth? The sum is little enough that it might be considered nominal, posing no problem of ability to pay. Again, experienced persons might caution that this amount could be viewed by a family in financial straits as more than nominal, and among such families a fair proportion are likely to be doubtful about the benefit of what CYS seems to be offering. Should we risk losing such youth? What if we added some simple measure of family ability to pay and decided that those with incomes at or below the poverty level would not be charged any fee? A two-tier fee policy can be established: one tier including those whose incomes fall below a certain level and who pay nothing, the other tier including all others, each of whom pays a flat fee. Now we shall estimate that incomes for one-fifth of the CYS client families will be below the minimum level; the remaining 676 must bear the burden of the fees, resulting in a charge of $11.20—still perhaps nominal (incomes estimate source: *Wall Street Journal*, "Census Poverty Rates," August 3, 1983).

Notice that we have had to consider the implications of fee charging in terms of motivation to continue, ability to pay, and other case-specific factors. Let us move on and think about the steps CYS would have to take to implement this policy. First, procedures must be set up and applied to all cases to find out family income levels. This would probably be easiest to do during Intake but will itself consume staff time and other resources—which must be reallocated to the task wherever it is performed. Second, procedures must be developed for explaining the fee policy and for collecting payments from the families considered able to pay. Again, extra resources must be allocated to these efforts. Third, policies and practices must be established to deal with families who fail to pay the fee when it is explained and due. If requirements were not explained to families earlier in their contacts with CYS, line-staff would now have to pause and present them—perhaps delaying further service until payment is made, or even requiring an additional contact solely for this purpose. And what is to be done when the payment is not made when due? Who should follow up with the "delinquent" families? How long should service be delayed, and with what effects on the youth's already problematic behavior?

Again, in microcosm, we can now see some of the complexities and difficulties of imposing user charges, including the additional resources that must be set aside for their collection. Because such small sums are involved in these alternatives, our discussion may appear to have trivialized the issues. But regardless of the specific amounts involved, all the elements applied to CYS are present when making decisions about client fee policies and practices and deserve careful consideration as agencies seek to introduce these arrangements.

Certain aspects of charging client fees require further examination, two of which have been lightly touched on: the additional efforts needed for determining family incomes and for collecting fees. Readers are familiar with related procedures from their own experiences in establishing credit at banks or stores and perhaps with obtaining loans, including tuition assistance in higher education, but some readers may also have experience with the eligibility determination methods used by various public agencies. All these require extra effort, form preparation, and review by the organization line-staff, as well as by some verifier. These tasks are tedious. They involve delays and inevitable errors and are sometimes humiliating. CYS might settle for simple evidence of family income, perhaps through a paycheck or other wage/salary record. The larger the numbers of clients, the more demanding the procedures. The more complicated the fee/charge schedule, the greater the time and resources that must be allocated to the procedures. The simple two-tier approach suggested for CYS minimizes some of this work, but more demanding procedures are necessary in many service organizations, often because of federal/state statutes and regulations.

Additional procedures will be necessary to obtain payments from clients (usually referred to as "billing") and, not infrequently, to follow up on those who are late or delinquent. One can now appreciate the amounts of additional resources—and time lags—that must be incorporated into plans for user charge systems. Two unfortunate consequences often result from all but the most simple procedures: (1) the routinization of processes, which both staff and clients come to regard as arbitrary, distasteful, and intrusive, and (2) the tendency toward "creaming" applicants or clients in order to maximize revenues from this source. Criteria and operational strategies that result in skewing selection toward the most likely to pay, known as "creaming," subvert program objectives while excluding those often most in need of the service. This risk increases as programs become more dependent on client/user charges. Sliding fee schedules, of course, are explicitly intended to allow for differences in ability to pay. But increasing strains on agencies' budgets can also have the effect of making them most hospitable to those likely to produce the highest revenues.

With these principles and cautions in mind, we recommend that readers develop criteria and methods of introducing client fees within the CYS program. Particular care should be taken to avoid adverse effects on disadvantaged clients or on service delivery and results. Any fee schedule must be set high enough to absorb some reasonable level of delinquency or nonpayment, perhaps up to 8 percent. Finally, it will be necessary to decide if the revenue from this source must also cover the staff time costs of implementing the procedures, and to devise methods that do not significantly deflect staff energies from their priority service tasks.

Reimbursement and Performance Contracting

All the premises and principles set forth for user charges are equally relevant when seeking revenues through purchase-of-services, reimbursements, and performance contracts. Such arrangements have certain common features: Agencies undertake formal agreements with external funding sources to provide services to designated persons, for which they will receive monies according to prearranged payment schedules. The external groups are often state agencies that purchase particular services on contract from not-for-profit or profit organizations for certain persons—hence the term purchase-of-service or service provider contracts. Similar practices are also used by health and other insurance systems, retirement and pension systems, and many other groups on behalf of their members. In all these situations, the body that contracts to pay for the service is known as the third party, the client or beneficiary being the first party, and the service enterprise being the second party (or service provider). (As we have already noted, under many of these systems the client/beneficiary is required to pay some portion of the total cost of the service—whether by absorbing a deductible amount, by prior contribution, or by paying for costs over a rate ceiling set by the third party.)

Payment is usually made through after-the-fact reimbursement by the third party for costs incurred and properly reported by the service provider. Almost all the procedures for determining who can receive the service, what services can be paid for (the "coverage"), what costs are allowable, how and when the payments will be made, and so on, are rigorously defined and implemented, partly because huge sums of money are often involved, partly because of public pressures for conserving tax-derived funds, and partly because most third parties have developed sophisticated cost analysis and reimbursement procedures.

The fundamental premise is that services will be paid for only when they are provided by whoever is specified, and as specified, in the contract, only upon evidence of the actual cost of the service, and only after proper reporting of these facts. The record-keeping, cost analysis, and reporting capabilities of the agency must be well developed to handle these arrangements. And it must be prepared for the not uncommon audits that will occur. Because of the considerable pressure in many sectors to keep costs down, service providers find that meticulous budgeting and cost containment practices are needed to recoup revenues to cover their expenses. Finally, the after-the-fact reimbursement schedules can cause cash flow problems for agencies with precarious revenue situations.

The amounts to be reimbursed are arrived at in several ways. By one method, now being extended by the federal government for medical services, a "prospective" rate or ceiling price is set for each service (usually by a service unit definition), and no costs over that rate are reimbursable. Organizations that cannot bring their actual service unit costs down to the established level must either make up the difference by drawing on other revenues or cease participating in these arrangements.[5] By a second method, the *kinds of costs* (or cost elements) that are allowable (that is, for which reimbursements will be made) are defined. Service providers, following this procedure, cannot obtain payments for any elements in their actual service costs that are excluded from the terms of the contract. Some combination of these two methods is also common: Only allowable costs are paid, and a ceiling is imposed; rates are set for certain cost elements but not for the total service unit cost; and so on. By a third method, the detailed terms of the service to

---

[5] Use of a flat or set rate may also allow some organizations to provide services at a "profit" if they are able to bring their actual expenses below the ceiling.

be provided are negotiated, followed by reimbursement for the full, actual costs incurred. This pattern allows the third party considerable voice *before* services are given in the nature of the services, how they will be given, and even at what cost levels for certain elements.

Cost reimbursement contracts also assure the funding source maximum control over which persons can be served, what characteristics or qualifications they must possess, and so forth. Control over both the nature of the service and the eligible persons are understandably interpreted by agencies as encroachments on their autonomy and independence. But they are usually voluntary participants in these funding arrangements—at least in a formal sense—and are not prohibited from providing the same, better, or more costly service to others of their own choosing, assuming they have other sources of revenue. In these conditions it becomes necessary for the provider agency to distinguish carefully all service and cost matters between the two sets of clients: those for whom purchase-of-service contracts apply, and all others. Separate entries must be made in all records and files, separate reports and billing statements submitted, and auditable evidence prepared documenting that the purchase-of-service clients received services as defined in the contract. (Many physicians routinely follow these practices for patients covered by Blue Cross/Blue Shield and other insurance plans.)

If CYS were to pursue this kind of supplementary funding during the coming year, it would need to maintain records to meet these requirements and to manage its operations and case flow in ways that conform to the terms of the new contract. Depending on the terms, this might impose differential selection, service patterns, and the like, on the additional youth accepted and paid for through this agreement. Further, the CYS fiscal records would have to demonstrate, through cost analysis methods, that it had "earned" the per client rate as defined in the reimbursement contract—that is, that it cost not less than this rate. In principle any expenses that exceeded the negotiated rate would have to be charged to some other funding source (here the original funder). Unless the purchase-of-service contract is negotiated to permit charging fees to the clients covered by the contract, this cannot be done. It would force CYS to institute a three-tier charge system: the two previously cited, and a third for clients covered by the contract, who would be charged nothing regardless of family income.

Supplemental Funding Through Performance Contracting.   In this discussion we combine two important matters: seeking additional revenues from another funder *and* obtaining them through reimbursement contracting that specifies major elements of program performance. As we have discussed, CYS plans to generate some revenue by instituting client payments with the start of the new FY. If its planners are able to resolve the issues pertaining to fee schedules and collections, this plan will entail no program modifications, no case volume beyond that already projected, and no obligations to another funder. Once the new year has begun and the decision is made to seek supplemental funding through a purchase-of-service contract, new issues arise that must be addressed. Now, however, *full* EOY expense and cost analysis information will be available, as well as updated line-item market costs, and so on.

Multisource funding involves two fundamental principles that are easily understandable: First, no changes can occur in the program or in reporting and accountability requirements that would infringe on the award as defined by the original funder—who is providing continuation support—at least not without difficult renegotiation about the award; second, all service activities undertaken with the additional revenues must be *full-funded*, that is, they must be conducted and reported in ways that assure that the expanded services are entirely supported by the new monies and that none of these costs will be absorbed by the first funder.

The eminently reasonable intent and effects of these conditions are to preserve program integrity and to honor all commitments already undertaken with the first funder. But, as discussed in earlier chapters, funders often impose differing requirements that impinge on many aspects of program and fiscal affairs. Assuming that the two sets of funders' requirements are compatible and not contradictory, the problem consists of carefully reconciling their variations. We know, at a minimum, that the purchase-of-service contract will be for a different fiscal period, that it will involve after-the-fact billing by CYS and later reimbursement, and that payments will be made only for the *full direct and indirect costs* of serving the additional clients.

Our simplified presentation here assumes no change in the character of CYS services or in the kinds of clients, only an increase in their numbers. Let us now also assume that the new funder will support service only for handling clients through S/I and Referral, and none through C/R, and that the contract will guarantee reimbursement for all costs involved in serving 100 more youth, beginning with the second quarter of the new FY. Finally, we also assume that a sufficient demand exists for CYS services so that no special efforts will be needed to recruit the additional clients.

Whether labeled service provider or purchase-of-service agreements, all performance contracting involves specification of support in terms of services (performance) to be rendered to designated clients. CYS would then face the critical question of a precise definition of the *services to be provided for the additional clients* who are to be handled through S/I and Referral only. Let us examine the possibilities that the JYC and CYS administrators would have considered before negotiating with the new funder.

One possibility is that S/I will process 100 additional youth. We know from the CYS case flow information that a proportion of these will not proceed on farther for various reasons. Applying the revised caseflow projections presented earlier in this chapter, this would mean that only 46 of the 100 additional youth would receive Referral service (519 ÷ 1,122 = 46.3%). The Chapter 8 case flow diagram reveals that only 84 percent of the Referral exits were successfully "placed" or connected with appropriate out-referral resources.[6] The "output" resulting from handling 100 more cases through S/I, then, can be estimated to be 39 more youth successfully linked to out-referral resources.

Is this what the new funder expects, and will it reimburse CYS accordingly? If the answer is yes, then the contract should specify that reimbursements will be made for the revised unit cost of S/I multiplied by 100 units, *plus* the 46

[6] Note that we use available continuation budgeting case flow projections, but must fall back on last year's *actual* case flow data where no new estimates have been made—here, for the proportion of Referral placements to exits.

service units multiplied by the revised unit cost of Referral (including full shares of the revised Mgt/Gen and Overhead costs, using one of the procedures in Chapter 9).

A second possibility is that the new funder wishes to pay the full costs of serving 100 more clients *through successful Referral placements*. Now reimbursement costs must be figured by working "backward." The ratio of successful Referral cases to the number exited from that center last year was 1:1.8 (divide 397 by 336). The cases routed to Referral as a ratio of all youth handled by S/I is now projected as 1:2.16 (divide 1,122 by 519). These calculations indicate that 255 more cases apparently must be processed through S/I in order to route 118 more cases into Referral, thus to assure 100 successful placements.

Both these options—and a funder may propose still others—contemplate contracting for payments based on estimated costs for given numbers of service units: the first for input/throughput units, and the second for input/throughput/output units. These options would result in radically different total contract costs, and each would necessitate radically different levels of staffing and resource allocations. The magnitude of either change for the CYS case flow, program, staffing, and budget can be grasped by making crude estimates of the changes as follows:

- The revised case flow already projected for the original funder will increase the S/I unit input by about 7 percent over last year.
- The first option cited above would increase this projected S/I unit input by about 9 percent.
- The second option cited above would increase the projected S/I unit input by about 23 percent.

Changes of these magnitudes would necessitate redesign of major components of the CYS program, because they present threshold differences in staffing demands, space arrangements, program–community relations, and other critical matters. The program and fiscal replanning required would go far beyond reallocation of current resources by cross-walking. The second option would seem impossible to plan and implement during the first quarter, or even first half, of the new FY, even if it seemed a desirable expansion for CYS. It would probably invalidate important features of the cost analysis information already developed, because it would lead to extensive changes in assumptions about the relation of input resources to output results.

Although the total additional revenues that could be generated by either option are also of great importance, readers should not become preoccupied with particular figures. The issues to be underscored have to do, on the one hand, with the implications of obtaining revenues that involve service or performance obligations, how these are defined, and the consequences of being unable to fulfill the terms of the contract; and on the other hand, with the implications of the kinds and degrees of necessary changes in the scope of the program, the level of its resources, and the difficulties of planning and implementing such changes. Finally, we must emphasize that failure to develop good, reliable cost estimates for service or performance reimbursement contracts can entail very great risks for the survival of the program.

Retrenchment Budgeting

We have distinguished between budget cutting, decremental budgeting, and retrenchment budgeting. Decremental budgeting is, in many respects, similar to figuring how to make cuts in the original budget request. We suggested earlier that the notion of retrenchment be confined to reduction in a continuation budget of more than *10 percent* of a current year's support. The distinction recognizes the *magnitude of change* represented by such resource reduction and the *discontinuity* this presents for planning. The current year's program and fiscal experience can provide less precedental guidance when planning for cutbacks on the order of 20 to 35 percent. A change of this magnitude invalidates most of the cost relationships that have been derived from the most recent analyses.

Retrenchment means that large, often radical changes must be made in the character and scope of program services for the coming year, perhaps also for the agency as a whole. As we discussed in Chapter 3, such changes are likely to focus on substantial redefinitions of program clientele and domain, type and range of services, community relations, and the like. Because personnel are the critical resource in service organizations, it is probable that large changes must be made in the size, composition, and even salary levels of staff. These shifts present serious problems for the stability of the program (and organization), which are beyond the scope of this book.

Our observations and experience—and fragmentary literature sources—indicate that budget reductions up through about 10 percent tend to be handled quite differently from those rising well above this figure. This is partly because many organizations operate with a certain amount of slack in their available resources. Up to this level program managers (or heads of responsibility centers) may be expected to recommend or impose cuts and related changes and to make strenuous efforts to maintain continuities in planning based on current and recent experience. Not every conceivable cost-cutting economy or efficiency change has yet been pursued, and they must now be instituted. This approach also represents an attempt to avoid the magnitude of *replanning* required to introduce more radical changes and to limit adverse effects to particular programs (Levine, 1980).

If planners have vigorously searched for ways to economize up to this time, it is probable that part of the impending cuts can be "absorbed" through enactment of all—not merely a few—of these alternatives. And if reductions in program support have occurred decrementally over several years, rather than suddenly between two years, planners should have been able to make cutbacks in a one-step-at-a-time sequence. Although the cumulative results of annual decrements also arrive at a drastically reduced level of funding, the deliberately phased downsizing of a program to accommodate to a smaller resource base can be effected more efficiently and often less painfully. For example, reduction of staff through "normal" attrition and gradual narrowing of the range of services or client eligibility can avoid some of the shock effects of large layoffs, abrupt service termination, jumps in user charges, and the like.

This chapter's discussion of the tasks of estimating and projecting from the present to the coming year indicates the precipitous rise in "decision costs" when substantial program and fiscal replanning is necessary. The desire to avoid incurring these high costs probably accounts for the tendency of some administrators to temporize, postpone replanning, and prolong the search for alternative replacement revenues. But development of new revenue sources takes considerable lead time, as well as strenuous effort, and is problematic in any event. Reliance on these delaying approaches is likely to result in forfeiture of many options that could have been selected if explored much earlier. It is exceedingly difficult to effect retrenchment budgeting in efficient, cost-effective, and less harmful or destabilizing ways when it must be done at the last minute. Administrators who delay cutback changes too long must often resort to across the-board reductions, sudden terminations, and other arbitrary solutions that could have been avoided through advance planning (Levine, Rubin, and Wolohojian, 1982).

Despite the fundamental discontinuities for planning imposed by retrenchment budgeting, all the standard procedures presented in previous chapters continue to be applicable. Basic principles and practices must still be followed, and accountability requirements must be honored. Skillful fiscal planning and management are even more important when the risks for service delivery, program integrity, and organizational survival are much greater.

It seems to us that not-for-profit organizations have shown great adaptiveness in weathering this chilly period, undoubtedly far greater than that possible for many of their former beneficiaries. We cannot forecast the future for these organizations but are convinced of two things: (1) that the affluence they enjoyed during the 1960s and early 1970s will not recur in this era, and (2) that the demands for prudent fiscal management and competent application of budgeting procedures will continue to engage our energies and challenge our abilities.

APPENDIX A
INITIAL AND FINAL DOCUMENTATION REQUIREMENTS

Program and Budget Applications

All funders require certain basic information and materials from applicant agencies seeking support. Those most commonly required are listed below: The first list pertains to the program applicant, and the second shows information required of the fiduciary organization responsible for the program. The information, forms, and documentation required by various funders have many similarities but also many differences. Therefore, applicants must be alert for important variations, nonuniform definitions, special clauses, and so forth. Funder requirements and application procedures are usually defined in guides, instructions, and other materials supplied on request, some of which may need further interpretation by a representative of the funder.

The burden of description, explanation, and documentation is typically greater for new service programs, and especially for new agencies that have not yet been able to demonstrate their capabilities. When continuation support is being requested for an ongoing program, it is customary to require additional concrete information about program operations, results, and costs for the most recent fiscal period.

Abbreviated Summary of Required
Program Documentation

PROGRAM IDENTIFICATION

Title; fiscal period; total cost
Summary or abstract of program
Statement of purposes
Expected clients or beneficiaries
Table of organization, staffing

PROGRAM DESCRIPTION (Narrative)

Information establishing problem, need for program
Full description of proposed program goals, services, benefits or results expected
Information about clientele: characteristics, numbers, locations, admissions statuses, etc.
Program staffing: position descriptions, manning table, credentials, etc.
Program timetable, schedule
Relevant performance measures, units of service
Evaluation component (if any)
Collaboration with other agencies/services; proof of cooperation
Agency capability to undertake this program, prior experience, etc.
Facilities available
Licenses; code certifications
Insurance coverages
Needed endorsements: parent or state agency, local or other reviews and clearances

BUDGET AND BUDGET NARRATIVE

Line-item summary of request budget
Functional budget detailed by services, cost centers
Budget explication and justification (by line-items and cost centers; estimation procedures; bases for allocations; other)
Indirect/Overhead costs (with explication)
Unit costs

Charges, fees, rates
Subcontracts
Cost-sharing, matching funds, in-kind
Payout schedule (if option given)
Other funding sources or revenues, with exact dollar amounts

Abbreviated Summary of Required Parent Agency Documentation

Name, location, domain/jurisdiction, etc.
Charter, governing board, financial officer
Table of organization
Administration of proposed program/budget
Support services
Other programs and services
Accreditations
Civil Rights, Fair Labor practice, equal pay, affirmative action, compliance statements, etc.
All sources funding (sometimes)
All federal funds (for federal fund applications)
Employer SSA and IRS identification numbers

Funders' Financial Reports

The profusion of forms, procedures, and requirements encountered when seeking support from a funder is matched by the variety of demands for retrospective, *post hoc* information about the whole fiscal period. Not only do the requirements for financial reports vary among different funding sources (federal, state, local, private), they often vary within the same source: Department X at the state level may well require documents different from Department Z.

Many attempts have been made to adopt broad, uniform financial reporting methods, especially at the federal level (see OMB Circulars A–87 and A–122). But programs must remain alert to modifications, additions, shifts, and so on. Here we can only outline the most common types of information usually called for in ongoing, periodic, and final financial reports.

As stewards of other people's money, not-for-profit organizations must prepare various of the final reports listed below, which call for breakouts of the same kinds of information we have stressed throughout the book. But a funder's final requirements should reinforce and shape the fiduciary organization's fiscal and record-keeping practices. Knowing what will be expected and demanded at the end of the year (and sometimes during the year) should profoundly affect how an organization sets up and maintains its ongoing accounting and reporting systems and how it assembles its own internal financial reports and lays the foundation for future audits.

1. *Final Expenditure Reports (direct and indirect costs)*
   Totals: by object costs[1]
             by functions, cost centers, services[2]
             by units of service[3]
             by activity or output measures[3]
             by direct/indirect/both costs per service units
             by dollars over/under budget/year
             by actual vs. budgeted amounts with/without indirect costs
             by percent over/under budget
             by percent over/under previous year
   Unexpended balances
   Cost-sharing
   Remaining obligations
   Adjustments between cash and accrual accounting

2. *Revenue Summary Information*
   Totals: by source(s)
             by types (fees, contracts, gifts, interest)
             by percent/dollars over/under actual/budgeted

3. *Other Reports*
   In addition to the standard cost information just listed, the federal government requires special documents for cost reimbursement. These include contractors' releases, property inventories, bank statements, insurance information, bonds, refunds, and tax certificates.

---

[1] Elements within objects may have to be further broken down by functions.

[2] Each function may have to be further broken down by every measure listed.

[3] These are considered "documentation of effort" and may also be required during the FY—often quarterly.

4. *Money Transaction Reports*

As part of the federal effort to achieve standardization, three forms have been developed to handle money transactions between grantor and grantee. Usually, however, small and midsize programs receive federal monies through an intermediary with fiduciary responsibilities: state or local governmental agencies, national umbrella organizations or their branches, regional councils. These larger units will have special staff able to handle this level of paperwork, but for the reader's information we briefly list the contents of these three forms, which may also have to be submitted at specified periods during the fiscal year.

1. Financial Status Report (by programs/functions/activities)
   a. Net outlays previous/present periods
   b. Total unliquidated obligations
   c. Federal share of a. and b.
   d. Income credits
   e. Total dollars authorized
2. Federal Cash Transaction Report
   a. Cash on hand end of previous period
   b. Total receipts
   c. Total cash available
   d. Gross/net disbursements
   e. Prior adjustments
   f. Cash on hand end of this period
3. Request for Advance or Reimbursement (by programs/functions/activities)
   a. Net outlays to date
   b. Estimated net outlays for advance period
   c. Federal share previously/now requested

Financial Position Statements

Financial position statements depict the service history of the program in quantified terms that can be audited; they render an account of stewardship and fiduciary responsibilities along with dollar accountability. They are required at the end of a fiscal year, but some or all may be required at a specified time or periodically during the fiscal period. The *Standards* (1974) explains in detail the purpose and requirements for these reports of financial position for nonprofit organizations.

Uniform Statements Complying With Accounting Principles

Four types of financial statements are considered essential to ensure that the financial affairs of a publically funded organization are satisfactorily disclosed.

1. A Statement of Support, Revenue, Expenses, and Other Changes for this year and the previous year
2. A Statement of Changes in Fund Balances (Current Funds, Building Funds, etc.) for this year and the previous year
(Statements 1 and 2 are often combined.)
3. A Statement of Functional Expenses, for this year and the previous year
4. A Balance Sheet, which summarizes and compares the assets and liabilities for every kind of restricted and unrestricted resource (Current Funds, Building Funds, Endowment Funds, etc.), for this year and the previous year

These statements are also used as the bases for audit review. Smaller programs and agencies should set aside resources to have them prepared by accounting specialists.

BUDGET
LINE-ITEMS

This outline contains a representative list of budget expense line-items as prescribed by federal and state agencies and departments, the United Way, and other funders. The order and classifications of the first three lines are standard, and the others vary among funders, but the range and substance of the information will generally be included somewhere in the budget documentation. For each line-item the two most consistently required components are presented: (1) the principal kinds of object costs within that category and (2) the most common measures for computing those costs. For example, personnel costs may be broken down by the kinds of staff subcategories needed (professional, clerical, maintenance, and so on); and the measures for computation may be shown as FTEs, workdays per month, normal work hours per week, and so forth. The range of elements customarily needed for cost estimating is included here to emphasize the connections between the nature and the measurements of line-item costs. Therefore, many of the details and specifications shown in this outline would generally be documented and explained in the text accompanying a budget summary form—not on the summary form itself. An analogous format is often used to detail a revenue budget. The use of code numbers for recording all expense and revenue financial transactions at every level (including journals, ledgers) allows the organization to identify and track the movement of resources (see United Way [1975] for excellent descriptions of all these matters). All organizations should try to adopt a code number system even if it is not required by a funder. The UWAACS system is suitable for practically every not-for-profit organization and is based on recognized principles of accountancy. In the outline we indicate the UWAACS code numbers for expense line-items in the lefthand column.

UWAACS Code No.	Line-Item No. & Title	Major Sub-categories	Common Alternative Costing Measures

7000–7099	1 Personnel Salaries/Wages	Executive/Administrators
		Professional staff
		Clerical
		Technicians
		Maintenance staff
		Temporary staff
		Other
		  COLA
		  Overtime/Shift differential
		  Hardship, etc.
			Annual or monthly salary rates by FTEs or hours per week or per month

7100–7199	2 Health and Retirement Benefits	Medical/Hospital plans Pension/Retirement plans Supplemental: food, housing, relocation Transport, etc. Insurance: life, accident Other	Percentage of salaries/ wages based on average actual cost of benefits or actual costs of benefits; estimated average costs
7200–7299	3 Payroll Taxes, etc	FICA Unemployment: state, federal Workers' compensation Disability insurance	Percentage of salaries/ wages based on average actual cost of benefits; or estimated average costs
8000–8099	4 Professional Fees (Consultants)	Legal Audit/Accounting Computer programmer Development/Public relations Medical/Dental/Psychological Subcontracts Other: testing, educating tutors, guards	Estimated actual per hour/day/month; contracts

(continued)

UWAACS Code No.	Line-Item No. & Title	Major Sub-categories	Common Alternative Costing Measures
8100–8199	5 Supplies	Office: standard supplies Duplicating/Reproduction Building and housekeeping (janitor supplies, paper, soap, etc.) Medical/Dental/Clinic Recreation/Vocational Food and beverages Laundry Other	Estimated actual or average per standard volume (gross of paper, per meal, per gallon paint, etc.)
8200–8299	6 Telephone/Telegraph (Communications)	Installation & purchase Local Long distance Leased services Teletype	Average number of calls per day/week/month times average cost per call; or average charge per month
8300–8399	7 Postage/Shipping	Postage/Parcel Post Freight Messenger delivery service	Estimated averages per week/month
8400–8499	8 Occupancy	Rental charges Utilities: gas, electric, water, oil Building/Grounds maintenance & supplies: contracts, cleaning, rubbish removal, etc. Mortgage interest Taxes: real estate, personal property Licenses/Permits	Actual per contract, lease, inquiry; or estimated averages per month/year based on experience, bids, etc., or contracts

Account	Category	Items	Calculation
8500–8599	9 Rental & Maintenance of Equipment	Assessments Other Office equipment Data processing equipment	Per lease or contract charge per month/year/item
8600–8699	10 Print & Publications	Printing Art work: photography (both fees & supplies) Informational items: films, newsletters, etc. Publications: one-time purchases Subscriptions (for agency itself) Other media charges	Estimated by bids/costs per page or per piece; or actual/estimated costs per item/year/contract
8700–8799	11 Travel	Local: bus, taxi, auto allowances Agency Vehicles: gas & oil, repairs, insurance, licenses, leasing costs, tires Out of town: fare, hotels, meals, incidentals	Mileage rates times estimated mileage; actual per contract/lease; average estimated per car/per trip/per month (by experience, bids); actual or estimated cost per number of trips times number of people (with destinations)
8800–8899	12 Conferences, Conventions (often included in Travel)	Space & Equipment rental Supplies Meetings: food/beverages for participants (for meeting conducted by agency) Honaria for speakers Registration fees	Estimated for each event per number of participants

(continued)

UWAACS Code No.	Line-Item No. & Title	Major Sub-categories	Common Alternative Costing Measures
8900–8999	13 Special Assistance to Individuals/ Clients	Medical/Dental/Hospital Shelter/Board Homemaker service Food/Clothing Transportation/Recreation Prosthetic devices Wage supplements	Estimated average for recipient (per day or total) based on experience tied to program objectives
9000–9099	14 Membership Dues	Individual Organization (must provide return benefits such as regular services, publications, supplies, etc.)	Actual cost (per person if appropriate)
9100–9199	15 Awards/Grants	Affiliated organizations Other individuals & organizations	Cost per award: include ultimate purpose
Not in UW Code	16 Equipment A. Current Expenses	Office Vehicles Furnishings Medical/Dental Recreation/Education Training Food service	Unit cost over a set level (often $150); per unit based on bids/market costs
	B. Capital Expenses	Same as above	Unit cost over a higher set level (often $500); per bid/market costs

9200–9299		
9300–9399		
	17 and 18 Open Categories for New Line-Items	
9400–9499	19 Miscellaneous	Moving/Recruitment Bonding insurance Medical malpractice (for clinics)	Actual or estimated per individual/ per group
9500–9599	20 Depreciation or Amortization (for buildings, equipment)	Equipment Leasehold Vehicles Building	Per unit per month/year per authorized rate (10 years, life of unit, etc.)

PERSONNEL MEASURES

Job Classification and Compensation

People employed in all but the smallest organizations fill positions designated by job titles, are expected to perform certain defined duties, and are paid salaries or wages considered appropriate to their jobs. These conditions are governed by two principal elements in personnel systems: job hierarchies and compensation or salary schedules.

Organizations usually establish one or more job classification hierarchies (e.g. Technical, Professional, Support), and each job in a hierarchy has a title (e.g. file clerk, investigator, department head), stated qualifications, and a description of tasks and responsibilities. In larger personnel systems jobs are designated by code numbers, and employees may also be assigned individual numbers if several persons have the same title.

Many job hierarchies are organized by graded or vertical categories of related jobs, which define ascending degrees of skills, qualifications, responsibilities, and salary ranges. Individuals may be promoted "up through the ranks," depending on skills, performance, or experience, but horizontal moves between categories rarely occur, because each category denotes different competencies and experiences. In general professional and nonprofessional jobs are segregated, because most professional jobs require specialized training.

Job titles, qualifications, and duties are closely interrelated in classification systems, but each has a distinctive meaning. The *job title* is a short label for each role, which may or may not correspond to titles for similar jobs in other organizations. The *qualifications* denote the characteristics, skills, and training required for a given job and are presumably necessary to ensure competency. The *job descriptions*, if well-written, detail the main duties, tasks, and activities of each job.

A compensation schedule specifies ranges of salaries or wages and is linked to the job classifications through designated *grade* levels. Jobs are ranked in ascending numerical order, with corollary maximum and minimum annual salary ranges for all full-time employees in each grade level, which typically has several steps denoting the annual increments for each job within that grade. Thus employees with the same job title may be paid differing amounts because of varying lengths of time on the job, meritorious performance, and so forth. Each employee's *salary rate* is the actual amount representing a year of full-time employment at his or her step level.

Persons may be employed full time or part time, permanently or temporarily, but always for designated jobs with titles and the rest. Part-time employees receive fractions of the full-time salary rates at their grade levels (three-quarter pay for three-quarter-time work), and temporary employees may be paid according to standard rates or on a separate hierarchy and schedule. Persons employed at a fraction between half time and full time usually receive most or all the fringe benefits, sometimes on a prorated basis. Those employed at less than half time may receive fewer or no fringe benefits (benefits are discussed in a later section).

Budgeting requires knowledge of all these elements so that cost estimating can be based on a realistic determination of personnel requirements. Program planners should specify the particular competencies and skills necessary for each job and include relevant tasks and responsibilities in the operational plan. In larger organizations, personnel specialists usually check to see that the staffing plan fits the job classification and compensation structures.

In conventional personnel and budgeting systems individuals engaged to perform services as independent vendors are *not* classified as employees. Thus professionals of all kinds may contract with an organization to provide a certain number of days (or parts of days) of service without being considered members of its staff. They are paid only for the days or hours actually worked and receive no fringe benefits; their costs are included in a separate budget category (Professional Fees, Contractual Services or Consultants).

Full-time Equivalents (FTEs)

A standard statistic is almost universally used as a measure of the level of personnel employed in organizations and programs, or employed with funds from particular budgets. The measure is stated as an *FTE*, that is, a *full-time equivalent*, and should be defined and used in specific ways.

The amount of paid service *equivalent* to that of a single full-time employee for a twelve-month period or fiscal year is called 1.00 FTE. In many agencies this amounts to a maximum of 260 days of service (5 work days x 52 weeks = 260 x 8 hours = 2,080 hours). *Actual* work time is less because of legal holidays and vacation or sick leave.[1]

FTEs are always stated in decimal form, and 1.00 FTE always means that the total amount of paid service is the equivalent of one person working full time for twelve months. Any figure less than 1.00 FTE always states the decimal *proportion* of a twelve-month full-time job for which a person or persons have been employed. For example, when referring to a single individual, .33 means service equivalent to one-third of full time for twelve months, or full time for four months, or two-thirds time for six months—each representing one-third of a full-time job for a year.

FTEs are additive and are generally comparable across organizations. Thus, 2.00 FTEs indicates paid services *equivalent* to that of two full-time employees for twelve months. A total of 2.00 FTEs can represent various numbers of individuals and dif-

[1] The following formula is used in this book to obtain the number of actual work/hours for the CYS program and other examples:

> 260 work/days minus
> 10 days vacation
> 7 holidays
> 5.5 sick days

equals 237.5 actual days or 1,900 work/hours.

fering amounts of time for each. Thus 2.00 FTEs may mean that one person was employed full time for a twelve-month period (1.00), and other persons were employed part time totaling 1.00 FTE for the year. The services of the part-time persons were *equivalent* to that of one full-time employee over the twelve months, but their services could have been engaged on a variety of bases. One person may have worked full time for the first six months, and another full time for the second six months; or two people may have each worked full time only for the first six months of the period; or one person may have worked half time throughout the year, another at half time during the first six months, and still another at half time for the second six months, and so on.

The FTE statistic has many applications in program planning, personnel management, budgeting, and analysis. It provides a simple, uniform, and easily calculated measure of employed personnel. *Within* programs or agencies, the total number of FTEs aggregates the paid service of all persons employed in all job classifications regardless of salary differences or part-time versus full-time statuses. FTEs are also generally comparable *between* programs and agencies (allowing for differences in length of work week, vacation policies, and so on). The measure is also useful for indicating resource balances such as staff/client ratios, ratios of contact or line staff to support staff, and the like (see Exhibit A).

What the statistic does *not* reveal is also important: It does not reflect the numbers of particular individuals whose employment proportions are aggregated into the total FTEs. It does *not* reflect the changing numbers of staff who may be employed at different times during a twelve-month period. It does *not* reflect the departures and arrivals of individuals employed in the same job during the period. And it does *not* state for individuals or for the entire staff the varying holiday, vacation, or sick leave days, which reduce the annual number of *actual workdays* of service in an agency.

Exhibit A. Illustrative Personnel Budget and Staffing Table

Job Code	Job Title	No. of Persons	FTEs	Salary Range	Total Salaries
156	Program Director	1	1.00	$26–28,500	$ 27,550
122	Section Heads	3	3.00	23–26,000	72,600
116	Supervisors	5	5.00	21–24,000	116,000
111	Contact Workers I	13	10.80	16–19,000	202,500
110	Contact Workers II	18	16.25	12–15,800	230,750
092	Secretaries I	12	9.50	8–11,000	97,375
	Totals:	52	45.55		$746,775

NOTES TO EXHIBIT A

1. Fifty-two different persons were employed during this year of operations, and their full-time equivalent total is 45.55—obviously some of the Contact Workers I and II and the Secretaries worked only part of the year or were employed less than full time.

2. The salary ranges for each position are given, but we know the exact salary only of the Program Director. For each of the other job lines we can divide the total salary amount by the total FTEs reported for that line to obtain the *average* salary per FTE. Take the Secretaries, for example: $97,375 divided by 9.50 FTE = $10,250. The midpoint of the Secretaries' salary range is $9,500, so the average per FTE salary of $10,250 is $750, or 8 percent higher than midpoint, indicating that some of these employees had more experience or were otherwise qualified for higher pay rates within the range.

3. The ratio of secretarial support staff to all other staff is 1:3.79, meaning that there was an average of one secretary for every 3.79 other staff. (The subtotal of all other staff is 36.05 FTE; divide this by 9.50 secretarial FTE to obtain 3.79.) If we arbitrarily define the Program Director, the Section Heads, and the Secretaries as "administrative staff" and consider all others as "on-line" staff, the administrative/on-line staff ratio is 1:2.37. Both these ratios are frequently used to examine balances among types of personnel resources.

4. If 2,500 clients were served by this agency and these staff during the past year, we can calculate that the staff/client ratio was 1:54.9, while the ratio of on-line staff to clients was 1:78.

Work/Hours, Work/Days, Work/Months

Related but different measures are used to overcome some of the limitations of the FTE statistic and to permit calculations focused on relatively short time periods. In making staff assignments, arranging workloads or weekly work schedules, and planning special projects, it is desirable to use smaller measures than an FTE. The smallest measure is usually the "work/hour"—sixty minutes of work time—even when staff members are required to

Exhibit B. Employee Activity Summary

Name: J. Jones

ACTIVITY SUMMARY FOR May 198X (23 work days)

Job: STAFF ASSISTANT

Activities	Planning Division		Project RED		Total Work/days	% Total Time
	Work/days	% time	Work/days	% time		
Project PERT plan	--	--	4.75	20.6	4.75	20.6
MIS review	3.25	14.1	--	--	3.25	14.1
Monthly stat. analysis	6.50	28.3	.75	3.3	7.25	31.5
Div. staff meetings	3.00	13.0	1.00	4.3	4.00	17.4
Conf. attendance	--	--	2.00	8.7	2.00	8.7
Misc.	.50	2.2	.25	1.1	.75	3.3
Sick days	1.00	4.3	--	--	1.00	4.3
Totals	14.25	61.9	8.75	38.0	23.00	99.9
					(1 work/month)	

Acc't no. 506853/See Project RED log

log their activities in fifteen-minute intervals.[2] Many programs expect that a specified number of work/hours for certain staff will be devoted to direct client contact, while other proportions of the workday will be devoted to noncontact activities. In forward planning it is frequently necessary to estimate or assign a certain number of work/days of effort for individual staff to specified duties (perhaps on particular dates). Since 1 work/day = 8 work/hours, and there are five in a normal work/week, careful use of these measures can avoid overloading staff on any given day or over a period of time.

Time studies, activity logs, and other procedures are used to determine reasonable or average amounts of time necessary to perform particular job duties. Calculation of duties in terms of work/hours (or fractions thereof) permits the deliberate construction of appropriate workloads and the avoidance of overload, fatigue, high rate of errors, and so on. Planned workloads are usually aggregations of work/hours to work/days and then to work/weeks or work/months of effort (see Exhibit B). If these were expressed in terms of FTEs, with 1,900 work/hours representing the total for a twelve-month period, a task requiring five work/hours would result in the FTE figure .0026; a task requiring as much as fifteen work/hours would result in the FTE figure .0079. Clearly, such figures are too unwieldly for practical use.

Note that here we are considering actual hours and days of work time, excluding weekends and vacation days. However, when discussing FTEs we took account of weekends but ignored the issue of holidays, sick leave, and vacations. Work/days, work/weeks, and work/months can be directly aggregated to FTEs (the respective figures are 260 [maximum], 52, and 12—all equal to 1.00 FTE), and FTEs can be directly disaggregated to these figures. This is sometimes done for budgeting purposes (as when calculating wages for employees paid on an hourly basis), but it is risky when planning concrete job workloads within ongoing programs or when planning complex forward projects. There are a number of useful ways to acknowledge the probable "missing" days due to holidays or vacations, and these vary among organizations. The important principle to keep in mind is that the twelve-

---

[2]Until recently the terms "man-hours" and "man-days" were used instead of "work/hours" and "work/days."

month full-time equivalent FTE statistic always *overstates* the actual number of work/days on the job. When counting "up" from work/hours and work/days it is necessary to allow for these "missing" days, which is usually done through adjustments in the weekly or monthly schedule (such as making arrangements to cover for absent staff).

For organizations that operate on a twenty-four hour, yearlong basis (e.g. hospitals, some crisis programs, police departments), 1.00 FTE also represents the equivalent of one employee working full time for twelve months. However, the *scheduling* of staff work/days and duties differs markedly from those organizations operating on the conventional eight-hour day, five-day week. In continuously operating organizations, a staff member's work/week is planned on a shift basis and bears little resemblance to the agency's full schedule of operations. To take account of variations when comparing FTEs across agencies, it is important to learn the particular definition of an FTE, the usual number of holidays and vacation days, and the procedures used for aggregating work/days into FTEs.

Budgeting for Personnel

FTEs and the related personnel measures are especially useful in agency budgeting and payroll procedures. Salary rates are generally established for all jobs (by grade and step) in terms of 1.00 FTE for each, that is, at 100 percent of the annual position salary rate for a full-time employee. Salaries for persons employed at less than 1.00 FTE are calculated at the appropriate FTE decimals (e.g. .75 FTE means 75 percent of the full-time rate).

Some examples will be helpful. A person employed full time at a salary rate of $13,000 will be paid as follows: 1.00 x $13,000 per year = 13,000 ÷ 12 = $1,083.33 per month. (Note that the cents are *not* rounded off these sums, since that would deprive employees of their full earnings and introduce errors into calculations of fringe benefits.) Suppose two persons are employed at the same job and at identical salary rates of $12,000 for 1.00 FTE, but for a total of 1.80 FTEs. One person is employed full time (1.00), the other is employed four-fifths time (.80): $12,000 ÷ 12 = $1,000 per month for the person employed at 1.00 FTE; $12,000 ÷ 12 = $1,000 x .80 = $800 per month for the person employed at .80 FTE.

Employed personnel may be assigned to more than one program and paid from more than one account, if that is how their duties are divided. A program evaluation specialist, for example, may spend all of one month working in connection with one program, then spend half time the next month on the same program and half time on a different project. This staff member is employed full time, and one payroll check for the full salary will be issued each month. All of the cost of this payment will be assigned to the program during the first month, but during the second month half the cost will be assigned to the program account and the other half to the project account (see Exhibit B). Similar variations may occur over other months affecting other programs and their accounts and may apply to part-time as well as full-time employees. It is obviously necessary to ensure that employees are carefully instructed about their changing duties, that accurate time recording is maintained, and that the costs are properly assigned each month to the appropriate accounts. The same procedures are used to assign all salary costs between functions or types of duties within a program, regardless of which accounts are involved.

Complications arise with step variations in salary rates for the same job (e.g. because of longevity), computation of fringe benefits (especially for part-time employees), differentials for income and other payroll taxes, and so on. Still other complexities are encountered in arranging for sick leaves with pay, educational or other leaves without pay, and the like. We shall only acknowledge these sources of variability, but there are standard procedures for handling them in both budgeting and payroll computations in accord with agency personnel policies, government regulations, and so forth.

Since the personnel and fiscal measures can be related to each other and can be aggregated and summarized, they are highly useful in all organizations, but especially in those employing large numbers of changing personnel in many positions. They permit examination of total personnel and total salary and wage costs in standardized terms that can aid in interyear comparisons within each agency, in comparisons between agencies, and in various kinds of fiscal and trend analyses. There might appear to be a loss of detail when summary FTE information is presented, e.g. proportions of part-time staff, intra-job salary variations, turnover of staff during a fiscal year, or fringe benefit fluctuations. However, because the summary statistics are *directly* based on both personnel and fiscal files, it is possible to generate and reconcile as much detail as may be needed.

Personnel Ratios

Ratios are used to express the relation between two groups of staff or between clients and staff. It is often desirable to examine the ratio of support to professional staff, for example, or to report the ratio of staff to clients.

A ratio states the relationship in quantity between two values or things. It is typically expressed with a slash (/) separating the two things being considered, or with a colon (:) when the numerical value of the ratio is being stated. For example, where there is one doctor for each 15 patients, the doctor/patient ratio is stated as 1:15. Note that the same *order* of the expression is maintained in both the text and numerical expressions of ratios.

A ratio is the result (quotient) of dividing one sum (the divisor or "base") into another sum (the dividend). The ratio of 15 to 27 is obtained by dividing 15 into 27: $27 \div 15 = 1.8$. In budgeting, the ratio expression is usually stated with a colon to indicate and separate the two figures, here 1:1.8. We shall restate this as follows: Where there are 15 FTE secretarial staff and 27 FTE professional staff, the secretarial/professional staff ratio is 1:1.8. This means that for the *equivalent* of each 1.00 FTE secretary there is the *equivalent* of 1.8 FTE professional staff. Again the order is maintained—secretarial then professional staff.

To check the accuracy of a ratio, we can *multiply* each of its elements by the base to obtain the original figures: 15 x 1 equals 15, and 15 x 1.8 equals 27.

There are several advantages in using ratios rather than raw numbers when reporting or assessing relations among personnel and other resources. Ratios simplify numerical data; they permit direct comparisons with other ratios based on different figures, and one of their figures is a multiple of the other, which helps with interpretation of the ratio measure. We shall consider these in order. First the relations of 15 to 27, or 180 to 324 or 750 to 1350, are more quickly grasped when stated as 1:1.8, which is the common ratio of each. Second, the same example illustrates how groups of personnel in programs of quite different sizes can be compared with respect to their secretarial/staff and other ratios. Despite the much larger staff cadre in the third program, the ratio tells us that it employs the same *proportion* of secretary to other staff as do the two smaller programs. The ratio can be used with similar effect to make comparisons between fiscal years for the same program despite changes in its staff complement.

Fringe Benefits

The line-item on budget forms known as Fringe Benefits is inextricably linked to the Salaries/Wages (Personnel) line-item. Fringe Benefits (Fringes for short) comprises two distinct subdivisions: Payroll Taxes and Employee Benefits. They may be shown in the budget either together or separately, depending on the funder's requirements, and are often expressed as percentages of total Salaries/Wages.

Most readers will be generally familiar with the kinds of costs included in Fringe Benefits. But it should be useful to list the most prevalent types of Fringe costs and to note who has the responsibility for which costs. A number of these items are mandated by law, some are required by union or other contracts, some result from parent organization negotiations or regulations, and a few result from policies of individual organizations.

Since Payroll Taxes and Employee Benefits contain distinctly different kinds of costs, we shall consider each separately. They are both inseparable from Salaries/Wages (Personnel) costs, so we shall begin by reviewing the major elements in a typical Personnel category.

1. Salaries/Wages (Personnel)
   a. Professional Staff
      Full time
      Part time
   b. Clerical and Other Nonprofessional Staff
   c. Technical and Maintenance Staff
   d. Temporary Staff
   e. Overtime/Shift Pay/Incentive Pay/Hardship Pay
   f. Cost of Living Adjustments (COLA)

2. Fringe Benefits
   2A. *Payroll Taxes*
      a. Social Security (FICA)
      b. Unemployment Insurance
         State
         Federal
      c. Worker's Compensation
      d. Disability Insurance
   2B. *Employee Benefits*
      a. Health Insurance Plans (Medical, Dental, Hospital)

b. Pension/Retirement Plans
c. Life Insurance
d. Accident Insurance
e. Supplemental Pension or Annuitant Benefits
f. Other Supplemental Employee Benefits
   (e.g. termination agreements; relocation allowances; meals, rooms, uniforms, if required; training, education grants; deferred compensation; supplemental unemployment)

In general this listing represents the contents of Fringe Benefits for most organizations. However, a few points must be clarified and underscored.

1. Items 1e and 1f (Overtime, etc., and COLA) are paid *directly* to staff in the form of salaries and wages; therefore, they properly belong in this line-item.

2. Vacations, holidays, and sick leave are reckoned as absorbed *within* salary costs. The very important consequences for managing work schedules were noted earlier, but other consequences, such as the need for additional temporary staff should be reflected here in the calculation of FTEs and in total Salary/Wage costs.

3. All items in the Payroll Taxes category are based on and determined by Salary/Wage costs. Social Security (FICA), Unemployment, and Worker's Compensation are mandated by law; other insurance obligations may be consigned to this category by the funder.

4. A few of the Employee Benefits may sometimes appear in other categories, depending on funder or parent organization regulations, or for other reasons. For example, Accident Insurance is sometimes included with Disability Insurance under Payroll Taxes. Also, some of the Other Supplemental Benefits (2B–f) may be included in full or in part under Salaries/Wages (e.g. termination, deferred compensation).

Now we need to focus on *who is responsible for paying which Fringe costs.*

1. Payroll Taxes

a. Social Security: the employee and the employer are each responsible for 50 percent of the total Social Security Tax. The employee's 50 percent share is taken out of each salary check, along with federal and state income taxes, and is accounted for on the year-end Wage and Tax Statement (W–2 Form). The agency (employer) is then responsible by law for depositing its 50 percent share, plus the employee's 50 percent share (that was withheld from the paycheck and is still in the employer's bank account) at designated banks or government agencies at designated times (usually quarterly).

b. Unemployment Insurance, Worker's Compensation, and Disability Insurance are almost always paid in full *solely* by the employer. In the rare instance where other policies are in effect, the employee's share would be taken out of the paycheck.

2. Employee Benefits. Responsibility for the costs in this category vary considerably among organizations. In some they are shared by employer and employee at contracted or negotiated levels. For example, employees may contribute agreed-upon percentages or specific dollar amounts to health, pension, or life insurance plans. In others some costs—like the health plan—will be paid solely by the employer, but the costs of the other benefits may be shared, and so on. If an employee is responsible for paying any part of any benefit, that cost will be taken out of the paycheck and noted either on the check stub or on some other form. The agency (employer) is always responsible for transmitting the total obligation to the proper insurer or pension fund.

Thus we see that in every instance the employer is responsible for collecting, handling, transmitting, and reporting all the costs related to Fringe Benefits. The employee is responsible only for understanding what has been taken out of the paycheck and why. Because all Fringes are linked to *individuals'* Personnel costs, differences in benefits among employees within one agency result from variances in their time proportions on the job or in their permanent or temporary status, and sometimes result from their election of certain benefits.

BIBLIOGRAPHY

AICPA. 1974. *Audits of Voluntary Health and Welfare Organizations.* Rev. ed. New York: American Institute of Certified Public Accountants.

————. 1978. *Statement of Position on Accounting Principles and Reporting Practices for Certain Nonprofit Organizations.* New York: American Institute of Certified Public Accountants.

American Hospital Association. 1968. *Cost Finding and Rate Setting for Hospitals.* Chicago: AHA.

ANTHONY, ROBERT N. 1974. *Management Accounting.* Homewood, IL: Richard D. Irwin.

ANTHONY, ROBERT N., and REGINA HERZLINGER. 1980. *Management Control in Non-Profit Organizations.* Rev. ed. Homewood, IL: Richard D. Irwin.

BRACE, PAUL, K.; ROBERT ELKIN; DANIEL D. ROBINSON; and HAROLD I. STEINBERG. 1980. *Reporting of Service Efforts and Accomplishments.* Research report by Peat, Marwick, Mitchell & Co. Stamford, CT: Financial Accounting Standards Board.

COPELAND, WILLIAM C., and IVER A. IVERSON. 1978. *Managing Federal Money for Children's Services, Manual 4.* New York: Child Welfare League of America.

DAUGHTREY, WILLIAM H., JR., and MALVERN J. GROSS, JR. 1978. *Museum Accounting Handbook.* Washington, D.C.: American Association of Museums.

DAVIDSON, SIDNEY; JAMES S. SCHINDLER; and ROMAN L. WEIL. 1975. *Fundamentals of Accounting.* 5th ed. Hinsdale, IL: Dryden Press.

379

ELKIN, ROBERT. 1980. *A Human Service Manager's Guide to Developing Unit Costs.* Falls Church, VA: Institute for Information Studies.

FERLIE, E., and K. JUDGE. 1981. "Retrenchment and Rationality in the Personal Social-Services." *Policy and Politics* 9, No. 3: 311–30.

FORMAN, JANE; PHYLLIS ELLIOTT; and ROBERT RIESETT. 1981. *Analyzing Costs in Human Services.* Vol. 1. Reprint. Washington, D.C.: Department of Health and Human Services, Office of Human Development Services.

Government Printing Office. Annual. "Guide to Record Retention Requirements." In *Federal Register.* Washington, D.C.: GPO.

GROSS, MALVERN J., JR., and WILLIAM WARSHAUER, JR. 1978. "Cost Accounting in Nonprofit Organizations." In *Handbook of Cost Accounting.* Ed. Sidney Davidson and Ronald L. Weil. New York: McGraw–Hill.

———. 1983. *Financial and Accounting Guide for Nonprofit Organizations.* Rev. 3rd ed. New York: Wiley.

HALL, MARY. 1977. *Developing Skills in Proposal Writing.* 2nd ed. Portland, OR: Continuing Education Publications.

HENKE, EMERSON O. 1980. *Introduction to Nonprofit Organization Accounting.* Boston: Kent.

HILL, JOHN G. 1960. "Cost Analysis of Social Work Service." In *Social Work Research.* Ed. Norman A. Polansky. Chicago: University of Chicago Press.

HORNGREN, CHARLES T. 1982. *Cost Accounting: A Managerial Emphasis.* 5th ed. Englewood Cliffs, NJ: Prentice–Hall.

LEE, ROBERT D., JR., and RONALD W. JOHNSON. 1977. *Public Budgeting Systems.* 2nd ed. Baltimore: University Park Press.

Legal Services Corporation. 1977. *Audit and Accounting Guide for Recipients and Auditors.* New York: LSC, with assistance of Arthur Anderson & Co.

LEVINE, CHARLES, ed. 1980. *Managing Fiscal Stress: The Crisis in the Public Sector.* Chatham, NJ: Chatham House Publishers.

LEVINE, C. H.; I. S. RUBIN; and G. G. WOLOHOJIAN. 1982. "Managing Organizational Retrenchment: Preconditions, Deficiencies, and Adaptations in the Public Sector." *Administration and Society* 14, No. 1: 101–36.

LEWIS, CAROL, and ANTHONY LOGALBO. 1980. "Cutback Principles and Practices." *Public Administration Review* 40 (March–April): 184–88.

LOHMANN, ROGER A. 1980. *Breaking Even: Financial Management in Human Service Organizations.* Philadelphia: Temple University Press.

LYNCH, THOMAS D. 1979. *Public Budgeting in America.* Englewood Cliffs, NJ: Prentice–Hall.

MAY, R. G.; G. G. MUELLER; and T. H. WILLIAMS. 1980. *A New Introduction to Financial Accounting.* 2nd ed. Englewood Cliffs, NJ: Prentice–Hall.

National Health Council, Inc.; National Assembly of National Voluntary Health and Social Welfare Organizations, Inc.; and United Way of America. 1974. *Standards of Accounting and Financial Reporting for Voluntary Health and Welfare Organizations.* Rev. ed. New York.

National Institute of Mental Health. 1972. *Cost-finding and Rate-setting for Community Mental Health Centers.* Methodology report by James E. Sorenson, David W. Thipps et al. Rockville, MD: NIMH.

NELSON, CHARLES A., and FREDERICK J. TURK. 1975. *Financial Management for the Arts: A Guidebook for Arts Organizations.* New York: Associated Council of the Arts.

Price Waterhouse & Co. 1980. *Effective Internal Accounting Control for Nonprofit Organizations.* New York.

Project Share. 1980. *Productivity in Human Services: Measurement, Improvement, and Management.* Rockville, MD: Project Share.

RICHARDSON, DAVID. 1981. *Rate Setting in the Human Services: A Guide for Administrators.* Rockville, MD: Project Share.

SALAMON, LESTER M., and ALAN J. ABRAMSON. 1982. *The Federal Budget and the Nonprofit Sector.* Washington, D.C.: Urban Institute Press.

SKIGEN, MICHAEL R., and EUGENE K. SNYDER. 1975. *Cost Accounting.* New York: Barnes & Noble.

STRECKER, SISTER MARY F. 1971. "Accounting for the Not-for-Profit Organization." *Management Accounting,* August.

STRETCH, JOHN. "What Human Services Managers Need to Know About Basic Budgeting Strategies." *Administration in Social Work* 4 (Spring): 88–97.

U.S. Office of Management and Budget. 1980. "Cost Principles for Nonprofit Organizations." Circular A–122. In *Federal Register* 45, No. 132 (July). Washington, D.C.

———. 1981. "Cost Principles for State and Local Governments." Circular A–87. In *Federal Register* 46, No. 18 (January). Washington, D.C.

United Way of America. 1974. *Accounting and Financial Reporting: A Guide for United Ways and Not-for-Profit Human Service Organizations.* Ed. Russy D. Sumariwalla. Alexandria, VA: United Way of America.

———. 1975. *Budgeting: A Guide for United Ways and Not-for-Profit Human Service Organizations.* Alexandria, VA: United Way of America.

Urban Institute. 1983. *Serving Community Needs: The Nonprofit Sector in an Era of Governmental Retrenchment.* Progress Report No. 3 (September). Washington, D.C.: Urban Institute.

WHITE, VIRGINIA P. 1975. *Grants: How to Find Out About Them and What to Do Next.* New York: Plenum Press.

WILDAVSKY, AARON. 1974. *The Politics of the Budgeting Process.* 2nd ed. Boston: Little, Brown & Co.

YOUNGQUIST, EMILY, and GUY FARRELL. 1980. *Effective Fiscal Management: Dollars and Sense, an Accounting Overview.* Falls Church, VA: Institute for Information Studies.

INDEX

INDEX